BODY, SOUL, AND LIFE EVERLASTING

BODY, SOUL,
and
LIFE EVERLASTING

• •

*Biblical Anthropology
and the Monism-Dualism Debate*

JOHN W. COOPER

WILLIAM B. EERDMANS PUBLISHING COMPANY
GRAND RAPIDS, MICHIGAN / CAMBRIDGE, U.K.

APOLLOS
LEICESTER, ENGLAND

© 1989 Wm. B. Eerdmans Publishing Co.

This edition published 2000
in the United States of America by
Wm. B. Eerdmans Publishing Co.
255 Jefferson Ave. S.E., Grand Rapids, Michigan 49503 /
P.O. Box 163, Cambridge CB3 9PU U.K.
www.eerdmans.com
and in the United Kingdom by
APOLLOS
38 De Montfort Street, Leicester, England LE1 7GP

Printed in the United States of America

05 04 03 02 01 00   7 6 5 4 3 2 1

Library of Congress Cataloging-in-Publication Data

Cooper, John W., 1947–
Body, soul, and life everlasting: biblical anthropology
and the monism-dualism debate / John W. Cooper.
p.   cm.
Includes indexes.
ISBN 0-8028-4600-9
1. Man (Theology) — Biblical teaching.
2. Man (Christian theology).   I. Title.

BS661.C68   1989
233'.5 — dc2089-35058
CIP

British Library Cataloguing in Publication Data

A catalogue record for this book is available from the British Library.
ISBN 0-85111-474-1

To my children,

John and Catherine,

who are not their own,
but belong, body and soul,
both in life and in death,
to their faithful Savior, Jesus Christ.
(HEIDELBERG CATECHISM, ANSWER ONE)

And to my mother,

Beatrice,

who is away from the body
and at home with the Lord.
(II CORINTHIANS 5:8)

Contents

CONTENTS

Contents

CONTENTS

CONTENTS

Acknowledgments

I wish to express my gratitude to a number of people who have contributed in various ways to this book. My former colleagues in the Philosophy Department of Calvin College discussed the first draft in its entirety, offering helpful comments and encouragement. I am especially indebted to Professor Richard Mouw, now of Fuller Seminary, without whose faithful prodding and good words this project might not have been completed. Thanks are due to my colleagues at Calvin Seminary as well, especially to the Theological Division, who read and commented on several chapters. Professor Raymond Van Leeuwen of Calvin Seminary, Professor Ronald Feenstra of Marquette University, Professor Gerald Vander Hoek of Dordt College, and my father, the Reverend John Cooper, offered good advice on particular chapters, for which I am grateful. Professor Theodore Plantinga of Redeemer College read and made helpful suggestions about the book as a whole. In addition, I must not fail to thank my students, both in Philosophical Anthropology at the College and Biblical Anthropology at the Seminary, whose interests and insights have helped shape this book. Some of their names are in footnotes. I am grateful to the Seminary and its Board of Trustees for the sabbatical during which I completed this work. Faculty Secretary Jylene Baas contributed in countless ways. Ms. Dawn Bush and others at the Calvin Computer Center were most helpful. And finally I wish to thank the people at Eerdmans Publishing Company who had a hand in the production of the book, especially its editor, Milton Essenburg.

1989   JOHN W. COOPER

Preface to the Second Printing

I. The Original Argument

It is fair to ask why a book a decade old and out of print for several years should be republished. The short answer is that it stands up well in addressing issues and arguments that continue to be widely contended. It presents a case that remains relevant, robust, and right on target. A lot has been written since the book appeared. But instead of revising it extensively to dialogue with current scholarship, I reintroduce it by surveying recent contributions to the monism-dualism debate and indicating how the original version is still engaging.

Body, Soul, and Life Everlasting was written to remind thoughtful Christians that some sort of "dualistic" anthropology is entailed by the biblical teaching of the intermediate state, a doctrine that is affirmed by the vast majority in historic Christianity. The book makes the case that as Holy Scripture progressively discloses what happens to humans when they die, it teaches not only that each of us will undergo bodily resurrection, but that believers continue to exist "with the Lord" until the resurrection. The Old Testament notion of ghostly survival in Sheol, eventually augmented with an affirmation of bodily resurrection, is developed by the Holy Spirit into the New Testament revelation of fellowship with Christ between each believer's death and the general resurrection at Christ's return. Thus the Bible indicates that humans do not cease to exist between death and resurrection, a condition sometimes euphemistically termed "soul sleep," or that final resurrection occurs immediately upon death.

Body, Soul goes on to argue that, given this teaching of Scripture, human nature must be so constituted that we — the very individuals who live on earth — can exist at least temporarily while our physical bodies or organisms do not. In other words, there must be enough of a duality in human nature so that God can sustain Moses, Paul, and my mother in fellowship with him even though they are currently without their earthly bodies. At the same time, I follow Scripture, most traditional theology, and almost all current thought in emphasizing the unity of human nature, its essential bodiliness, and resurrection as the final Christian hope. All things considered, therefore, the biblical view of the human constitution is some kind of "holistic dualism."

The argument of the book is mainly exegesis and theological reflection on Scripture, only touching on some of the philosophical aspects of the body-soul or mind-body problem. It does not endorse a particular philosophical anthropology, such as that of Augustine, Thomas, Descartes, or Kant. But it does identify a condition that a philosophical account of human nature must meet in order to be consistent with what most of the holy catholic church affirms as a teaching of Scripture. To challenge the soundness of the book's conclusion about the constitution of human nature would require a strong, fully elaborated historical-exegetical-theological case against the claim that the Bible envisions an intermediate state between humans' death and their bodily resurrection.

II. Recent Affirmations of the Traditional Christian Position

One recent piece of evidence that the traditional doctrine still thrives among large numbers of faithful Christians is found in *The Catechism of the Catholic Church.*[1] Consider its exposition of the Apostles' Creed's article on the resurrection: "In death, the separation of the soul from the body, the human body decays and the soul goes to meet God, while awaiting its reunion with its glorified body" (par. 997). The duality required by this doctrine of the afterlife is clearly stated, while the unity of human nature is also strongly emphasized: "The human person, created in the image of God, is a being at once corporeal and spiritual" (par. 362). "The unity of soul and body is so profound that one has to consider the soul to be the

---

1. *Catechism of the Catholic Church* (Mahwah, NJ: Paulist Press, 1994).

'form' of the body; . . . spirit and matter, in man, are not two natures united, but rather their union forms a single nature" (par. 366).

The historic doctrine is still articulated by leading theologians. For example, Joseph Ratzinger, now Cardinal and head of the Roman Catholic Magisterium, has done so extensively in *Eschatology: Death and Eternal Life*.[2] This work briefly surveys the same biblical and intertestamental texts considered in *Body, Soul* and comes to virtually identical conclusions. It strongly defends the intermediate state and the reunification of human nature in the final resurrection at the return of Christ.

This reading of the relevant texts and their historical background remains standard fare in biblical scholarship. For example, E. P. Sanders has recently affirmed that the same variety of beliefs about personal eschatology that were identified in *Body, Soul* as background for the New Testament can be found in Judaism during the first century A.D.[3] Tom Wright makes a similar point, identifying three standard views: The first, held by the Sadducees, denies the afterlife. The second was held by Hellenistic Jews, influenced by Plato, who affirmed the immortal soul and sometimes also the resurrection. The third group, the majority, "speak of the bodily resurrection of the dead and frequently address the problem of an intermediate state. . . ."[4] The evidence from intertestamental Judaism crucial to *Body, Soul's* reading of the relevant New Testament texts continues to be recognized by leading scholars.[5]

Scripture commentators follow suit. To take one important text, for example, recent exegeses of Jesus' promise of Paradise "today" to the dying thief in Luke 23:43 still treat it as a clear reference to an intermediate state.

2. Joseph Ratzinger, *Eschatology: Death and Eternal Life*, trans. M. Waldstein, ed. A. Nichols (Washington, D.C.: Catholic University of America, 1988). The German original, of which I was unaware, was published in 1977. The English translation appeared a decade later, too late for me to consider in *Body, Soul*. Its impact on English-speakers has occurred during the 1990's.

3. E. P. Sanders, *Judaism: Practice and Belief, 63 BCE-66 CE* (London: SCM Press, and Philadelphia: Trinity Press International, 1992), esp. "Life after Death," pp. 298-303.

4. N. T. Wright, *The New Testament and the People of God* (Minneapolis: Fortress Press, 1992), p. 331; see also "The Renewal of the World, of Israel, and of Humans," pp. 320-34.

5. See John Collins, "Resurrection and Eternal Life" in *Apocalypticism in the Dead Sea Scrolls* (London and New York: Routledge, 1997), pp. 110-29. See also Charles Hill, "Some Observations on New Testament Eschatology," and "Millenium and Intermediate State," in *Regnum Caelorum: Patterns of Future Hope in Early Christianity* (Oxford: Clarendon Press, 1992), pp. 154-162 and 178-181.

According to Robert Stein, it is a "temporary state of . . . conscious experience with Jesus in paradise."[6] Whatever doctrinal inferences are made from such texts, historical evidence for the traditional reading has not been eroded or successfully reinterpreted in recent scholarship.[7] An example from Paul's epistles is Ben Witherington III's exegesis of 2 Corinthians 5:1-10, a classic text for the intermediate state: "Paul speaks of three states: the present condition in the tent-like frame, the intermediate state of nakedness . . . and the future condition . . . the resurrection body."[8] The historic interpretation of Scripture continues to flourish.

The traditional view of human nature has also been embraced and defended in different ways by Christian philosophers during this decade. Alvin Plantinga,[9] Richard Swinburne,[10] and Keith Yandell[11] continue to affirm substance dualism. Charles Taliaferro has published a philosophical defense of "integrative dualism" in extensive dialogue with current alternative views.[12] Stephen Davis has endorsed and defended dualism in an extensive apologetics for the resurrection.[13] Gary Habermas and J. P.

6. Robert H. Stein, *Luke, The New American Commentary*, Vol. 24 (Nashville: Broadman Press, 1992), p. 593. See also Luke Timothy Johnson, *The Gospel of Luke, Sacra Pagina Series*, Vol. 3 (Collegeville, MN: Liturgical Press, 1991).

7. Joel B. Green, who does not believe that Luke or the New Testament teaches the intermediate state, nonetheless admits that "Jesus' promise of Paradise 'today' is in keeping with Luke's understanding of the immediacy of salvation." He also recognizes that Luke's portrayal of the afterlife in the parable of the Rich Man and Lazarus (16:19-31) has "many analogues in contemporary Jewish literature." *The Gospel of Luke* (Grand Rapids/Cambridge, UK: Eerdmans Publishing, 1997), pp. 823, 607.

8. Ben Witherington III, *Conflict and Community in Corinth: A Socio-Rhetorical Commentary on 1 and 2 Corinthians* (Grand Rapids: Eerdmans Publishing, 1995), p. 391.

9. Alvin Plantinga, "On Heresy, Mind, and Truth," *Faith and Philosophy* 16/2 (April 1999), p. 186. "Now I should confess up front that I accept dualism. . . ." He goes on to say that dualism was accepted by St. Paul and is entailed by what the Creeds teach.

10. Richard Swinburne, "Body and Soul," in *The Mind-Body Problem: A Guide to the Current Debate*, ed. R. Warner and T. Szubka (Oxford and Cambridge, MA: Blackwell, 1994), pp. 311-316; "Dualism Intact," *Faith and Philosophy* 13/1 (January 1996), pp. 68-77. Swinburne's views are surveyed in Chapter Ten of *Body, Soul, and Life Everlasting*.

11. Keith Yandell, "A Defense of Dualism," *Faith and Philosophy* 12/4 (October 1995), pp. 548-566.

12. Charles Taliaferro, *Consciousness and the Mind of God* (Cambridge: Cambridge University Press, 1994). On page 245 he writes, "In general, I think the Christian understanding of the afterlife is best served by assuming a dualist view of human nature." See also "Animals, Brains, and Spirits," *Faith and Philosophy* 12/4 (October 1995), pp. 567-81.

13. Stephen Davis, *Risen Indeed: Making Sense of the Resurrection* (Grand Rapids: Eerd-

Moreland have done the same in their multidisciplinary case for immortality.[14] Moreland and Scott Rae have elaborated a lengthy exegetical and philosophical defense of body-soul dualism in relation to contemporary ethical issues.[15] Substance dualism is not such an intellectually discredited or outdated view that competent philosophers are unwilling to defend it.[16]

Other Christian philosophers, influenced by the Thomistic tradition, have elaborated more substantially holistic views of human nature that affirm a duality sufficient to allow for temporary personal existence apart from the body. David Braine uses contemporary philosophical tools to articulate a concept of humans as language-using animals that is a holistic alternative both to substance dualism and materialism and yet accounts for the possibility of personal transcendence of biological death.[17] Eleonore Stump has developed an explicitly Thomistic anthropology in dialogue with current philosophy, brain science, and genetics.[18] Jeffrey Boyd, a practicing psychiatrist and Episcopal clergyman, has recently advocated a similar view of the human constitution as necessary for promoting emotional-spiritual health, as well as for maintaining the Christian view of the afterlife.[19] The Thomistic tradition has generated substantive contributions to recent discussions of the body-soul question.

The first edition of *Body, Soul* also considers the possibility that John Cobb, who embraces process philosophy in the tradition of Whitehead and Hartshorne, might provide a view of human nature that is holistic and yet dualistic enough to allow for personal survival of death. This "process" approach to the body-mind problem has since been developed more fully

---

mans, 1993). Although he also defends a physicalist account of the resurrection for apologetic purposes, he endorses holistic dualism as his own view: "Introduction," xi, note 10.

14. Gary Habermas and J. P. Moreland, *Beyond Death: Exploring the Evidence for Immortality* (Wheaton, IL: Crossway Books, 1998).

15. J. P. Moreland and Scott Rae, *Body and Soul: Human Nature and the Crisis in Ethics* (Downers Grove, IL: InterVarsity Press, 2000).

16. John Foster, *The Immaterial Self: A Defense of the Cartesian Dualist Conception of the Mind* (London and New York: Routledge, 1991) is an extensive philosophical work that does not consider Christian doctrine.

17. David Braine, *The Human Person: Animal and Spirit* (Notre Dame: University of Notre Dame Press, 1992). See pp. 542-45 for his treatment of "The Question Raised by Death."

18. Eleonore Stump, "Non-Cartesian Substance Dualism and Materialism Without Reduction," *Faith and Philosophy* 12/4 (October 1995), pp. 505-531.

19. Jeffrey Boyd, *Reclaiming the Soul: The Search for Meaning in a Self-Centered Culture* (Cleveland: Pilgrim Press, 1996).

by David Ray Griffin.[20] Although my original questions about the consistency of process anthropology with an intermediate state have not been answered, his work deserves to be noted.

One position that was mentioned in *Body, Soul* but not given serious consideration is emergentism. This is a version of materialism that is arguably consistent with the possibility of an intermediate state. According to this theory, human beings begin to exist as purely material organisms, but the person with all of his or her mental-spiritual capabilities normally emerges as the organism develops and grows. Thus the human person is an entity that is distinct from his or her organism, generated by it and interacting with it, but that cannot naturally exist or function without it. At death, however, God supernaturally maintains the person with her mental-spiritual capacities in existence until the resurrection. William Hasker continues to promote this solution to the mind-body problem.[21] Although I still have reservations about it, I think that emergentism, if philosophically tenable, could offer a materialist philosophy of human nature that is consistent with the traditional Christian doctrine of the afterlife. If so, this is a significant development in the millenia-old debate.

III. Recent Affirmations of Alternative Positions

In spite of the fact that beliefs in an intermediate state and the separability of persons from their earthly bodies are currently defended by leading biblical scholars, theologians, and philosophers, sincere and thoughtful Christians continue to challenge these beliefs.

Some standard works on the New Testament simply ignore the traditional view. They present intertestamental Jewish and New Testament eschatology in terms of a straightforward alternative between the "Greek" idea of the immortality of the soul and the "biblical" idea of the resurrection of the body, failing even to consider the evidence for a third position, belief in an intermediate state that would combine aspects of the other views.[22]

20. David Ray Griffin, *Unsnarling the World-Knot: Consciousness, Freedom, and the Mind-Body Problem* (Berkeley, Los Angeles, and London: California University Press, 1998).

21. William Hasker, "Concerning the Unity of Consciousness," *Faith and Philosophy* 12/4 (October 1995), pp. 532-47.

22. See, for example, Bart D. Ehrman, *The New Testament: A Historical Introduction to the Early Christian Writings* (New York: Oxford University Press, 1997), p. 277.

Other scholars directly challenge the traditional view. The most extensive recent biblical-theological case for an alternative position is Samuele
Bacchiocchi's *Immortality or Resurrection?*[23] Evangelical theologian Clark
Pinnock has given an enthusiastic endorsement in the *Foreword*.
Bacchiocchi defends the Seventh-Day Adventist appropriation of the
"soul-sleep" eschatology inherited from a Reformation Anabaptist tradition. This book, perhaps the best defense of its position to date, is extensively documented and generally well-argued. Its emphases on the unity of
human nature, the essential goodness of the human body, and the inclu-
sion of the renewed earth in God's everlasting Kingdom highlight important biblical themes. But in my judgment the book's case against the intermediate state is invalidated by several factors. The entire argument
proceeds from the assumption that the immortality of the soul and the
resurrection of the body are mutually exclusive, which is a false dilemma.
It also fails to do full justice to the Old Testament belief that Sheol is a real
place of the dead and avoids the hard data that some intertestamental Jews
affirmed a conscious intermediate state, even referring to it as "sleep."
Consequently it does not take full measure of the evidence that some New
Testament texts most likely imply an intermediate state or refer to the human soul or spirit as existing apart from the body. In the final analysis
Bacchiocchi's biblical-theological argument for "soul sleep" does not so
much challenge the case for the traditional teaching as skillfully reassert an
alternative view.

Joel Green has published several works in which he argues that "the
dominant view of the human person in the New Testament is ontological
monism" and rejects the claim that it countenances a "separable soul."[24]
He admits that intertestamental Judaism displays a variety of views of the
afterlife and that the dualist reading of the New Testament has some textual basis. But he does not consider this evidence sufficient to justify the
traditional position. While I agree with Green on many points of exegesis

23. Samuele Bacchiocchi, *Immortality or Resurrection? A Biblical Study on Human Nature and Destiny* (Berrien Springs, MI: Biblical Perspectives, 1997).
24. Joel B. Green, "'Bodies — That Is, Human Lives': A Re-Examination of Human Nature in the Bible," in *Whatever Happened to the Soul? Scientific and Theological Portraits of
Human Nature,* ed. Warren Brown, Nancey Murphy, and H. Newton Malony (Minneapolis:
Fortress Press, 1998), pp. 149-173, 173. *The Theology of the Gospel of Luke* (Cambridge:
Cambridge University Press, 1995). His commentary on the Gospel of Luke was noted above
in connection with the exegesis of Jesus' promise of Paradise to the dying thief.

and on his theological affirmation of the holism of our final hope, I find his arguments for an alternative to the traditional position incomplete and unsound. For instance, he criticizes *Body, Soul* for claiming that the parable of the Rich Man and Lazarus in Luke 16 teaches the intermediate state[25] even though I am careful to say that this text on its own is not a prooftext for the intermediate state, but is about wealth and love for neighbor. I return to draw from it only after establishing that Luke does affirm an intermediate state in 23:43, Jesus' promise of Paradise to the dying thief. In making his own case, however, Green first denies that Luke 16 suggests anything at all about an intermediate state and then avoids the topic when commenting on 23:43,[26] thus failing to engage the debate about this important aspect of Luke's eschatology. Another example of an insufficient argument is his alternative reading of 2 Corinthians 5:1-10.[27] In attempting to avoid a disembodied intermediate state in this text, Green fails to consider 2 Corinthians 5:6-9, 12:2-4, and Philippians 1:20-24, where Paul, although he does not use the words "soul" or "spirit," explicitly refers to his own personal existence ("I") separated from his body. In general, Green plays down the evidence for the intermediate state and dualism in Scripture instead of either refuting it or providing an alternative reading that is shown to be as comprehensive and coherent as the traditional view. Nonetheless, anti-dualists find in Green exegetical justification for a materialist view of human nature and the afterlife.[28]

Such views have been articulated and defended by a new generation of Christian philosophers. Most of them have adopted materialism for philosophical reasons, mainly problems with dualism and scientific advances in correlating mental activities with brain functions.[29] However, many have

25. Green, *Gospel of Luke,* p. 606; "Bodies," p. 168, note 52.

26. *Gospel of Luke,* p. 823.

27. "Human Nature in Paul," in "Bodies," pp. 169-72.

28. "Bodies" is the main exegetical chapter in *Whatever Happened to the Soul?*, an interdisciplinary collection of essays devoted to the propagation of a Christian monistic, physicalistic view of human nature. It includes two chapters by philosopher Nancey Murphy, discussed below. Murphy also credits Green with having shown that physicalism is compatible with Scripture and Christian teaching in "I Cerebrate Myself: Is There a Little Man Inside Your Brain?," *Books and Culture* 5/1 (Jan.-Feb. 1999), p. 24.

29. Two influential books that take this philosophical-scientific approach are Patricia Smith Churchland and Terence Sejnowski, *The Computational Brain* (Cambridge, MA: MIT Press, 1992) and Daniel Dennett, *Consciousness Explained* (New York: Little, Brown, 1991). An excellent overview of the primarily materialist approach to the philosophy of mind dur-

also asserted that their views are consistent with Scripture because it teaches bodily resurrection, not the immortality of the soul or temporary disembodied survival. Their greatest challenge has been explaining how the resurrection person/body is identical with the original person/body.[30]

Peter van Inwagen marked this path at the beginning of the decade in *Material Beings*, where he gives a materialist ontology of everything in nature, including all of human nature.[31] He has searched for accounts of bodily resurrection consistent with his position.[32] He has also argued that dualism and the intermediate state are more in the minds of Platonistic readers of Scripture than in the biblical text itself, fully aware of the significance of his allegation that the entire Christian tradition is mistaken.[33]

A number of philosophers have followed van Inwagen's lead. Lynne Rudder Baker has argued that a materialist approach to human existence is more consistent with the Bible's view of humans as psychophysical unities and its promise of bodily resurrection. She surveys several scenarios for what follows death, claiming that "many different philosophical positions are consistent with the scant clues to be found in the Bible."[34] Interestingly, she even suggests that if there is an intermediate state, an interim body could account for it. Kevin Corcoran has developed similar ideas, claiming that persons are not identical with their bodies but "constituted" by them. He suggests that at death a kind of "fission" might occur whereby the earthly body becomes two things: a corpse and a bodily-person that could exist in an intermediate state.[35] Trenton Merricks affirms that human persons are essentially physical-bodily beings and argues that a person's resur-

---

ing the past several decades is Jaegwon Kim, "The Mind-Body Problem After Fifty Years," in *Current Issues in Philosophy of Mind*, ed. Anthony O'Hear (Cambridge: Cambridge University Press, 1998). An excellent collection of essays by major philosophers on all sides of the dualism-materialism debate is Richard Warner and Tadeusz Szubka, ed., *The Mind-Body Problem: A Guide to the Current Debate* (Oxford, UK, and Cambridge, MA: Blackwell, 1994).

30. This topic is treated briefly in *Body, Soul*, Chapter Eight.

31. Peter van Inwagen, *Material Beings* (Ithaca, NY: Cornell University Press, 1990).

32. Peter van Inwagen, "The Possibility of Resurrection," reprinted in *Immortality*, ed. Paul Edwards (New York: Macmillan, 1992), pp. 242-46.

33. Peter van Inwagen, "Dualism and Materialism: Athens and Jerusalem?" *Faith and Philosophy* 12/4 (October 1995), pp. 475-88.

34. Lynne Rudder Baker, "Need A Christian Be a Mind/Body Dualist?" *Faith and Philosophy* 12/4 (October 1995), pp. 498-504, 502.

35. Kevin J. Corcoran, "Persons and Bodies," *Faith and Philosophy* 15/3 (July 1998), pp. 324-40.

rected body can be the very same body as her earthly body even though there is a temporal gap in its existence. He gives reasons for rejecting dualism and an intermediate state and considers a number of texts in claiming that Scripture is on his side.[36] Though not materialists, Stephen Davis and Dean Zimmerman have offered different accounts of how materialists might explain the numerical identity of earthly and resurrected humans in spite of a gap of nonexistence between death and resurrection.[37]

Perhaps the best-known and most popular philosopher currently promoting Christian anti-dualism is Nancey Murphy. She regards the body-soul question as one of many debates within the Christian tradition that involve false dilemmas resulting from wrongly polarized philosophical starting points.[38] She advocates a more "holistic" approach, which in the case of human nature is neither substance dualism nor standard materialism but *non-reductive physicalism*. This is the view that "the person is a physical organism whose complex functioning, both in society and in relation to God, gives rise to 'higher' human capacities such as morality and spirituality."[39] She has co-edited and contributed two chapters to *Whatever Happened to the Soul?*, a collection of essays by Christian biologists, psychologists, ethicists, philosophers, and theologians, defending and articulating physicalism.[40] She has promoted it among the broader community of thoughtful Christians in the review journal, *Books and Culture*.[41] She contends that "Christians can get along quite nicely with a view of the human being as a purely physical creation — one whose capacities for con-

36. Trenton Merricks, "The Resurrection of the Body and the Life Everlasting," in *Reason for the Hope Within*, ed. Michael Murray (Grand Rapids/Cambridge, UK: Eerdmans, 1999), pp. 261-86.

37. Stephen Davis, "General Resurrection and Physicalism," in *Risen Indeed*, mentioned above with dualistic views. Dean Zimmerman, "The Compatibility of Materialism and Survival," *Faith and Philosophy* 16/2 (April 1999), pp. 194-212.

38. Nancey Murphy, *Beyond Liberalism and Fundamentalism: How Modern and Postmodern Philosophy Set the Theological Agenda* (Valley Forge, PA: Trinity International Press, 1996), esp. pp. 149-51, "Body, Mind, Soul, Spirit."

39. Nancey Murphy, "Human Nature: Historical, Scientific, and Religious Issues" in *Whatever Happened to the Soul?*, pp. 1-30, 25.

40. Warren Brown, Nancey Murphy, and H. Newton Malony, eds., *Whatever Happened to the Soul? Scientific and Theological Portraits of Human Nature* (Minneapolis: Fortress Press, 1998).

41. Nancey Murphy, "I Cerebrate Myself: Is There a Little Man Inside Your Brain?" *Books and Culture: A Christian Review* 5/1 (January-February 1999), pp. 24-26.

sciousness, social interaction, moral reasoning, *and relationship with God* arise as a result of the incredible complexity of the brain."[42] With respect to dualism and the afterlife she asserts that "In the Hebrew Bible, human life is regularly understood monistically rather than dualistically, and this unified being is a physical being." "New Testament writers recognize a variety of conceptions of the composition or makeup of the human being but do not *teach* body-soul dualism." "Original Christian hope for life after death is based on bodily resurrection, patterned after that of Jesus, not on immortality of the soul."[43] Physicalism is acceptable because it is compatible with Christian belief, she assures us, and it is superior to dualistic views in matters of philosophy and science, especially epistemology, neurophysiology, and psychology.

IV. *Body, Soul* and the Traditional Position Once Again

The monism-dualism debate among Christian thinkers continues unabated, perhaps more vigorously now than when *Body, Soul* first appeared. Having reviewed recent contributions to the dialogue, I reassert my original position, then offer a concession, and finally propose an addition to terminology.

I must reaffirm my claim that the New Testament teaches an intermediate state of fellowship with Christ for believers. None of the exegetical and theological works on this topic or the *ad hoc* efforts of non-theologians have come close to offering an alternative explanation of the evidence or refuting it. Recent discussions continue to suffer from the same deficiencies as their predecessors. One typical mistake is the assumption that the (temporary) existence of a person without a body and bodily resurrection are mutually exclusive alternatives. This is simply false. An intermediate state ought not to be confused with a Platonic notion of "the immortal soul," as amply demonstrated in *Body, Soul*. A second typical mistake of commentators and theologians is failure to take all the relevant intra- and extra-biblical data into consideration when making pronouncements about biblical texts. The Gospels cannot be read apart from the eschatology of first-century Judaism. No Pauline text can be exegeted with-

42. "I Cerebrate Myself," pp. 24-25.
43. "I Cerebrate Myself," p. 24.

out considering everything Paul had to say about being "apart from the body," the time of the resurrection, and his own education in Jewish orthodoxy and Greek thought. My reading of recent discussions has not found anything that seriously challenges the case for the intermediate state made in *Body, Soul.*

Thus I continue to believe that the intermediate state is a teaching of Scripture. I still recognize that it is not a primary doctrine, such as Jesus' resurrection and ours, which are clearly and frequently asserted by Scripture and confessed by Christians universally in the Apostles' and Nicene Creeds. But although there is less evidence and emphasis, I do not think that Scripture is silent or confused or polyvocal on the issue. The cumulative testimony of the Bible is consistent, relatively unambiguous, and sufficient to assert the intermediate state as doctrine, just as the great majority of teachers in Christian tradition have done. Since Christians ought to believe what the Bible teaches, we ought to believe that there is an intermediate state. Although we may find views of human nature incompatible with this doctrine to be attractive or advantageous for other reasons, we ought to eschew them. One must have sufficient reason for denying or completely revising what the historic Christian church has affirmed as the teaching of Scripture and proclaimed to comfort millions of people who have mourned at gravesides: Our loved ones are with the Lord until the resurrection. None of the recent biblical and theological discussions are nearly sufficient to justify the wholesale revisionism or agnosticism that some propose.

Are recent philosophical and scientific discussions sufficient? In a word, no. Although great advances have been made in understanding the functions of the brain and their correlation with various mental states, there is no conceptual need to abandon a doctrinally required dualism in favor of monism. Nancey Murphy is candid about this. After surveying the advances in brain science she admits: "it is still possible to claim that there is a substantial mind and that its operations are neatly *correlated* with brain events. . . . It follows, then, that no amount of evidence from neuroscience can *prove* a physicalist view of the mental."[44] This point, made in *Body, Soul,* still holds.[45] Christian philosophers and scientists need not adopt conceptual paradigms that implicitly contradict sound doctrine.

44. Nancey Murphy, "Nonreductive Physicalism: Philosophical Issues," *Whatever Happened to the Soul?,* p. 139.
45. See "Brain Physiology" in Chapter Ten.

But now I must make a concession of sorts. Perhaps there are physicalistic theories of human nature that are compatible with an intermediate state. In *Body, Soul* I argue for "dualism" in the sense that persons must be able by God's power to exist temporarily without their earthly organisms, which become corpses.[46] I do not claim that substance dualism is the only way to meet this condition. However, I do not seriously consider whether a materialist anthropology could meet it. I now concede this possibility. Earlier in this introduction I noted William Hasker's emergentism, the view that persons are distinct from though generated by their organisms.[47] On this account, God's supernatural power could maintain persons in conscious existence apart from their bodies until the resurrection. Also mentioned above is Kevin Corcoran's hypothesis, that at death the physical body "divides" into a corpse and a bodily-person who exists during an intermediate state. Both theories are forms of physicalism and both allow the possibility of personal existence apart from the earthly body between death and resurrection. At the same time, however, both theories are kinds of dualism as defined in *Body, Soul* since both posit a "dichotomy" at death between the organism and the subsistent person. I do not know whether these theories are philosophically tenable all things considered and whether they are consistent with other Christian doctrines. I find them to be counter-intuitive and no less conceptually problematic than dualism is alleged to be, since they are almost kinds of substance dualism in disguise. My own philosophical position continues to waffle between substance dualism and the soul-matter holism of the Thomistic tradition. But I must concede that these versions of physicalism are *prima facie* consistent with traditional eschatology. If I am correct, this is a significant development that may bear fruit in the monism-dualism debate.

Finally, let me propose an addition to terminology. *Body, Soul* promotes "holistic dualism," a term chosen to capture both the unity of human nature and the possibility of personal existence without a body. John Kok, a Christian philosopher at Dordt College, suggested to me that "dualistic holism" might be more consistent with the biblical picture, which emphasizes the unity of human nature as created and redeemed by

---

46. See especially "The Intermediate State and Dualism" in Chapter Eight.

47. Hasker's view is mentioned in Chapter Ten, footnote 27, where his emergentism is also labelled "dualistic interactionism" because person and organism are distinct and reciprocating.

God and which treats death and temporary disembodiment as an unnatural privation. Kok has a point. I concede that "dualistic holism," if not a better term, is at least as good. The position I propose is open and flexible enough to bear both labels. If "dualistic holism" seems better to those who wish to emphasize unity instead of duality, I am pleased to endorse it.

Body, Soul, and Life Everlasting remains a relevant and substantive contribution to the monism-dualism debate. It sketches the contours of a view of human nature that reflects the entirety of biblical teaching, preserves the doctrine of Christian tradition, is consistent with the best philosophy, and is open to the most recent scientific discoveries. I am grateful for the interest that has led to its republication.

Introduction

The Body-Soul Question:
Still a Vexing Problem

Why another book on the body and the soul? Isn't this a dead issue, an old-fashioned theological topic which no one cares about anymore? Isn't it one of those purely academic questions which has no bearing on anything important in life? What is the point of raising it again?

As a matter of fact the nature of the human soul is far from being an irrelevant question or dead issue. Many in the academic community have taken a clear position on the body-soul question which they continue to assert with conviction. And if what they are saying is true, then two disturbing conclusions immediately follow. First, a doctrine affirmed by most of the Christian church since its beginning is false. A second consequence is more personal and existential — what millions of Christians believe will happen to them when they die is also a delusion.

What exactly is the body-soul question and how does it bear on our personal beliefs and hopes? The central issue is whether the soul can survive and function apart from the human body. In other words, is human nature constructed in such a way that at death it can "come apart," the conscious personal part continuing to exist while the organism disintegrates? Traditional doctrine and the beliefs of millions of Christians have answered these questions positively. God does hold the human self, person, soul, or spirit in existence between death and the final resurrection. But if this is so, then the person or soul cannot be the same as a living active human body or necessarily tied to such a body. There must be enough of an ontological difference between the person or soul and the body that they are not only distinct from each other, but also separable at

1

death. Philosophers have typically labelled this view of the human constitution "anthropological dualism." Human beings are an ontic duality of body and soul.

An intellectual and personal crisis for Christians who affirm the traditional view of the afterlife has been generated by the massive assault on anthropological dualism by modern scholars. Philosophers have attacked traditional arguments that the soul is an immortal substance. They have proposed alternative theories of human nature according to which the soul is really an aspect of the body or essentially correlated with the body. In neither case could the soul survive the death of the body. Scientists have undermined belief in the soul's separability by uncovering numerous ways in which consciousness is dependent on and influenced by the brain. In addition, computerized robots which read, think, speak, and answer questions seem to suggest that the existence of a spiritual substance is wholly unnecessary for such higher mental functions to be carried out. The word "soul" may still refer to such capacities, but human souls are then the mental capabilities of the computer-like human brain, not separable entities. Neither philosophy nor science has strengthened the case for traditional Christian anthropology or personal eschatology — beliefs about what happens to individuals after death. Quite the opposite.

To confuse matters even more, the attack on dualism has not been launched by modern atheists and unbelievers alone. Some antidualist philosophers and scientists are sincere Christians. Furthermore, for at least a century developments in Christian theology and biblical scholarship themselves have largely been hostile to traditional anthropology. Biblical scholars have argued that ancient Hebrew and even New Testament writers did not operate with a dualistic view of human nature, but with a monistic or holistic one. Thus scholars cast serious doubt on whether Scripture teaches the existence of souls apart from bodies after death. Historians of theology supported these contentions by claiming that both dualistic anthropology and belief in disembodied souls are tenets of Plato's philosophy which were brought into Christian theology by the church fathers after the completion of the New Testament. This explained why these beliefs became so central in Christian thinking even though they are not found in the Bible itself. These conclusions motivated liberal and even some conservative Christians alike to reject traditional anthropology. Liberals rejected it as old-fashioned and no longer intellectually tenable. And some conservative Protestants argued that since we ought to follow Scripture alone and not human traditions, if anthropological dualism is a human tradition not based in Scripture, we ought to reform our confessions and purge them of such accretions of the Greek mind. The body-soul distinction has come under attack from many different directions.

Abandonment of traditional dualistic anthropology is not without its costs, however. The most obvious is that the beliefs virtually all ordinary Christians have about the afterlife must also be jettisoned. If souls are not the sort of thing which can be broken loose from bodies, then we do not actually exist between death and resurrection, either with Christ or somewhere else, either consciously or unconsciously. That conclusion will cause many Christians some level of existential anxiety. A more general cost is the loss of another plank in the platform of traditional Christian belief, pried loose and tossed into the shredder of modern scholarship. Not without reason, ordinary Christians are wary of the modern academic enterprise. The nature and status of Scripture, the person and work of Christ, and most other historic Christian beliefs have been undermined by modern scholars. The academic assault on dualism only increases the tension and suspicion.

This tension is felt by educated Christians as well and is handled in various ways. Some pastors, theologians, and scientists openly assert their modern anthropological conclusions and are prepared to live with the consequences. If their assertions bring confusion or anxiety to their students and parishioners, or evoke a hostile reaction from them, so be it. This is considered a necessary part of education and growth in the church.

I am personally acquainted with others who embrace the modern view but who choose not to reveal that fact. I once visited a dying person with an elder who did not believe the traditional account of the afterlife. When I asked what he intended to say, he responded that we should simply tell the dying woman what she had always believed. There was no point in upsetting her on her deathbed with the truth. It would make no difference anyway. There are other scholars and religious professionals who handle the tension between traditional and modern anthropology as this elder did.

Still other reflective Christians feel the tension within themselves. They are inclined to accept the standard teachings of the church but also find the arguments against dualism to be persuasive. They may understand the Bible to suggest a temporarily disembodied afterlife but be convinced that the findings of science strongly support the brain-bound character of conscious existence. They find themselves in a real dilemma. In dealing

3

with it they might continue to affirm both positions and suffer from the perpetual guilt of intellectual bad faith. Or they might resort to some sort of two-levels-of-truth theory to resolve the dilemma. And a few might even exult in the discovery of yet another paradox between the truths of revelation and the testimonies of reason. But all members of this group are aware of the apparent incompatibility between traditional eschatology and antidualistic anthropology.

Finally, there are those who do not seem to sense the tension. I have heard a number of preachers and professors who in the very same sermons and lectures both denounce the body-soul distinction as an unbiblical Greek idea and nevertheless affirm that believers fellowship with the Lord between physical death and the final resurrection. They seem blissfully unaware that they are deploying contradictory assertions. Very often their parishioners and students are aware of this problem, however, and are confused if not upset by it. This, too, I know from personal experience. Unless this topic wholly transcends logic — in which case we can say nothing about it at all — it is not possible both to affirm and deny that persons can exist apart from bodies.

Far from being a dead or irrelevant issue, the body-soul question is alive and troubling for many Christians today. There is a pervasive sense of tension between what the church has taught and what numerous educated Christians think they ought to believe. My own experience of this conflict has motivated me to an in-depth study of the matter, the results of which are set forth in this book. I have become convinced that the dilemma is a false one. There is a way of making the body-soul distinction which is faithful to Scripture, upholds the traditional teaching of the church about the afterlife, and is perfectly consistent with the "assured results" of contemporary science and philosophy. Making this case is the purpose of this study.

Chapter One presents the outlines of traditional Christian anthropology and identifies the various sorts of objections which have been lodged against it. Thus the positions in the debate are set forth and we can proceed to evaluate them and to search for the truth of the matter.

The next six chapters examine the biblical material itself. The basic issue in the debate is the nature of biblical anthropology. Does Scripture portray the human constitution dualistically, as the tradition has claimed? Or is it really monistic or holistic, as modern scholars are urging? This is at least an interesting academic question. For Christians who believe that

Scripture ought to inform our thinking and living at the basic level, it is more than an academic question. The answer, if we can arrive at one, is normative for our own beliefs about life after death and for our view of human nature during this life — both in academic and practical pursuits.

Chapters Two and Three concentrate on the Old Testament, the former on its holistic emphasis and the latter on the evidence adduced for dualism. Chapter Four examines the anthropology of Jewish eschatology between the Testaments, for this is crucial in understanding the continuity as well as the differences between the Old and New Testaments. Chapters Five through Seven focus on the anthropology and eschatology of the New Testament. Chapter Five sets forth the issues involved in evaluating the debate among exegetes of the New Testament. Chapters Six and Seven analyze the key texts in the non-Pauline and Pauline writings. By this point a coherent biblical picture has emerged.

The last three chapters elaborate and defend the results of this study of Scripture. Chapter Eight uses philosophical categories to clarify and examine some anthropological implications of biblical eschatology. Chapter Nine answers some of the practical and theological objections often raised against my understanding of the biblical material. And Chapter Ten examines my conclusions about biblical anthropology in the light of contemporary science and philosophy. By that point I hope to have convinced the reader that this is a view of the human constitution which flows out of Scripture, preserves the heart of the church's historic doctrines, and can provide a framework for respectable participation in the modern intellectual world.

The book surveys a great deal of material gleaned from a number of different disciplines. I have attempted to organize and present it in a way which is both popularly accessible and academically sound. Speaking of academics, my own graduate training is in philosophy, with a major focus in anthropology. I have also benefited from a sound theological seminary education, including exegetical work in the biblical languages. I hope that my arguments will stand up to the scrutiny of readers who are experts in the fields in which I have dabbled and that they will find my conclusions suggestive. Most of all, however, I hope that this book is helpful to nonexperts, to interested laypeople, college and seminary students, and pastors and teachers who are curious about the body-soul debate or troubled by modern approaches to it. For I am convinced that a clearheaded analysis of the topic, proceeding from the belief that the Bible is the abidingly informative and supremely normative word of God, can be of significant intellectual and pastoral value to the general Christian community. And that seems to me to be sufficient justification for yet another book on the body and the soul.

Chapter One

Traditional Christian Anthropology and Its Modern Critics

I. Early Christian Views of the Afterlife

From earliest times Christians have affirmed continuing personal existence after biological death.[1] Members of the early church believed that when the body dies, persons do not completely cease to exist, even temporarily. Rather, they survive in some form or other to enjoy the blessing of God or to suffer his judgment.

The particular details attributed to the afterlife varied somewhat according to time and place. Some early Christians assumed that souls are immediately transported to their final destinations, either hell or the heavenly kingdom of God. However, most believed that there is some kind of interim location and period of waiting between death and the final resurrection, the return of Jesus, and the final kingdom of God.[2] Gradually more ideas about this "intermediate state" were developed. It was not thought to be located in heaven, but Hades, the realm of the dead. In Hades there are different areas, some for the blessed, others for the damned. Gradually the divisions of Hades were given more detailed descriptions. Purgatory, an idea already

---

1. Louis Berkhof, *The History of Christian Doctrines* (Grand Rapids: Eerdmans, 1937; reprint, Baker, 1975), pp. 259-261; J. N. D. Kelly, *Early Christian Doctrines*, rev. ed. (New York: Harper and Row, 1960, 1978), pp. 459-489; Harry Wolfson, "Immortality and Resurrection in the Philosophy of the Church Fathers," in K. Stendahl, ed., *Immortality and Resurrection* (New York: Macmillan, 1965), pp. 54-96.

2. Justin Martyr was among the first to defend an intermediate state and reject an immediate assumption to heaven. Cf. Berkhof, p. 259.

found in Augustine, was supposed to be an area in which those who were to enter heaven were cleansed of their remaining sins through suffering. *Limbus patrum* was said to be the place where the Old Testament saints awaited redemption through Christ. *Limbus infantium* was later postulated as a permanent dwelling, neither blessed nor cursed, for children who had not been baptized. By the high middle ages the picture was well developed indeed, as can be seen from Dante's *Inferno*. Not all Christians shared these ideas about the intermediate state which emerged during the first centuries of the faith. But all seem to have taken it for granted that persons continue to exist after physical death.

We also discover a variety of beliefs about the resurrection, a doctrine virtually all Christians affirmed.[3] Some, like Origen, held a rather spiritualistic view, asserting that the resurrection body does not consist of matter or flesh, but of a spiritual substance suited to the presence of God. Jerome, on the other hand, spoke for many in claiming that the resurrection body would be literally identical with the earthly body, including the very same hair and teeth. Most were like Augustine, however, allowing for modifications and perfections of the earthly body while still insisting that what will be raised is the same body as the one which died.

In spite of this diversity of opinion on specific issues, there was consensus on basic features of the resurrection. Virtually all Christian writers, even Origen, were adamant about defending the intrinsic goodness of the body as created by God against the anticorporeal doctrines of Gnosticism. In addition, very early the belief that the resurrection will be a general future event correlated with the return of Christ became the common Christian expectation. And virtually all early Christians seem to have agreed that persons both survive physical death and are resurrected to some form of bodily existence.

Implicit in this belief that persons can survive organic decease is the idea that human beings are so constituted that they can "come apart" at death. When the body dies the person retains her existence and most likely some kind of consciousness as well. A separation or rending of that which was so intimately joined in life occurs at death. The person or self or soul or spirit survives the death of the body. Early Christians, in other words, assumed that human nature is such that personal existence is not necessarily tied to the organism of earthly life.

3. Berkhof, pp. 265-266; Kelly, pp. 469-479; Wolfson, pp. 63-73.

But even at this point there are interesting differences of opinion. While all agreed that persons can come apart, there was no consensus on the number of ontological ingredients or dimensions in terms of which God created humankind. Some held that humans consist of three parts — body, soul, and spirit. They are called "trichotomists," since they divide human nature into three components. Spirit is the essential human self which relates to God. Soul is that dimension of persons which mediates and conjoins the spirit with the material body. The trichotomistic view was more popular among the Greek and Alexandrian church fathers who were influenced by Plato, among them Clement of Alexandria, Origen, and Gregory of Nyssa.[4]

It is the other option, "dichotomy," which emerged as the more dominant and eventually orthodox view. It was popular from the beginning among the Latin fathers and given lasting status by Augustine. It is the view that humans consist of two dimensions or components, body and soul/spirit. Dichotomists generally take "soul" and "spirit" as synonyms. Death cuts body and soul apart. Hence the term "dichotomy." Since this view entails that human beings consist of two metaphysically different and separable components, philosophers label it "dualism." This became the standard doctrine in Western theology and philosophy for more than a thousand years.

Although dualism triumphed over trichotomist views, and although not all Christian teachers agreed on the details of the intermediate state or the definition of the resurrection, it is important to see that all were working with a common anthropological assumption: human existence can be broken up by death and conscious persons nonetheless survive. In fact apologists commonly opposed those like the Epicureans who argued against the existence of separated souls.[5] The idea that persons survive apart from their bodies is an essential element of early Christian teaching about the last things.

---

4. Louis Berkhof, *Systematic Theology* (Grand Rapids: Eerdmans, 1941, 1976), pp. 191-192.

5. Cf. Wolfson, pp. 72-84. "The conception of the soul common to all the Fathers is essentially Platonic. The main characteristic of that Platonic conception of the soul is its separability from the body" (p. 79). He then goes on to specify the differences between dichotomist and trichotomist Platonists.

II. Dualistic Anthropologies

A. Augustine

The fact that Augustine had been a Platonist before his conversion is evident in his Christian doctrine of human nature. He criticizes Platonism for holding that souls are not created but are by nature self-sufficient and have existed eternally. And he rejects the opinion that the body is intrinsically antithetical to the good. These Platonic doctrines directly contradict the teachings of Scripture.

Given these qualifications, however, Augustine's anthropology is recognizably Platonistic. For one thing, he identifies the essential self with the soul rather than the body-soul composite and conceives of the soul as operating the body. Armand Maurer puts this succinctly:

> He often uses expressions like the following: "I, that is, my soul." And he defines man, with Plato and Plotinus, as "a rational soul, using a mortal and earthly body." Again, he calls the soul "a certain substance, sharing in reason and suited to the task of ruling the body." In short, the true man is the soul, and the body is its instrument.[6]

Nevertheless Augustine insists on the unity of human nature. Some of his later works emphasize that man is not just a soul, but a soul-body unity.[7] Further, he views the soul as permeating the body, not merely contacting it at a single point such as the heart or brain: "But the soul is present as a whole not only in the entire mass of a body, but also in every least part of the body at the same time."[8]

Nevertheless the soul is superior to the body because it alone bears the image and knowledge of God. The body tends to divert the soul from spiritual things and to tempt it with sinful desires. And the soul is superior because it alone is immortal. Its immortality is conferred by God, to be sure.

---

6. *Medieval Philosophy* (New York: Random House, 1964), p. 8. The first two quotations are from *On the Doctrines of the Church*, I,27 and 52. The last is from *On the Greatness of the Soul*, XIII,22.

7. Cf. Augustine, *The City of God*, XIX,3, where he commends Varro for "regarding man as neither the soul alone nor the body alone but the combination of body and soul" and for valuing both body and soul as intrinsically good.

8. Augustine, *On the Immortality of the Soul*, XVI,25.

But that is because God has created it as a simple spiritual substance. Given this qualification, Augustine considers the Platonic argument that the soul is by nature immortal to be correct after all. For simple substances do not decompose. The soul survives bodily death. The body is created from matter and thus tends toward degeneration unless prevented by God. The resurrection body, however, will live forever.

Augustine's anthropology is a two-substance dualism. Human beings are composed of spirit and matter intimately conjoined so that the soul permeates and animates the entire body. Whereas the body depends for its existence and activity upon the soul, the reverse is not true. Augustine's view of the human constitution dominated Christian thought in the West unchallenged until the thirteenth century, as did his views on many theological topics.

B. *Thomas Aquinas*

While some commentators present Thomas Aquinas as a Christian Aristotelian who asserted himself against Augustinian Platonism, that picture is too simple, especially as it pertains to his anthropology. It is more accurate to say that he cleverly combined important features of the Aristotelian body-soul relation with a basically Augustinian dualistic framework. Thomas uses Aristotle to emphasize the unity of human nature and to account for the intimate correlativity of soul and body on every level of existence. But he remains with Augustine in affirming that the soul is a distinct substance which can survive biological death.

In Book I, Question 75 of *Summa Theologica*, Thomas proceeds "to treat of man, who is composed of a spiritual and of a corporeal substance." Although his view of the material-spiritual composite differs somewhat, Thomas' concept of the soul is clearly in line with Augustine. With Augustine he holds that "the soul of man is a principle both incorporeal and subsistent." It is a substance because it has its own proper operation for which it does not need the body — the complex, multidimensional operation of the intellect.[9] The body is not needed to think, wish, will, hope, or love. But it is needed for awareness of the earthly objects of these operations, which are mediated through the bodily senses. One cannot think

---

9. Thomas Aquinas, *Summa Theologica*, I,75,3.

about trees without having seen trees, and seeing requires body and brain. The soul is also incorruptible according to the nature with which God endowed it at creation.[10] Consequently, "the human soul retains its own being after the dissolution of the body."[11] All of this is perfectly Augustinian.

Thomas even considers himself faithful to the Doctor of the Church in emphasizing the unity of human nature. He objects to Plato's notion that a human person is a soul using a body. Instead he insists that humans by nature are soul, flesh, and bones in intimate unity. It is that intimate unity which walks, sees, and — at least during this life — thinks. Having a body is part of the nature or essence of a human being as a rational animal. The soul is only part of that nature. Therefore a disembodied soul is not a complete person.[12] The Platonic preference for disembodiment is clearly contradicted by the Christian account of humans as essentially bodily creatures of God.

It is in accounting for the unity of human nature that Thomas relies on Aristotle. Aristotle's metaphysics is somewhat different from Plato's. Instead of positing matter and spirit as two substances, he held that there are two metaphysical principles, form and matter, which combine to constitute single substances — the actual things which exist, such as rocks, trees, and humans. Human beings are thus single entities constituted by form and matter, neither of which can exist on its own. Matter is that of which we are made — earth, air, fire, and water. Form or soul is the principle which organizes the matter into a human being with typically human structure, capacities, and purposes. Form is what constitutes matter as the sort of thing an entity is — a flower or a person. For it is the essence or nature as well as the principle of actuality. Important to notice here is the fact that the soul actualizes all human functions and capacities — biological, psychological, rational, volitional, and cultural. The soul is not the seat of some capacities, the body of others. The form-matter unity is the subject of all human operations. So the human form or soul is an organic-sentient-rational soul. There are not two or three souls in humankind or just one soul which uses a body. Over against these variations of Platonism, Thomas sides with Aristotle in emphasizing the substantial unity of human nature and in providing a more holistic or integrated account of

10. *Summa Theologica*, I,75,6.
11. *Summa Theologica*, I,76,1.
12. *Summa Theologica*, I,75,5.

12

human functioning. It is the psychophysical unit as such that digests food, senses the world, thinks about itself, and loves God.[13]

A completely consistent Aristotelianism is untenable for Christians, however. For Aristotle's soul is only the form of the body and not a substance as such. Therefore it cannot survive death as an individual entity. At most its rational capacity might be reassimilated into the eternal universal reason like a drop of water into the ocean. As we have seen, at this point Thomas abandoned Aristotle and held that the soul is both the form of the body and an intellectual substance in its own right. It can exist separate from the body, but it is then deficient in two ways. Metaphysically it is only potentially, not actually the form of the body. And functionally it cannot be conscious in any way that would require bodily organs. Whether Thomas is successful in his synthesis of Augustine and Aristotle is still a matter of debate.

C. John Calvin

The tradition of Augustinian Platonism was maintained by the Protestant Reformation. According to Calvin, for example, of the ancient philosophers "hardly one, except Plato, has rightly affirmed [the soul's] immortal substance."[14] But Calvin appropriates considerably more than the soul's immortality from Christian Platonism:

> Indeed, from Scripture we have already taught that the soul is an incorporeal substance; now we must add that, although properly it is not spatially limited, still, set in the body, it dwells there as in a house; not only that it may animate all its parts and render its organs fit and useful for their actions, but also that it may hold the first place in ruling man's life, not alone with respect to the duties of his earthly life, but at the same time to arouse him to honor God.[15]

Here in quick succession are all the markings of the Augustinian conception of the soul and its relation to the body.

---

13. *Summa Theologica*, I,76, "The Unity of Soul and Body."

14. John Calvin, *Institutes of the Christian Religion*, trans. F. L. Battles (Philadelphia: Westminster, 1960), I,xv,6, p. 192.

15. Calvin, I,xv,6, p. 192.

Calvin does not consider himself a philosopher. He adopts this position because he believes it is embedded in Scripture, both in the biblical language of body and soul and in its teaching about the afterlife. But he is also willing to use philosophical arguments in defense of the metaphysical body-soul distinction and the soul's immortality.[16]

Calvin's doctrine of personal eschatology is that immediately after death the souls of believers enjoy rest and fellowship with Christ until their resurrection at his second coming. Then they enter God's new creation. That Calvin not only defended the intermediate state but conscious fellowship with Christ is evident in his tract *Psychopannychia,* where he attacks the idea of "soul-sleep."

Calvin's doctrine of the afterlife not only remained a guidepost for subsequent Reformed theology and philosophy. It also shaped the beliefs of millions of faithful Christians. Consider, for example, Question and Answer 57 from the Calvinist *Heidelberg Catechism:* "How does 'the resurrection of the body' comfort you? Not only will my soul be taken immediately after this life to Christ its head, but even my flesh, raised by the power of Christ, will be reunited with my soul and made like Christ's glorious body."[17] What this expresses is not exclusively Calvinistic, however. It is still taken as literally true by millions of Christians in various ecclesiastical traditions.

D. René Descartes

Even Descartes, the father of modern anthropological dualism, considered himself to be a Christian philosopher in the Augustinian line. Although using seventeenth-century views of matter and physiology, he held the Augustinian doctrine that body and soul are each constituted from a different kind of substance. The body is matter, that is, extended substance. The soul is wholly incorporeal, consisting of conscious or thinking substance. It is the essential self or ego.

For Descartes, too, we find the possibility of the soul's survival of death a reason for his articulation of a dualistic anthropology: "it is certain

16. Calvin, I,xv,2, pp. 184-186.
17. *The Heidelberg Catechism, A New Translation* (Grand Rapids: Christian Reformed Board of Publications, 1975).

that I am truly distinct from my body, and can exist without it."[18] In fact, he grounded his belief in the afterlife not on philosophical reason, but solely on revelation. Philosophy cannot prove that the soul is inherently immortal and thus apart from divine power it might cease to exist when the body dies. But "since [God] has revealed to us that this will not happen, there should not be even the slightest doubt remaining."[19]

During this life body and soul interact. The soul causes the body to move, and the body delivers sensations of itself and the external world to the soul. The transactions occur in the pineal gland, where "animal spirits" rarify and condense, thereby bearing information back and forth from soul to body.[20] Thus Descartes's anthropology is called "dualistic interactionism."

Although the contact of soul and body seems to be concentrated at a single point, Descartes nevertheless maintained that they constitute a unity: "I am not lodged in my body merely as a pilot in a ship, but so intimately conjoined, and as it were intermingled with it, that with it I form a unitary whole."[21] For him the fact of metaphysical dualism does not conflict with the phenomenological unity of existence.

The standard themes of Augustinian anthropology — substantial dualism, temporal unity, and divinely conferred immortality of the soul after death — are all present in Descartes's dualistic interactionism. Although its details have been modified, it has remained a paradigm for dualistic anthropology into the twentieth century.

E. Conclusion

Since the beginning Christians have embraced anthropological dualism (or trichotomy) because they believed that persons survive bodily death. The Christian defense of the body-soul distinction has in large part been motivated by the doctrine of the afterlife. Both this anthropology and personal eschatology have been considered to be biblical teaching. Thus these doctrines have been confessed by the faithful, insisted upon by church

18. Descartes, *Meditations*, VI.
19. Descartes, *Objections and Replies to the Meditations*, II,7.
20. Descartes, *The Passions of the Soul*, XXXI, XXXII, XXXIV.
21. Descartes, *Meditations*, VI.

councils, and defended by Christian philosophers and theologians right on into the twentieth century.

This is not to say that consensus has ever been achieved on the details. Roman Catholics and Protestants have disagreed about Purgatory in the intermediate state. Not all have understood the resurrection body in the same way. And philosophers have debated the definitions of body, soul, and their relation. In particular, the unity of human nature is a topic on which thinkers in the Aristotelian-Thomist tradition have criticized Christian Platonists as deficient. For Thomists the unity is essential, whereas it appears accidental for Augustinians and Cartesians. Church councils, too, have objected to some anthropologies which they judged as denying the unity of human nature. On the key issue of the survivability of the individual soul after death, however, there has been virtual consensus.[22] It has been a mark of orthodoxy.

III. Nondualistic Philosophical Anthropologies

A. Thomas Hobbes and Materialism

As the authority of church and traditional theology waned after the Reformation, alternative approaches to philosophical anthropology were introduced. One dominant modern challenge to dualism is materialism, the view that human beings, both body and soul, consist solely of matter and its functions. Its first modern spokesman was Thomas Hobbes, a contemporary of Descartes.

Hobbes held that all creatures consist of only one substance — what Descartes called "extended substance" or matter. Things, including human beings, are bodies. The notion of an incorporeal substance is incoherent, according to Hobbes. Persons are not some combination of matter and spirit, but are wholly corporeal beings.[23]

But what then is consciousness and how does it arise? Thoughts and sensations are really the internal effects of external stimuli operating upon

22. I recognize that there has not been absolute consensus on this issue. Some Anabaptists have affirmed "soul-sleep," for example. Cf. also Norman Burns, *Christian Mortalism from Tyndale to Milton* (Boston: Harvard University Press, 1972), for an account of English Christians who have not affirmed an intermediate existence of the soul.

23. Thomas Hobbes, *Leviathan*, XXXIV.

the body's sense organs and from them on the brain and heart. Psychological states and events are produced in us by the motion of the body's complex machinery.[24] Consciousness is not the essential feature of an immaterial substance, but the result of the conjunction of all these effects of the body's internal motions.

But if the soul is a set of bodily effects and not a substance, what happens when death occurs? It is clear that a disembodied soul cannot exist; thus Hobbes considers the intermediate state to be nonsense.[25] His view of the afterlife is that "the souls of the faithful, are not of their own nature, but by God's grace, to remain in their bodies from the resurrection to all eternity."[26] In other words, people do not exist after physical death. But in raising up their bodies at the resurrection, God will be raising their souls as well. The time between death and resurrection is one of nonexistence.

Hobbes even considers his position to be based in Scripture. He argues that the biblical words for "soul" and "spirit" do not suggest that they refer to incorporeal substances, but to living, bodily creatures: "The soul in Scripture signifieth always either the life or the living creature; and *the body and soul* jointly, the body alive." He argues that animals, too, are called "souls" in Scripture, but they do not survive death.[27] So Hobbes challenges the dualistic exegesis of traditional Christian orthodoxy, which he calls "pernicious Aristotelian nonsense."

Hobbes's positions on anthropology are not very extensively or clearly elaborated. But his strategies are prototypes for a great deal of subsequent thinking both in exegesis and in philosophy of mind. His attack on the traditional dualistic reading of Scripture prefigures contemporary biblical scholarship, which still polemicizes against the misunderstandings of the biblical view of humanity that Greek assumptions have generated.

The descendants of his materialistic account of human nature and the human spirit are still alive and numerous, if not well, in the twentieth century. Behaviorism defines thoughts and intentions as the dispositions of bodily beings to react to external circumstances in particular ways. The mind-brain identity theory holds that thoughts and sensations are just events in the brain. Epiphenomenalism believes that thoughts and sensa-

24. *Leviathan*, I.
25. *Leviathan*, XLVI.
26. *Leviathan*, XXXVIII, XLII.
27. *Leviathan*, XLII.

tions are directly generated by the brain. For all these schools of thought the mind and soul are no more than the combination of these brain-caused states. These theories are more sophisticated versions of the same basic idea that we find in Hobbes. All forms of materialism are head-on competitors of dualism and the belief that persons can exist apart from their bodies.[28]

B. Baruch Spinoza and Dual-Aspect Monism

Materialism is not the only contemporary challenge to dualism, nor was it the only alternative to Descartes in the seventeenth century. The Dutch Jewish philosopher Baruch Spinoza postulated another possibility — what has come to be called "dual-aspect monism."

His ontology is monistic because reality as a whole is defined as one absolute substance. But this single whole can be considered two ways, thus displaying two aspects or modes of existence. Viewed one way reality is God; viewed another, it is Nature.[29] That single substance, therefore, is neither exclusively spirit nor matter but possesses the properties of both, each available to human apprehension from a different standpoint.

Human beings are but manifestations of that absolute substance. As such they are neither purely spiritual nor material, nor a combination of two substances. Humans are single finite entities which bear both physical and mental characteristics. Soul and body are neither entities nor distinct substances but aspects of a deeper unity. They are modes of being.[30] At bottom they are really the same thing. As Spinoza himself puts it: "the mind and the body are one and the same thing, conceived at one time under the attribute of thought, and at another under that of extension."[31] Whereas Descartes took thought and extension to be so different that they must be properties of distinct substances, Spinoza considers them properties of a single, basic substance. Body and mind are not distinct things. They are aspects of something else more basic. To speak of body and soul,

28. For a general account of the several contemporary forms of materialism see Keith Campbell, *Body and Mind*, 2nd ed. (Notre Dame, IN: Notre Dame University Press, 1986), or Jerome Shaffer, *Philosophy of Mind* (Englewood Cliffs, NJ: Prentice-Hall, 1968).

29. Spinoza, *Ethics*, I, Prop. XXIX; *God, Man, and His Well-Being*, I, Chs. 8 and 9.

30. *God, Man, and His Well-Being*, II, Appendix II.

31. *Ethics*, III, Prop. II, Note.

then, is to refer to abstractions from a whole, not to refer to separable realities. Hence the label "dual-aspect monism."

But if the soul and the body are the same thing, the soul obviously cannot survive physical death. The mind of the individual person operates only as long as it is one with a particular body. But since the mind of God contains the idea of each individual entity, and because the individual soul can know and love the eternal intelligible contents of the mind of God, there is truth in the belief that the soul is immortal. It becomes one with the eternal mind of God, that is, with the absolute single substance itself, and thus "lives forever."[32] Although the vocabulary might be the same, this is hardly the orthodox view that self-conscious individual persons continue to exist after organic death.

Spinoza is the modern parent of the second philosophical challenge to Cartesian body-soul dualism. He was upheld as a hero by such notable thinkers as Hegel and Schelling for his system as a whole. But we can distinguish his solution to the body-soul question — dual-aspect monism — from his metaphysical pantheism. This general approach to anthropology can be found in a variety of contemporary thinkers as a popular antidualist alternative to materialism. The idea that body and soul or the physical and the mental-spiritual-personal are just different aspects of a single entity or whole is endorsed by most followers of the existential-phenomenological approach to anthropology which has been popular in Europe.[33] It is the strategy of P. F. Strawson's influential theory that persons are single entities with both physical and mental properties.[34] In different ways it is evident in the process philosophies of A. N. Whitehead and Teilhard de Chardin. And it is behind a great deal of the "perspectivalism" advocated by psychologists and biologists who wish to assure us that they are not attempting to reduce human nature to that aspect which their science studies. Humans are single wholes, they say, but within us there are different "levels" or functional aspects. The various sciences focus on different functional aspects of the whole person, who is actually a psychophysical unity. As a guard against scientific reductionism this is helpful. But as an approach to the ontology of human nature it is a

32. *Ethics*, V, Props. XXX-XLII.

33. Cf. Herbert Spiegelberg, *Phenomenology in Psychology and Psychiatry* (Evanston, IL: Northwestern University Press, 1972), and C. A. Van Peursen, *Body, Soul, Spirit* (London: Oxford, 1966).

34. P. F. Strawson, *Individuals* (London: Methuen, 1959), Ch. 3; cf. Shaffer, pp. 52-57.

form of dual- or multiple-aspect monism whose prototype was devised by Spinoza.[35]

C. Conclusion

Hobbes and Spinoza are the patriarchs of the two major alternatives in contemporary philosophy to the substantial dualism of Christian anthropology.[36] Both are forms of monism, the theory that humans consist of one substance. Hobbes advocates materialistic monism, whereas Spinoza presents a "neutral" monism in that his substance is more basic than matter or spirit. With great sophistication and refinement their approaches to the body-soul question are still being elaborated and defended at present. Many of the best-known philosophers between then and now can be located in one general category or the other, although we cannot trace this history here.

These alternatives have challenged traditional Christian anthropology

35. This is the strategy of Donald MacKay, a well-known scientist and Christian. Cf. his *Brains, Machines, and Persons* (Grand Rapids: Eerdmans, 1980), Ch. 1. Cf. also David Myers, *The Human Puzzle* (San Francisco: Harper and Row, 1978), pp. 67-69, for a fine statement of the case that science is not reductionistic (unfortunately it is located in his section on the ontology of the body-mind problem).

36. Spiritual or idealistic monism, sometimes called panpsychism, is an alternative which I have chosen not to introduce at this point. It is the view that humans consist of just one sort of metaphysical element — soul, mind, or spirit — and that bodies are manifestations of that element. In different ways Berkeley, Hegel, and perhaps Husserl represent this view. Whitehead is both a panpsychist and a dual-aspect monist. It seems to be expressed by the Old Testament scholar Johannes Pedersen when he states that "soul and body are so intimately united that a distinction cannot be made between them. They are more than 'united': the body is the soul in its outward form." *Israel, Its Life and Culture* (London: Oxford, 1926), Vol. I, p. 171. I have chosen not to introduce it because, although it is an alternative to substantial dualism, at least some of its adherents have recognized the possibility of disembodied existence after death. If body is just a manifestation of soul, perhaps soul can exist without it. Though not substantial dualism, this is nevertheless an anthropological dualism in that the soul is an entity separable from the body. An example of this position will be presented in the last chapter. Those who deny that the individual human soul and body are separable, as Hegel probably did, see them as necessarily correlative aspects of a deeper unity and thus end up taking Spinoza's position. Because idealistic monists fall in line either with dualists or dual-aspect monists on the separability of the soul, I am not treating them as offering a distinct kind of anthropology here.

in at least two ways. First, they have exposed a number of problems in the arguments for the immortality of the soul used by major Christian thinkers. Some Christian dualists, including Descartes, were already aware of weaknesses on this flank, however. More seriously, the alternatives challenged the arguments on which the substantiality of the soul was based. They claimed that it is not necessary to suppose that the soul, mind, or spirit is a distinct substance in order to recognize that it can know God, grasp eternal truths, reason, and do other sorts of things which the animals cannot. This sort of attack at least relativized the credibility of dualism.

For Christians who took philosophy seriously and who believed that reason and revelation ought to assert the same truths, traditional anthropological dualism became a position to examine critically rather than to defend as dogma. And if the problematic status of dualism raised further questions about traditional views of the afterlife, those, too, required re-examination. But philosophy was not the only source of trouble for the orthodox doctrine of humanity.

IV. The Scientific Challenge to Dualism

Although philosophers had long attempted to understand the causal connections between the body and soul, not a great deal was known about this topic before the development of brain physiology, experimental psychology, and scientific psychiatry in the nineteenth century.[37]

Brain physiologists and psychiatrists noticed the direct causal influence of cerebral functioning on states of consciousness. Mental capacities such as thought, memory, understanding, and even the use of the senses were found to be correlated with specific areas of the brain. Damage to these areas causes loss or malfunction of a person's mental capacities. Furthermore, the introduction of electrical impulses and chemical compounds into the brain has marked influences on mental and emotional states. And a number of mental illnesses which in previous centuries had been traced to such causes as moonbeams and evil spirits were discovered

37. For excellent overviews of these developments see Franz Alexander and Sheldon Selesnick, *The History of Psychiatry* (New York: Harper and Row, 1966), Ch. 10; and Gardner Murphy, *Historical Introduction to Modern Psychology* (New York: Harcourt, Brace, 1949), Part II.

BODY, SOUL, AND LIFE EVERLASTING

to result from malfunction or injury of the brain. All of this scientific evidence seemed to point in one direction. Consciousness, mental capacities, and personality characteristics are rooted in the brain and the organism, not in some immaterial substance or unobservable entity called the soul or mind.

On another front, the rapid acceptance of the general theory of evolution after Darwin undermined belief that the soul is a distinct substance. For if more complex forms of life developed from less complex ones, then the mentality of higher primates and humans gradually emerged from organisms which were virtually unconscious or mindless. There was no longer a need to postulate a spirit or immaterial substance to account for the psychological and intellectual capacities of human beings. At every level of evolution, mental capacities are a function of the operations of the neuro-cerebral system. Simple nervous systems operate organisms without the medium of consciousness. Complex brains generate and operate in part through consciousness. The notion of a separate spiritual substance seemed wholly gratuitous in the evolutionary scheme of things.

Similar positions were emerging in experimental psychology. Whereas classical psychology had always claimed the soul and its faculties as its proper object of study, pioneers of the new scientific psychology such as William James and Wilhelm Wundt preferred to speak of consciousness and its functions. Psychologists no longer took themselves to be dealing with the operations of a distinct entity, but a dimension of the organism closely tied to the brain. When John Watson began to articulate his behavioristic approach to psychology, there was a psychologist who actually denied the significance of consciousness altogether. Watson held that thoughts are identical with internal physiological speech movements. Humans are organisms whose behavior is determined wholly by habituated responses to external stimuli, not by thoughts, desires, commitments, and values and certainly not by mental states housed in some mysterious incorporeal substance. Even appeal to states of consciousness is unnecessary in explaining human behavior. The development of modern psychology, like the other human sciences, seemed to undermine traditional dualistic anthropology completely.

Thus the modern scientific study of human nature challenged dualism in two ways. First, it uncovered a great deal of evidence that what takes place in the mind is directly dependent on what takes place in the brain. The earlier belief that mental events are caused by faculties and powers of the soul was widely discredited. Secondly, this evidence removed much of the justification for positing the existence of the soul itself. If all the events in the soul are caused by events in the brain, why hold that there is a distinct entity such as the soul in the first place? Mind itself, as well as individual mental events, can be conceived as a result of brain activity. Without certain brain functions, there is no conscious mind or personality whatsoever. These arguments are still widely regarded as scientific disproof of the existence of a substantial soul.

V. The Challenge to Dualism from Biblical Scholarship

Already in Thomas Hobbes we have encountered the judgment that traditional dualism has systematically misinterpreted the biblical picture of human nature. By the early twentieth century this theme had become a commonplace among biblical scholars. Christian Platonists have understood the terms "soul" and "spirit" in Scripture as referring to an incorporeal substance, the core person or true self, capable of existing without the body. But scholars now argued that this reading is wholly mistaken. An unbiased analysis of the biblical text itself, especially the Old Testament, will reveal that "soul" and "spirit" (Hebrew: *nephesh* and *ruach*; Greek: *psychē* and *pneuma*) have quite different meanings than they do in Platonic circles.[38] They are used of animals and humans alike and have more to do with the power of life and breath in the earthly creature than anything remotely connected with immortal existence after death. Similarly, the words for "body" and "flesh" contain no hint that they refer to anything metaphysically distinct from soul and spirit. Those connotations are foreign to the Bible. In this way the straightforward, uncritical dualistic reading of the anthropological terminology in Scripture was directly attacked,

---

38. Cf. H. Wheeler Robinson, *The Christian Doctrine of Man* (Edinburgh: Clark, 1911). He asks the reader, p. 5, to "put aside the interpretation natural to an Augustine or a Calvin . . . and to read the Old Testament in its original sense" . . . "which may sometimes reveal crude and primitive ideas that repel us." After explaining aspects of Hebrew notions of the soul and the bodily organs he asserts, "No clearer proof could be given that the term 'dualism' is inappropriate and misleading in relation to Hebrew psychology" (p. 21). And on p. 69: "the Hebrew conception of personality on its psychological side is distinctly that of a unity, not of a dualistic union of soul (or spirit) and body." Cf. also Johannes Pedersen, *Israel*, Vol. I, pp. 99-181, "The Soul, Its Powers and Capacities."

the interpretation which had been the basis of the body-soul distinction's doctrinal status throughout the history of the church.

Popular assumptions about the afterlife received similar treatment. Many Christians not only envisioned everlasting spiritual existence as their own eternal reward, but assumed that this is taught in the Old and New Testaments. As recently as the 1950s Oscar Cullmann generated a controversy by challenging this belief in favor of the New Testament emphasis on the resurrection of the body.[39] It was an even more bitter pill for the faithful to swallow when scholars claimed that Old Testament saints really did not look forward to much of an afterlife at all.[40] Death for the Hebrews was the virtual end of personal existence — a passing into the land of forgetfulness, the place of oblivion which is cut off even from God. This assertion by students of the Old Testament was backed up by numerous quotations from Scripture itself, passages which had escaped the notice of traditional Christian Bible-readers. Such claims could not therefore so easily be dismissed as the heretical ravings of perverse modernists. They could be substantiated from Scripture just as easily as orthodoxy had allegedly proven the body-soul distinction and the life everlasting.

Modern biblical scholarship provided a greater threat to traditional Christian anthropology and eschatology than philosophy and science. The latter could be ignored as part of the kingdom of Satan or at best the deceptive results of attempts to discover truth by fallen reason alone. But biblical scholarship was unpacking the contents of God's word in Scripture itself. Those results had to be reckoned as truth. Of course much biblical scholarship had been produced by individuals who denied the authority of Scripture as God's infallible word and instead affirmed modern scientific rationalism. The writings of these "higher critics" could safely be ignored. But the problem remained. For a simple, straightforward, noncritical reading of the text would justify many scholarly claims about the body-soul distinction and the doctrine of the afterlife as they are found in Scripture. Their distortion by the exegetical efforts of Christian dualism could be documented. The Bible itself was summoned to witness against traditional orthodoxy.

---

39. Oscar Cullmann, "Immortality of the Soul or Resurrection of the Body?", first published as "Unsterblichkeit der Seele und Auferstehung der Toten," *Theologische Zeitschrift* (1956).

40. Pedersen, pp. 460-470; Robinson, pp. 39-42, "The Eschatology of the Individual."

VI. The Historical-Theological Challenge to Dualism

If the dualistic understanding of the body-soul distinction does not come from the Bible, what is its source? How is it that Christians for eighteen hundred years had counted this belief as true as the gospel itself? Historians of Christian doctrine had ready answers for these pressing questions.

Since the eighteenth century, historians had studied various ancient civilizations carefully and were increasingly impressed by the uniqueness and diversity of individual cultures. The idea that human nature is everywhere and always the same seemed a naive prejudice of the Western mind. Historians of Christianity were struck in particular by the differences between the worldview of the Hebrew people and those of the classical Greek and later Hellenistic and Roman civilizations. These differences touched not only their views of nature, the spiritual realm, and human social and moral existence, but the very structure of human beings themselves.[41] Whereas the Greco-Roman outlook perceived human existence dualistically as a tragically contradictory mix of the material and spiritual realms, the Hebrews had a much more positive and holistic view of humans as the valued earthly creatures of God.

Problems for Judaism and Christianity arose, according to this account, when the dominant Hellenistic ideas began to seep into the biblical worldview and gradually alter it.[42] Jews in the diaspora began to assimilate Greek ideas about the body and the soul. The same thing occurred in the early church when Hellenistic thinkers were converted to Christianity. Scholars like Justin Martyr and even Augustine were Platonists before they became Christians. While they were willing to give up whatever their new faith required of them, they believed that Greek thinkers, especially the Platonists, had uncovered some truths about human nature. Among them was the idea that human beings consist of an immortal soul and a material

---

41. Cf. James Barr, *Semantics of Biblical Language* (London: Oxford, 1961), Ch. 2, "The Current Contrast of Greek and Hebrew Thought."

42. Barr, p. 13, summarizes this popular analysis as follows: "Greek thought is supposed to have been productive of splits and distinctions unknown to the Hebrews — being and becoming, reality and appearance, time and eternity, body and soul, spirit and matter, group and individual. The use of these distinctions is supposed to have remained common in European culture, and some at least of them have worked their way into Christian theology, where they have created problems which would never have arisen if the Jewish basis of Christian thinking had been kept in mind."

body. Thus faithful Christians did not need to renounce anthropological dualism. For they found this position to be the teaching of the Bible as well. In this way their exegetical and theological works, which became almost canonical in the history of Christian doctrine, systematically read the Greek mind into the Scriptures and elaborated it as theological orthodoxy.[43] Given its authoritative position, the Platonic body-soul distinction was uncritically accepted for more than a millennium until modern historical awareness and suspicion of Christian tradition motivated scholars to a fresh reading of the Bible. Only then was the difference between holistic Hebrew and dualistic Greek anthropology finally exposed.

Modern theologians responded to this widely accepted analysis in two ways. Some, for example the Hegelians, considered the marriage a good thing. God has worked through history to forge Christianity from both the Hebrew soul and the Greek mind. Together they have faithfully expressed the truth of divine revelation in history. Others, like Adolf von Harnack, regarded the historical synthesis of the biblical and Hellenistic outlooks as a distortion of the Christian faith and called for the systematic elimination of Greek influences from Christian theology. Whether positive or negative about the history of doctrine, modern theologians agreed that the age of Christian anthropological dualism is over.

VII. The Challenge to Dualism
from Christian Orthopraxis

So far the objections to the traditional body-soul dualism have been mainly academic and intellectual, generated by philosophers and scientists, theologians and biblical scholars. But there is another sort of objection which has become very popular and persuasive in the context of the contemporary elevation of effective practical action over mere knowledge and belief. This is the charge that body-soul dualism hampers authentic Christian orthopraxis — proper and effective living. Many Christians who are vitally concerned about obedience to the whole gospel and implement-

---

43. A very influential source of this idea is Adolf von Harnack, *Outlines of the History of Dogma*, trans. Edwin Mitchell (1893; reprint, Starr King Press, 1957). Although Harnack concentrates on how Greek thinking hardened faith into dogma, not on anthropology as such, his thesis applies to anthropology as well and was documented by many scholars.

ing the holistic biblical vision of life have developed a strong aversion — almost a "dualophobia" — to traditional anthropology, for they believe that the body-soul distinction implicitly sunders the unity of human life. It posits a dichotomy in human nature which leads to other dualisms, dichotomies, and illegitimate separations of what God has joined together. These false distinctions are not just bad theory. They have led to all manner of attitudes and practices among Christians and non-Christians which have harmed countless individuals, promoted destructive social and cultural dynamics, and distorted the church's witness of the gospel itself.

Since the dualistic anthropology of historic Christianity is implicated in so many distorted and harmful attitudes and practices, they argue, it must be rejected in favor of a holistic view of human nature. Only then will it be possible to implement the holistic biblical vision of religion and of the integration of our individual, social, and cultural life. Since the body-soul distinction has been an important factor in many of our diseases, its removal is a therapeutically necessary step in their healing.[44]

The list of evils in which anthropological dualism is implicated is truly sobering. Some commentators charge that it has been instrumental in the rise of modern secularism and the progressive erosion of Christian influence on society and culture. According to this analysis, the body-

---

44. The writings of the Dutch Reformed philosopher Herman Dooyeweerd associate the body-soul or body-mind distinction with many false dichotomies. See, for example, *In the Twilight of Western Thought* (Nutley, NJ: Craig, 1965), pp. 157-195 and *Roots of Western Culture* (Toronto: Wedge, 1979), Chs. 5 and 6. He views the history of Western civilization as animated by a series of unbiblical "ground-motives," each of which contains an inner contradiction. The Greek dilemma was between form and matter, the medieval Christian was between nature and grace, and the modern humanist is between nature and freedom. These ground motives have shaped culture fundamentally — generating all sorts of false dichotomies — and are expressed in anthropological ideas as well. The dualistic anthropologies of these eras have been implicated with unbiblical ground motives. Thus Dooyeweerd sometimes leaves the impression that a body-soul distinction itself is necessarily symptomatic of an unbiblical perspective. This is how he has been taken by almost all of his followers, at least in North America. A biblical dualistic anthropology is in principle impossible. This analysis is the source of much of the antidualistic polemic within Reformed circles in North America. Almost none of the Dooyeweerdians has explored the other option which he suggests: interpreting the ontic body-soul distinction within a genuinely biblical worldview. As will be shown in the last chapter, Dooyeweerd himself has an anthropology in which body and soul/spirit/self/ego/heart separate at death. Cf. G. C. Berkouwer, *Man: The Image of God* (Grand Rapids: Eerdmans, 1962), pp. 255-263.

soul distinction of Thomas Aquinas, stemming from the Greeks, is correlated with his nature-grace distinction, the idea that humankind has a natural and a supernatural end. While grace is required for humans to attain the supernatural goal of salvation, reason is sufficient for living the natural life of this world. Thus the scholastic body-soul distinction allowed for life to be divided into two dimensions and thereupon the nature-grace distinction permitted the assertion of the autonomy of reason and the independence of life in this world from the distinctives of divine revelation. This in turn has led to the secularism of public life and privatization of religion in the modern world.[45] It has generated the belief, held by Christians and non-Christians alike, that Christianity should not be expected to have anything distinctive or normative to say about science and technology, academics and education, business methods and economic systems, social and political issues, or general culture and public values. These areas ought to be addressed through a religiously neutral public philosophy which can include all interested participants. The body-soul distinction is partly to blame for this tragic loss of an active, robust Christianity.

Since the body-soul distinction has inclined Christians to surrender vast areas of life and knowledge to the forces of secularism, Christian educators, for example, fault it for the lack of a genuinely biblical approach to classroom management, teaching methods, and curricular content even in the nation's Christian schools. Donald Oppewal argues that holism must replace body-soul dualism as the foundation for developing a truly biblical notion of learning, teaching, and knowing.[46] David Myers, a Christian psychologist, makes a similar point. Whereas the tradition has treated knowledge intellectualistically, elevating ideas over actions and orthodoxy over orthopraxis, Myers favors a more integrated approach: "The contrasting biblical view of knowledge follows from its view of the person as a whole entity, not as a dichotomy of mind and body."[47] Traditional dualism must be abandoned if we are to regain wholesome views of knowledge and learning.

45. An excellent overview of the way in which the body-soul distinction, beginning with Plato, is associated with the rise of modern secularism and the spiritualization of Christianity is found in Brian Walsh and Richard Middleton, *The Transforming Vision* (Downers Grove, IL: InterVarsity, 1984), Ch. 7, "The Development of Dualism."

46. *Biblical Knowing and Teaching* (Grand Rapids: Calvin College, 1985), pp. 2-3.

47. *The Human Puzzle*, p. 125.

Anthropological dualism is also associated with other destructive tendencies of the modern mentality. Descartes's thesis that humans consist of a thinking substance and a material substance has reinforced the dichotomy between human subjectivity and the natural world and facilitated human domination of nature. "While man was a free, conscious, rational agent, all nature was but a grand machine, the realm of dead matter, functioning by ironclad laws of cause and effect which man could understand and exploit to human benefit." This in turn "lent support to the impunity with which autonomous humanity could manipulate and exploit the natural world for its own ends."[48] So the body-mind distinction has both contributed to man's sense of alienation from the universe and abetted the rape of the environment.

It has also led to the exploitation of human beings themselves. According to Theo Witvliet, "Christian dualism in respect of slavery in the New World could look back on a long tradition." This stretches back to the early church, where "the dualism of body and soul, internal and external, eternal and temporal, to be found in Hellenistic culture, took over Christian teaching and life-style. The freedom of the children of God was understood as an inner, spiritual freedom which left existing social circumstances untouched."[49] So the body-soul dualism of tradition has contributed to the justification for slavery and the oppression of various classes of people.

Elisabeth Schuessler Fiorenza has emphasized the connection between the subordination of women, the Mary myth, and

> the body-soul dualism of the Christian tradition. Whereas man in this tradition is defined by his mind and reason, woman is defined by her 'nature,' i.e. by her physical capacity to bear children. Motherhood, therefore, is the vocation of every woman regardless of whether or not she is a natural mother. However, since in the ascetic Christian tradition nature and body have to be subordinated to the mind and the spirit, woman because of her nature has to be subordinated to man. This subordination is, in addition, sanctioned with reference to Scripture. The body-spirit dualism of the Christian tradition is thus projected on women and men and contrib-

48. Walsh and Middleton, p. 123.
49. *A Place in the Sun* (Maryknoll, NY: Orbis, 1985), trans. John Bowden, pp. 53-54. Instead he prefers the holistic vision of African theologians "which contrasts sharply with the Western dualism of body and soul, matter and spirit, secular and sacred" (p. 93).

utes to the man-woman dualism or polarity which in modern times was supported not only by theology but also by philosophy and psychology.[50]

Here the charge is explicit: the body-soul dualism has directly contributed to the oppression of women.

Along similar lines Bishop Desmond Tutu suggests that the Western matter-spirit, body-soul distinction must be rejected if African Christians are to develop a theology which is faithful to the Bible and is compatible with their own cultural heritage as well as with the demands of true human community and social justice.[51] Repudiation of the Western body-soul distinction and the other dichotomies associated with it is a common theme among Third-World theologians and churches.[52]

But North American Christians are saying the same things. Anthropological dualism has truncated the gospel message. It has isolated the salvation of the individual soul from the redemption of the whole creation. According to Walsh and Middleton, when evangelicals "speak of caring *both* for the body *and* the soul, *both* the physical life *and* the spiritual life," they are "acknowledging a dualism" which "cripples our social action because such involvement is always subservient to the 'higher' calling of evangelism."[53] David Myers offers the solution: "Breaking down the cleavage between soul and body also reconciles the cleavage between the personal and social gospel. If matter and spirit are separate, then we may despise the material dimension, neglect it, abuse it, pollute it."[54] But holism promotes the proper attitudes and actions. These authors obviously consider an ontological body-soul distinction to be a major factor in the distortion and impoverishment of the Christian witness to the world.

The list of charges implicating anthropological dualism with harmful

50. "Feminist Theology as a Critical Theology of Liberation," *Theological Studies* (1975), reprinted in Gerald Anderson and Thomas Stransky, eds., *Mission Trends No. 4* (Grand Rapids: Eerdmans, 1979), pp. 188-216, quoted from pp. 206-207.

51. Desmond Tutu, "Black Theology/African Theology — Soul Mates or Antagonists?" (1975), in Gayraud Wilmore and James Cone, *Black Theology, A Documentary History, 1966-1979* (Maryknoll, NY: Orbis, 1979), and Deane William Ferm, *Third World Liberation Theologies* (Maryknoll, NY: Orbis, 1986), pp. 256-264.

52. Witvliet, p. 17, reports that a conference of missionaries and Third-World churches at Bangkok in 1972/73 pleaded for an alternative approach to "the Western dualism of body and spirit, thought and action, theory and practice."

53. Walsh and Middleton, p. 102.

54. Myers, p. 88.

attitudes and patterns of actions could be expanded at length. I have heard preachers blame it for scholasticism and irrelevance in theology and for quietism in the piety of church members. Evangelists and missionaries have faulted it for the church's failure at truly effective cross-cultural ministry. Psychologists and pastoral counselors have suspected it in the failure of some individuals to achieve integrated personalities. It has been associated with the resistance of some physicians and psychologists to considering psychosomatic factors in the treatment of their patients.

The litany could continue, but the point is established. Many people are convinced that the body-soul distinction must be rejected because it is incompatible with Christian orthopraxis and healthy human existence in general. Dividing humans into body and soul has promoted all manner of other false dualisms and dichotomies in human life. Successfully treating a disease requires the elimination of its root causes.

VIII. Conclusion

Traditional Christianity has held fast to an ontological distinction between body and soul mainly because it follows from the doctrine of the intermediate state. Historically both beliefs have been taken by the overwhelming majority to be the teaching of Scripture itself. But in modern times body-soul dualism has come under a series of attacks mounted both by Christians and non-Christians. Philosophers have criticized traditional arguments for the substantiality and immortality of the soul and have proposed nondualist theories of human nature. Scientists have turned up a great deal of evidence demonstrating the dependence of mental and psychological states on the brain, thereby undermining the basis for considering the soul a separate substance. Biblical scholars have subjected anthropological terms and texts to careful analysis and have concluded that the biblical view of human nature is not dualistic at all, but is quite emphatically holistic. Historians of Christianity have confirmed that the roots of traditional anthropology are nourished by the soil of the Hellenistic worldview, not by Scripture as had always been assumed. And finally, many Christians who devote themselves to radical obedience and witnessing the whole gospel for all of life have charged that the body-soul distinction of traditional Christianity is one of the root causes of the many ways in which the faith has been distorted and prevented from effecting the complete salvation of humanity and the whole creation.

All these charges are voiced from different directions, but they all conclude the same thing — dualism is out, holism or monism is in. As David Myers puts it: "the truth is that we do not *have* bodies, we *are* our bodies. On this important concept scientific research and biblical scholarship seem to be approaching a consensus."[55]

Altogether this represents a truly formidable cumulative case against anthropological dualism. If it stands up, or even if some of the individual charges are accurate, there is very good reason for repentance from dualism and conversion to monism-holism.

But thus far we have heard only from the prosecution. The evidence certainly seems incriminating. But is there a defense? Have philosophy and science falsified dualism? Does a body-soul distinction really lead to the distortion of Christian faith and practice? These are crucial issues, and we will consider them in the final chapters of this book. But the most fundamental issue of all for those who regard biblical teaching as authoritative is whether historical Christianity has really just read anthropological dualism into Scripture where it is not present at all. Christian belief must be normed by biblical teaching. For this reason the next six chapters will be devoted to evaluating the debate between monists and dualists regarding the correct interpretation of biblical anthropology.

55. Ibid., p. 88.

Chapter Two

Old Testament Anthropology:
The Holistic Emphasis

I. Introduction: The State of the Debate

A. Traditional Christian Dualism

There is little question that traditional exegetes have viewed the Old Testament picture of human nature through the lenses of Christian Platonism. The truth of the idea that human beings consist of a material body and an immaterial soul or spirit was simply taken for granted. People read the Old Testament as saying the same thing, never thinking to inquire whether this is in fact the case. Thus, for example, when Genesis 2:7 says that "the LORD God formed the man from the dust of the ground and breathed into his nostrils the breath of life," it was simply assumed that here God is depicted as implanting an immaterial substantial soul into a material body. And just as earthly life was thought to begin with the incarnation of a spiritual substance in a physical substance, it ends when the two are separated. For Ecclesiastes 12:7 states that ". . . the dust returns to the ground it came from, and the spirit returns to God who gave it." That verse seemed quite clearly to express a body-soul dichotomy. Although the body decomposes into physical matter, the individual substantial soul survives and ascends to dwell with God. In these cases as well as many others in the Old Testament, it seemed perfectly natural to read the text in terms of the body-soul distinction as articulated by Christian Platonism.

Consider Calvin, for example. "It would be foolish to seek a definition of 'soul' from the philosophers," he writes. "Of them hardly one, except

33

Plato, has rightly affirmed its immortal substance."[1] His self-conscious partiality toward Plato is evident in his definition of the soul and in his reading of the Old Testament:

> Now I understand by the term "soul" an immortal yet created essence, which is his nobler part. Sometimes it is called "spirit". . . . [W]hen the word "spirit" is used by itself, it means the same thing as soul; as when Solomon, speaking of death, says that then "the spirit returns to God who gave it" [Eccl. 12:7].[2]

Calvin's approach is a paradigm of traditional exegesis.

This reading, it should be admitted, is not wholly without basis in the text, at least in the vocabulary of the Old Testament. The Hebrew words *nephesh* and *ruach*, for example, were frequently translated already in the Septuagint as *psychē* and *pneuma,* the Greek words which in turn were often rendered quite comfortably as "soul" and "spirit" in English. Thus the King James Version of Genesis 2:7 reads that "man became a living *soul*" where the Hebrew term is *nephesh*.

B. Modern Christian Antidualism

In more recent times, as we have seen, the pendulum has swung to the opposite side. The scholarly community has become highly suspicious — almost paranoid — of the presence of Platonic dualism in the traditional interpretation of Scripture. Nowadays most biblical scholars strive to outdo one another in emphasizing that Hebrew anthropology, like the Hebrew mind and Hebrew worldview in general, is decidedly antidualistic and enthusiastically holistic or monistic.[3] As Russell Aldwinckle observes:

1. John Calvin, *Institutes,* I,xv,6, trans. F. L. Battles (Philadelphia: Westminster, 1960), p. 192.

2. Calvin, I,xv,2, p. 184. Precisely the same exegesis of Gen. 2:7 and Eccl. 12:7 is given by Aquinas, *Summa Theologica,* I,75,6, Rep. Obj. 1.

3. A fine example of this is M. E. Dahl's chapter "The Semitic Totality View," in his book *The Resurrection of the Body* (London: SCM, 1962). He explores the Hebrew mind in general and then infers that its anthropology, like everything else, is holistic. Cf. also the statement of A. R. van de Walle, *From Darkness to the Dawn* (Mystic, CT: Twenty-third Publications, 1985), p. 152: "Semitic thought saw human beings predominantly as indivisible unities. It imagined them as it saw them, as bodies. Anachronistically, one could call this Se-

It has become a dogma of much so-called biblical theology in our time to stress the sharp distinction between the Hebrew doctrine of man and the dualist Greek view which divides man into body and soul. What has been called the "Semitic totality concept" is taken to mean that man for Hebrew thought is conceived of as a unitary being to which such a dualism could not possibly apply.[4]

It is not always clear precisely what is meant by "holistic" and "monistic" in the writings of Old Testament scholars. But in anthropological contexts the terms almost always imply that the Israelites viewed human nature as a "unity" of personal and bodily existence. Soul and body, the mental, physical, and spiritual, are so essentially tied together that were they somehow separated, a human being would not only cease in every way to function, she would actually cease to exist. In fact, body, soul, and spirit do not refer to mere parts at all, but in different ways connote the whole human person.[5] Thus holism and monism mean at least this, that no part or aspect or dimension as such can survive intact the dissolution of the whole. Whereas in Greek dualism the real self or essential person can survive and perhaps even flourish apart from organic existence, for Hebrew holism personal existence apart from bodily existence is a flat impossibility. It is inconceivable to the Hebrew mind. As Otto Kaiser observes: "For some decades there has been a cherished hypothesis in theology that says that according to the Old Testament perspective, with a person's death it is all over."[6]

Of course it is considered a truism that the Hebrew mentality is not "theoretical" or inclined toward systematizing abstract ideas. But if one were to ask hypothetically which philosophical tradition is most compatible with the Israelite worldview if it were theoretically articulated, vitalism or even materialism would be the answer of many contemporary scholars. Consider M. E. Dahl's comments on the anthropology of Genesis 2:7: "It is

mitic view of the human being monistic." Even Reinhold Niebuhr cannot refrain from referring to "the monism of the biblical view" in *The Nature and Destiny of Man* (New York: Scribner's, 1941), Vol. I, p. 13.

4. *Death in the Secular City* (Grand Rapids: Eerdmans, 1974), p. 72.

5. Cf. G. E. Ladd, *A Theology of the New Testament* (Grand Rapids: Eerdmans, 1974), p. 457: "Recent scholarship has recognized that such terms as body, soul, and spirit are not different, separable faculties of man but different ways of viewing the whole man."

6. Otto Kaiser and Eduard Lohse, *Death and Life* (Nashville: Abingdon, 1981), p. 41.

not so much that man is *made of* 'dust of the earth'; he *is* dust, which presumably means that, in man, matter has, by the in-breathing of God, acquired the characteristics of self-conscious being."[7] Humans are purely material entities, but God has endowed human matter with the typically human higher capacities. The influence of contemporary materialism is unmistakable in this interpretation.

But monistic materialism is not the only contemporary philosophy the Hebrews are taken as foreshadowing. Their concern with living an active life in community rather than with abstract contemplation suggests to some an anticipation of the social practicalism of Marxism and Deweyan pragmatism. And as with the existentialists, their awareness that this present earthly existence is all there is allegedly fuels the drive toward "authenticity" in life so characteristic of Hebrew religion.[8] If there is anything common to most of the philosophical schools since Kant, it is antidualism or anti-Platonism, especially in anthropology. And in that respect, most contemporary intellectuals would agree that the ancient Hebrews have more in common with romanticism, Hegelianism, Marxism, pragmatism, materialism, existentialism, and process philosophy than with traditional Christian Platonism.[9] In general, the Hebrew mentality is considered more akin to contemporary than to classical Western philosophy.

C. Some Questions

But is that true? Have we really arrived at a correct assessment of the situation after eighteen centuries of philosophically induced misperception? Or is it possible that the modern mind has its own blindnesses and prejudices, its own tendency to create the past in its own image?[10] Further, may it be assumed that Platonic dualism and some sort of monism are the only al-

---

7. Dahl, p. 71. Cf. also van de Walle, p. 37: "All in all, using an anachronistic term, we might call the Israelite understanding of humanity a materialistic one."

8. Cf. Maurice Friedman's remarks in the anthology he edited, *The Worlds of Existentialism* (University of Chicago Press, 1964), pp. 18-21. Similar views are expressed by William Barrett in *Irrational Man* (Garden City, NY: Doubleday Anchor, 1962), pp. 73-79.

9. Aldwinckle, p. 72, asks contemporary scholars somewhat sarcastically whether Hebrew man "was only a B C anticipation of a Marx or a Ryle or a modern behaviourist?"

10. Aldwinckle, p. 72, warns against allowing the "emotivist use of the word dualist to settle the issue out of hand."

ternatives? Or is it possible to hold a position somewhere in the middle which coherently affirms insights of Platonism as well as holism? Such questions cannot be avoided if we are to assess honestly the claims of both sides in the debate over who faithfully represents the anthropological legacy of the Old Testament people of God.

My own conclusion is that the truth combines elements of the two extremes — that the Hebrew view of human nature strongly emphasizes living a full and integrated existence before God in this world, but that it unquestionably also includes the belief in continued existence after biological death. If I am correct, then Old Testament anthropology is both holistic and dualistic in senses yet to be explicated. This chapter will present the evidence for Hebrew holism. The next will demonstrate why Old Testament anthropology must also be classified as a form of dualism.

II. The Holistic Emphasis of the Old Testament

A. Antidualist Emphases

The biblical scholarship of at least the last hundred years has produced an enormous amount of material which undermines the Platonic-dualistic reading of Old Testament anthropology. Consider two main emphases of traditional Christian Platonism: that human beings consist of a material body with its physical-biological needs and functions and a substantial immaterial soul with its conscious mental and spiritual functions; and that the life to come is more real, more purely spiritual, and hence more God-glorifying than our present earthly pilgrimage. Neither of these emphases is found in the Old Testament, and both can almost certainly be ruled out by what it does stress.

With respect to the second — the refined spirituality and superiority of the afterlife — there is no basis at all. In fact the opposite is true, as will be demonstrated below. The Old Testament is resoundingly this-worldly. The fullest possible existence for a human being is to live an earthly life as God created it to be lived. Health, sufficient material goods, enjoyment of marriage and family, meaningful work, standing in the community, freedom from one's enemies, and above all walking in integrity with the God of the covenant — the Israelite who enjoyed these blessings could exclaim, "It doesn't get any better than this!" When the prophets look forward to

BODY, SOUL, AND LIFE EVERLASTING

the eschatological future, they do not envision heaven for the individual. Their hope is for a New Jerusalem and a new earth, a place where the existence of the Lord's people will again be what it was created to be in the beginning. Human life is tied to the earth. There is no "pie in the sky by-and-by" for the individual at death, no heaven for the liberated soul. What could express this more clearly than the book of Ecclesiastes? The afterlife, if it can be called that, is hopelessly pale and dull in comparison with the *shalom* of a full earthly life. This emphasis is diametrically opposed to the melioristic views of postmortem existence affirmed in some Greco-Roman religions and even in Paul's statement "to die is gain." The personal eschatology of Christian Platonism finds only counterevidence in the Old Testament Scriptures.

The yield of modern biblical scholarship is no more promising for the traditional Platonistic body-soul dualism. Numerous studies of Hebrew anthropological terms all point in the same direction. In the first place, there is such variety in the way the terms are used that it is impossible to arrive at a single, theoretically clear model of human nature from the Old Testament. But second, insofar as a nontheoretical depiction or general impression of the human constitution is present, it points away from the idea that the human soul is an immaterial entity of some sort. And it clearly neither limits biological functions to the body nor mental-spiritual capacities to the soul or spirit. In fact, soul and spirit seem to have biological functions and what we would take as bodily organs are considered seats of higher conscious capacities. This points away from dualism toward some sort of holism.

B. Old Testament Anthropological Terms

It will be worth our while to review the most important Hebrew anthropological terms in the light of recent scholarship to see just how strong the anti-Platonist tendencies of the Old Testament are. Although a great deal of literature is available, the state of the art can be found in Hans Walter Wolff's *Anthropology of the Old Testament*.[11] What he presents is virtually

---

11. Trans. Margaret Kohl (Philadelphia: Fortress, 1974). Other surveys of Old Testament anthropological terms can be found in H. Wheeler Robinson, *The Religious Ideas of the Old Testament* (New York: Scribner's, 1913), pp. 79-83; George Ladd, *A Theology of the New*

undisputed among scholars of various theological persuasions, and I will rely on it here.

1. *Nephesh*

Although *nephesh* has frequently been translated as "soul," it has a variety of meanings.[12] In places it must be read anatomically as "throat," "neck," or "stomach." Psalm 105:18 says, "his *nephesh* was put into irons." Similarly, *nephesh* has the bodily desire or appetite for food and drink, breath, and sex. Often it simply means the vital principle or life-force: "the *nephesh* of the flesh is in the blood" (Lev. 17:11). *Nephesh* is used of animals as well as people in the sense of "living creature." And occasionally it even means "dead person" (Num. 5:2; 6:11). Of course it is also the seat of emotions and moral dispositions. It can praise the Lord and hate the neighbor. Although it could be translated as "soul" in such contexts, it might more sensibly be read as "person" or "self" or by such personal pronouns as "I" and "myself." In those cases it is correct to suppose that the term stands for the whole person rather than for some immaterial part or aspect. "My *nephesh* will praise the Lord" simply means "I will praise the Lord." In sum, this crucial term is as different from as it is similar to the Platonic sense of "soul."

2. *Ruach*

Ruach[13] is a term which refers to wind or moving air and thus, like *nephesh,* is at times associated with breath. But it is also translated as "spirit," and it actually refers to the spirit of God more frequently than to the human spirit. When indicating the breath of a living creature *ruach* is often parallel to another important term, *neshama,* "the breath of life" (Gen. 2:7). "If he should take back his *ruach* to himself, and gather to himself his breath *(neshama),* all flesh would perish together, and man would return to dust" (Job 34:14). So *ruach* is a vital force or power or energy

Testament, pp. 458-459; and Anthony Hoekema, *Created in God's Image* (Grand Rapids: Eerdmans, 1986), pp. 210-213. A more comprehensive treatment which anticipates Wolff's is Walter Eichrodt, *Theology of the Old Testament,* 2 vols. (Philadelphia: Westminster, 1961, 1967), Vol. II, Ch. XVI.2, "The components of human nature."

12. Wolff, Ch. II; Eichrodt, pp. 134-142.

13. Wolff, Ch. IV, "*ruach* — Man as he is Empowered"; Eichrodt, pp. 131-134.

which animates living creatures.[14] This is very graphically depicted in
Ezekiel 37's vision of the dry bones. After the bones, tendons, muscles, and
skin all come together to reconstitute human bodies, they still require
ruach from the Lord before they live. *Ruach* is not an immaterial substantial soul, but a vital force, the power of life. It is not generated by the bodily
organization itself, but is externally conferred on the organism by God.
But *ruach* in humans is not merely biological energy; it empowers humans
to do whatever they were created to do. Our ordinary powers of thought,
will, and response to God are energized by the gift of *ruach*. In addition
there are extraordinary gifts of wisdom, prophecy, artistry, and the like
which are produced in us by a special spirit. This is not just the Holy Spirit
of God, but creaturely power which comes from the Creator. In view of
these enabling capacities it is not surprising that *ruach* also becomes the
seat of various conscious dispositions and activities. The spirit can reason,
deliberate, choose, will, rebel against God, hate one's neighbor, be de-
pressed or courageous, and err or lie. It seems to be the locus or source of
all the higher subjective human capacities. In sum, *ruach* is used in a wide
variety of ways in the Old Testament, some of them coinciding with
nephesh. But none of them clearly points to an immaterial subsistent self.
Once again Platonism is left without much foundation.

3. *Basar*

Hebrew anthropological vocabulary goes beyond such "spiritual" terms as
nephesh and *ruach* and includes a number of physiological words as well.
Basar is frequently translated as "flesh" and has a variety of meanings.[15] It
can refer to the muscle tissue in distinction from bones, fat, tendons, and
sinews, as illustrated in Ezekiel 37. (In spite of their nontheoretical, holistic
mentality the Hebrews were able to distinguish "parts" of the body which
taken together constitute the whole human organism.) The term *basar* can
refer to the human body as a whole, although it is never used to mean
"corpse." It can also signify various kinds of human relationship — the
"one flesh" bond between husband and wife, the blood ties of kinship, and

14. *Nephesh, ruach,* and *neshama* thus all intersect around the connotation of "life-
force" or "animating principle." Eichrodt discerns a difference between *ruach* and *nephesh* in
that *ruach* refers to the general life-force which comes from God whereas *nephesh* is always
individuated, the life of a particular creature; cf. Eichrodt, p. 135.

15. Wolff, Ch. III, "*basar* — Man in his Infirmity."

the "all flesh" solidarity of the whole human race. And frequently the term has the connotation of vulnerability, weakness, frailty, and contingency — utter dependence upon God. "All flesh is grass," confesses the prophet Isaiah (ch. 40). But never is *basar* used in a way which would imply a metaphysical distinction between living physical matter and nonphysical substantial spirit.

4. *Qereb*

In addition to anatomical structures which shape the body, the Hebrews also spoke of *qereb*, the "inner parts" or "bowels."[16] What is striking about the stomach, liver, bile, bowels, kidneys, and heart is not so much their physiological functions, which the Israelites knew little if anything about. It is rather that they are the locations and sources of the higher human capacities. As Wolff observes, "The inner parts of the body and its organs are at the same time the bearer of man's spiritual and ethical impulses."[17] The kidneys are an instructive example. Proverbs 23:16 pledges: "My kidneys will rejoice when your lips speak what is right." They are organs which can discern wisdom and rejoice in response. In this they actually parallel the heart, as in Psalm 73:21: "Then my heart was embittered, I was sharply pricked in my kidneys."

5. *Leb*

Of course the heart, *leb* or *lebah*, is the best known of the inner organs, occurring 814 times in the Old Testament.[18] At the outset it is important to belabor what might seem to be the obvious — whatever else it is and can do, the heart is the fleshy organ which beats in the chest. Jeremiah cries out, "Oh the agony of my heart! My heart pounds within me" (4:19). It has the same general location and status as the stomach and kidneys. I stress this over against post-Enlightenment romantic and idealist tendencies to discover a "noumenal self" or "transcendental ego" of some sort in the Old Testament concept of the heart. The Calvinist philosopher Dooyeweerd, for example, claims to capture the biblical view of the heart in his concept

16. Wolff, Ch. VII, "The Inner Parts of the Body"; Eichrodt, pp. 145-147.
17. Wolff, p. 66.
18. Wolff, Ch. V, "*leb(ab)* — Reasonable Man"; Eichrodt, pp. 142-145.

of a prefunctional, supratemporal ego or religious self.[19] Such a metaphysical construct may be a useful piece of contemporary philosophy, but it is not exactly the beating bundle of flesh in the breast of Jeremiah.

What Dooyeweerd and many modern philosophers of the heart are right about, however, is the fact that the heart in Hebrew thought is not significant primarily for its role in organic existence, but as the hidden control-center of the whole human being. The entire range of conscious and perhaps even unconscious activities of the person is located in and emanates from the heart. It experiences emotions and moods, it has personality and character traits, it is the locus of thought and deliberation, choice and action, and it is above all the source of love or hate of God and neighbor. It may be hidden from other people and perhaps even from oneself. But God searches its depths and knows it altogether. So, as with *nephesh* and *ruach,* there arc significant ways in which the biblical idea of the heart and modern notions of the ego, person, or deep self do overlap. But the fact that it is not disassociated from the organ located in the chest counts strongly against all attempts to idealize or transcendentalize it, whether devised by Christian Platonists or post-Kantians. But neither is it a merely physical organ which generates the mental powers, as contemporary materialists would suggest.[20]

One other observation about the heart is worth making. It is the locus of all higher human functions alike. Thus it is not primarily an organ of feeling and intuition and only secondarily and unnaturally the source of thought and rationality. Modern attempts to romanticize, psychologize, or irrationalize human nature are no more consistent with the Old Testament than classical rationalism is. No rationalist himself, Wolff feels compelled to warn against contemporary irrationalistic interpretations of the heart: "We must guard against the false impression that biblical man is determined more by feeling than by reason. This mistaken anthropological direction is all too easily derived from an undifferentiated rendering of *leb.*"[21] Each of the capacities and modes of human subjectivity has its own important and correlative place in human life as a whole. The entire pack-

19. Herman Dooyeweerd, "What Is Man?" in *In the Twilight of Western Thought* (Nutley, NJ: Craig, 1965), pp. 181, 186, 189.

20. Aldwinckle, p. 72, draws the line against materialistic interpretations: "Because heart, liver, kidney and bowels acquired a psychical use in Hebrew, this does not mean that the psychical was nothing more than the movements of these physical organs."

21. Wolff, p. 47.

age, often represented by the heart, is ultimately employed either in faithfulness to the God of the covenant or else in rebellion against him. And as a matter of fact, there is a great deal more stress in the Old Testament on "getting a heart of wisdom" than on having certain feelings or preconceptual intuitions, no matter how positive and uplifting they are.

C. Preliminary Results for the Holism-Dualism Debate

So we come to the end of our brief survey of the more prominent Hebrew anthropological terms. What if anything can be concluded for the holism-dualism debate? That depends on what each side defends. Suppose we accept rough-and-ready popular definitions of the terms. Let's say that holism means something like this: human beings are single entities all of whose capacities and functions are interrelated and integrated as a systemic unity. And let's suppose that dualism means what is popularly understood as Platonism or Cartesianism — humans consist of the conjunction and interaction of two wholly different substances each with its own distinct set of functions. If these are the options, then Old Testament anthropology is obviously holistic.

In the first place, the variety and interchangeability of terminology simply do not provide a footing for a clearly dualistic reading. There are no texts in which soul or spirit or person must be interpreted as an immaterial substance which functions independent of the body. No uses of organic, bodily terminology suggest that bodily functions are purely biological, much less independent of soul functions. Dualism is scarcely suggested by the Hebrew mode of speaking about human existence.

But second, the Old Testament picture of humanity positively seems to rule out dualism. Soul and spirit, *nephesh* and *ruach,* seem either to refer to the whole psychophysical person or otherwise to the energizing life-force given by God. Neither use refers to an immaterial entity. And regarding the division of labor among the various capacities of human nature, there is no systematic distinction between physical and spiritual organs whatsoever. Feeling, knowing, thinking, willing, loving, recognizing moral demands, keeping commitments, as well as praising and praying — the entire roster of higher human capacities — are sometimes attributed to the "spiritual" organs *nephesh* and *ruach*. But at least as often they are attributed to the heart, a bodily organ, and occasionally to the kidneys and viscera. Furthermore, *nephesh* and *ruach* cannot be treated as exclusively spiritual to begin with. For *nephesh* can refer to the body's throat or its breath, the latter meaning shared by *ruach,* the vital force. So if drawing any systematic conclusion at all is warranted, it appears that both "spiritual" and "physical" organs have both "spiritual" and "physical" functions. This scheme certainly suggests the functional integration or unity of the psychophysical totality rather than the compartmentalization of the soul's functions and the body's functions.

A third factor which points away from dualism toward holism is the highly publicized frequency of synecdoche in the Old Testament. That is a figure of speech in which a word which sometimes refers to a part of something is used to signify the whole. English examples are "All hands on deck!" or "She is a real brain." In neither case is the expression meant literally, asking that palms be placed on the floor or equating a person with her brain. Rather, the whole person is referred to by a part-term which calls attention to some specific characteristic, that sailors are manual laborers or that the woman is highly intelligent. In just this way, as numerous commentators have pointed out, *basar, ruach, nephesh,* and *leb* are often used to refer, not to specific parts, but to whole persons. Thus the personal pronoun would be a fully adequate translation. "My *nephesh* cries out" simply means "I cry out."[22] Surely this points away from dualism toward holism. The whole person, not just an immaterial ego, calls upon God.

A word of caution regarding synecdoche is in order, however. Some scholars, perhaps in fits of antidualist enthusiasm, seem to imply that all instances of Old Testament anthropological terms are cases of part-for-whole expressions. Typical is van de Walle's generalization: "All the terms, body . . . *ruach* and *nephesh,* do not refer to independent elements in a human being but to the one, total, indivisible human being."[23] Perhaps the referents of these words are not independent, but we have seen that often they do have different meanings and frequently they do pick out parts of persons, not the whole. *Nephesh* can be "throat" or "breath." *Ruach* does not include bones and kidneys. The variety of linguistic usage in the Old Testament defies any simple generalization, however rhetorically compelling. Hebrew anthropological terms do refer to distinct parts, aspects, and

22. Cf. Wolff, pp. 21-25, on *nephesh* as referring to the whole person and translated by personal pronouns.
23. van de Walle, p. 38.

particular features of persons. This fact can be recognized without danger of falling into dichotomies and dualisms. Holism need not entail the denial that wholes contain distinguishable parts. So the claim that Hebrew anthropology is holistic seems well established and Platonic-Cartesian dualism appears excluded.

III. Philosophical Reflections

A. *The Old Testament, Holism, and Monism*

But what follows from this conceptually? If the Old Testament is anti-Platonist, does that mean it is pro-monist or pro-materialist? Does holism entail a monism of any sort?

In the first place, I do not believe that on a purely conceptual level holism entails monism, materialist or otherwise. And with respect to the Old Testament, in the second, there is as much to rule out both materialism specifically and monism in general as there is against Platonism.

First, the definition of holism I have been using does not by itself entail monism. Holism, as suggested above, affirms the functional unity of some entity in its totality, the integration and interrelation of all the parts in the existence and proper operation of the whole. It views an entity as a single primary functional system, not as a compound system constructed by linking two or more primary functional systems. It recognizes entities as phenomenological and existential unities. It implies that the parts do not operate independently within the whole, and that they would not necessarily continue to have all the same properties and functions if the whole were broken up.

This sort of holism does not necessarily imply that the whole is at bottom a single homogenous substance or "stuff," that is, a metaphysical monism of matter or spirit or some other neutral and indefinable kind of substance. A holistic entity could conceivably be constituted out of any number of metaphysical substances or principles. And holism does not necessarily imply that if the whole is broken up, all parts disintegrate into chaos or nothingness. Secondary systems might continue to exist, although without all the properties and capacities they had when integrated within the whole. An organism is a prime example of a holistic entity, and under the right conditions organs can survive separation from their organisms. Hydrogen and oxygen atoms can survive separation from water molecules even though the breakup alters them. On this view, souls, spirits, minds, or persons might be able to exist without organisms, although they would be deprived by the loss. Let's call what I have been describing here "functional holism." My point is that it affirms phenomenological, existential, and functional unity, but does not conceptually entail monism or personal extinction at death.

In distinction from functional holism, however, another concept of holism seems to be employed by many who discuss Old Testament anthropology. This I will call "ontological holism." It defines the very being of an entity and its constituents in terms of their systematic unity. A thing in its totality is simply a particular holistic organization. The parts, aspects, and dimensions of the thing have being only in virtue of their status within the whole. Their existence, their nature, and their identity all depend on the whole. So if the whole breaks up, the parts cease to be what they were. No parts can survive the dissolution of the whole intact. They must either cease to be or become something else than what they were. In anthropology this means that a human person is a single integrated totality of psychophysical functions. If the totality is broken up, neither soul nor body nor person continues to function or exist.[24] For none of these is a separable entity, but all are merely "aspects" of a single whole.[25] Ontological holism is apparently the version of holism which is employed by those

24. Cf. John Hick, *Death and Eternal Life* (San Francisco: Harper and Row, 1976), p. 278: "The prevailing view of man among both contemporary scientists and western philosophers is that he is an indissoluble psycho-physical unity. . . . On this view there is no room for the notion of soul in distinction from body; and if there is no soul in distinction from body there can be no question of the soul surviving the death of the body." Cf. also Wolfhart Pannenberg, *What Is Man?* trans. D. Priebe (Philadelphia: Fortress, 1970), pp. 47-48: "The distinction between body and soul as two completely different realms of reality can no longer be maintained. . . . [T]he separation between physical and spiritual is artificial. . . . Still further, the distinction between body and soul even presupposes an original unity. . . . Both are abstractions. . . . This removes the basis for the idea of the immortality of the soul."
25. Thus ontological holism has the same consequence as dual-aspect monism, defined in Chapter One. Both view soul and body as two dimensions of a single thing. Much contemporary ontological holism is a species of monism in which the single basic category is not material or mental substance, but structure or organization. It is structural rather than substantial monism. Aristotle's hylomorphism is also an example of ontological holism as I have defined it, but it is a kind of dualism as well. Form and matter are distinct metaphysical principles, but they exist only in things, never separate. Aristotle's metaphysics is a dual principle version of ontological holism. Cf. p. 55.

who claim that the Old Testament depicts humans as "indissoluble unities" and on that basis deny personal survival of death. This denial is shared with materialistic and dual-aspect or neutral monism.[26]

Functional holism does not entail ontological holism. Ontological holism goes beyond functional holism in making the existence of the whole functional system a necessary condition for the continued self-identical existence of the parts of the whole. Whether Old Testament holism is merely functional or ontological cannot be settled on a priori conceptual grounds. This is a question of fact which can only be determined by discovering what the Hebrews thought about death and survival, the topic of the next chapter.

A second issue is the conceptual relation between Hebrew holism and philosophical monism. Quite apart from the conceptual anatomy of holism as such, it is clear that if Old Testament anthropology were philosophically elaborated, it would not lead to any sort of substantial monism — materialist, idealist, or neutralist. For in its own nonphilosophical way, the Old Testament picture of human nature repeatedly and consistently represents humankind as constituted from two different and mutually irreducible sources, elements, ingredients, "stuffs," or principles.[27] First, Adam is *adamah*, from the earth, the dust (*'apar*) of the ground. That is the case in Genesis 2 and throughout the Old Testament. Earth is the "stuff" or substance, if you will, of which our bodiliness is made. Ezekiel 37 presents a graphic image of how bones, flesh, sinews, and skin come together from the earth to form a human body. But that body is still lifeless. Thus a second ingredient must be added: the *ruach* or *neshama*, the life-force or power of breath which comes from God. When God withdraws the vital

26. As suggested in Chapter One, a third kind of monism — idealism or panpsychism — can allow that persons survive bodily death if personhood is located in the individual spirit. The body is considered a derivative mode of spiritual existence. The spirit continues even when the bodily mode ceases. The problem with this view, of course, is what to do with the corpse. Why doesn't the body instantly disappear once disconnected from the soul? That is what one would expect if body were wholly a form or product of soul, just as one would not expect mind to continue even for an instant after brain death if materialistic monism were true. If the material component of what was once a living body continues to exist, that component does not seem to be a mere extension of the soul. Thus some sort of spirit-matter dualism instead of consistent idealistic monism would seem to be indicated.

27. Cf. H. Wheeler Robinson's similar conclusion: "Man's nature is a product of the two factors — the breath-soul which is his principle of life, and the complex of physical organs which this animates" (p. 83).

force, the body becomes lifeless and disintegrates into the dust from whence it came. This second element, *ruach,* is not a thing — an individual entity which exists apart from living creatures. And so it is not a Platonic soul or an individual spirit. It is more like a kind of created energy produced by God and continuously flowing from him to the individual creature. When he withdraws it, that particular extension of *ruach* ceases to exist. It is not immortal. But it is a vastly different sort of thing than the dust of the ground. Whatever technical label — substance, element, principle, constituent — is attached, we must recognize that two kinds of ingredient are put together by God in order to create one holistic living creature. Perhaps the dust is a kind of substance in the sense of "stuff" and the life-force is an empowering principle or kind of energy. They do not both seem to be "substances" in the same sense of the word. Aside from their both being created by God, dust and life-breath may have no properties whatsoever in common. But whatever each is, they amount to a mutually irreducible duality which God puts together to get one person. And that picture does not look as though it could be philosophically elaborated into monism — materialist, idealist, or neutral.

Most certainly it is not a primitive form of materialism. A materialist view of life and human nature, whether crude or sophisticated, holds that the energy of biological life and of all the higher human capacities is identical with or is somehow generated by the physical energy contained in matter. Matter organized one way has the power of digestion and reproduction. Organized into more complex systems, it is self-conscious and capable of religious experience. To state materialism using Old Testament language, in other words, *ruach* would be contained within the dust itself and the dust would need only to be formed in a human way in order for *ruach* and *nephesh* to emerge and begin to function. But that is not the Old Testament picture. However it happens, human existence is created only when God puts the power to exist and function into the formed dust from the outside. Existential power is not inherent in the dust itself. God simply did not make the dust that way. Materialism is no more adequate for conceptualizing Old Testament images of humanity than is Platonism.

A parallel argument could be constructed against claims of finding idealistic monism or dual-aspect monism in Hebrew anthropology. The former views matter and the body as forms or expressions of ideal or spiritual substance. The latter holds that soul and body — spirit and matter, the mental and the physical — are aspects or manifestations of a more basic substance. The fact that the dust of the earth from which a human is formed is not a manifestation of *ruach* counts against idealism. Just as clearly, dust and *ruach* are not two sides or aspects of a third more primordial creaturely substance, a fact which rules out neutral or dual-aspect monism. So the Old Testament account of the human constitution, though nonphilosophical, does not seem compatible with any form of substantial monism. Our conclusion is that although Hebrew anthropology is functionally holistic, it cannot be construed as a primitive, nonphilosophical form of monism.

In summary, then, we have discovered that although the Old Testament clearly represents existential-functional holism, it does not entail substantial monism of any sort nor does it necessarily imply ontological holism. What it does suggest — at least the biblical data we have considered thus far — is a functional holism constituted from a duality of sources or ingredients without suggesting that the "spiritual" component is an immaterial entity such as Plato or Descartes would hold. Whether this functional holism turns out to be ontological holism will depend on whether human persons were thought to survive biological death.

B. The Old Testament and Philosophical Anthropology

If Platonic dualism and all varieties of substance monism are apparently inconsistent with Hebrew anthropology, are there no philosophical options left? Is the Old Testament view of humanity supraphilosophical, so special that it is philosophically ineffable? I suspect that some readers might delight in that conclusion. For they view philosophy as utterly antithetical to the mystique of the Hebrew mind. As a Christian philosopher, however, I would be deeply troubled by that result, for then the Old Testament would be completely irrelevant to the project of constructing a philosophical theory of human nature.

So I am very gingerly, cautiously, and tentatively going to experiment with a philosophical elaboration and interpretation of the material we have considered up to this point. (My hypothesis is provisional at this stage merely because it does not consider the implicitly dualistic data of the next chapter.) Let me suggest that there are some striking similarities between the anthropology of Aristotle and that of the Old Testament, acknowledging immediately that there are also deep differences. Aristotle was neither a

49

Platonic dualist nor a monist but a sort of "soft dualist" and an ontological holist.

According to Aristotle, all earthly things including human beings are constituted by two metaphysically different elements or principles, form and matter. Thus his ontology is called "hylemorphism" (matter-formism). Neither form nor matter is a substance (in the sense of "existing entity"); only the actual things they together constitute are substances — rocks, trees, birds, and people, for example. Matter is the stuff of which things are composed: earth, air, fire, and water. Form in no way arises out of matter. It is metaphysically *sui generis*. But neither does it exist as a separate or separable substance, as is claimed by Plato. Form is what organizes matter into actual beings, gives them their purposes for existing, provides the power or energy for doing what by nature they are supposed to do, and as the principle of order or rationality, renders them capable of being understood by intelligent beings. Thus, for example, it is the form or "soul" of a plant which gives it the shape of a plant, aims it at the purposes of growth and reproduction, energizes the functions of growth and reproduction, and renders it intelligible as a plant. The same is true for human beings. The human form or "soul" shapes the human bodily organism, gives it the purposes of biological, psychological, rational, social, cultural, and moral existence, and provides the biological, psychological, rational, and volitional powers to function in all the ways proper to human nature. Neither form nor matter is an independent substance. Neither soul nor body has its own independent functions. Rather, soul-form and matter together constitute a single rational-animal substance, a psychophysical unity which as a whole is the proper subject of all human activities, from the growth of the toenails to the construction of philosophical theories. Aristotle's ontology and anthropology represent an ontological holism of two irreducible principles.

The parallels between Aristotle's account and the Old Testament picture are not hard to see. The dust of the ground is something like Aristotle's matter, which in fact includes earth. *Ruach* shares some features of soul or form — it is the source of all the varieties of energy and purpose in human life but is neither matter nor an immaterial entity. Human *ruach*, you recall, is not just biological energy but supplies us with our emotional, rational, volitional, moral, and religious capacities as well. Ignoring other features of Aristotle's metaphysics, some of them (such as the uncreated nature of matter and form) obviously incompatible with the Old Testa-

50

ment, we have a philosophical anthropology which in interesting ways parallels the Hebrew view. Two distinct sorts of ingredients together constitute a holistic unity, the nonmaterial ingredient energizing and directing the entire entity. And neither ingredient as such can function or even continue to exist as a substantial entity once the whole is destroyed.[28]

I am not attempting to ground Aristotle in the Old Testament or assuming that the Israelites were philosophers or suggesting that Aristotle's ideas are fully symmetrical with Hebrew anthropology. I am merely noting the parallels in their two-principle holisms. It is at least interesting to speculate that Solomon, had he engaged in philosophy and been familiar with later Greek thought, might have been more sympathetic to Aristotle than to either Plato or Democritus.

But before baptizing Aristotle or designating the Israelites as proto-Aristotelians, we must consider whether all the data from the Old Testament have been taken into account. One implication of Aristotle's ontological holism is the impossibility of an individual afterlife. At most the spark of rationality inherent in human form might be reassimilated into the cosmic intelligence. But the individual person no more survives death than a drop of water does when it falls into a lake. As noted above, many people nowadays seem to believe that existence after death is not part of the Old Testament world-picture, that with death it is "all over." If the Hebrew view were fully consistent with Aristotle's — simply a two-principle ontological holism — then annihilation at death would indeed be entailed. But as a matter of fact, the Israelites did believe in existence after death. That complicates the picture considerably.

---

28. Unlike Aristotle's form, however, the Old Testament life-principle does not apparently give the body its structure. In Gen. 2:7 *neshama* is added to a formed body. The same is true of *ruach* in Ezekiel 37.

Chapter Three

Old Testament Anthropology: The Dualistic Implication

I. The Old Testament View of Existence after Death

A. Introduction: The Rephaim in Sheol

Although it has become commonplace for many intellectuals and students of religion to consider "nothingness" or annihilation the Hebrew view of what awaits us at death,[1] this idea was derived neither from reading the Old Testament nor from following the discussions of biblical scholars. To the best of my knowledge, in fact, no recognized Old Testament scholar has ever made that claim. In fact there is virtual consensus that the Israelites did believe in some sort of ethereal existence after death in a place called Sheol. Consider the following quotation from H. Wheeler Robinson's classic work *The Religious Ideas of the Old Testament*, written early this century:

> The dead are thus supposed to go on existing in some sense or other, even by the early thought of Israel. But it is an existence which has no attraction for the Israelite. . . . It is not his soul that survives at all; the dead are

---

1. Consider, for example, these remarks on the afterlife by the preeminent process philosopher, Charles Hartshorne, in *Omnipotence and Other Theological Mistakes* (Albany: SUNY Press, 1984), p. 32: "Only the ancient Jews and some of the ancient Greeks were nearly free from this flight from what, for all we really know, is the human condition [subjective nonexistence]. In the sublime Book of Job, where the human destiny is reflected upon with great depth and nobility, there is not a word about survival of death."

called "shades" *(rephaim)*, not "souls" in the Old Testament. The subterranean place of their abiding is called Sheol, and in many particulars it is like the Greek Hades.[2]

Aside from a quibble about the word "soul," this statement would be endorsed by anyone knowledgeable of the Hebrew scriptures.[3] As far as I know, the general description is undisputed among Old Testament scholars.

For our purposes it will be useful to take a brief look at the Old Testament picture of Sheol itself, what existence in Sheol is supposed to be like, the nature of the term *rephaim* and those whom it signifies, and whether there is any hope for the individual beyond Sheol in Israel's eschatology. Once we are clear on what the Old Testament actually says, it will be possible to suggest how that might be construed in categories relevant to philosophical anthropology. Perhaps then we will be able to adjudicate more fully the dualism-monism-holism debate.

But even before the details of the Old Testament texts are considered, a couple of things are obvious. The first is that some sort of ontic duality or dualism is entailed, even if that is non-Platonic. For if something of personal existence survives biological death, then personal existence is separable from earthly, bodily life. The dead survive apart from their flesh and bones. Earthly existence is holistically constituted, but some identifiable part, aspect, or dimension of earthly existence continues beyond the dissolution or dichotomization of the whole. That is not ontological holism as defined above, but some sort of dualism yet to be determined.

My second preliminary observation pertains to a tactic employed in the historical monism-dualism debate. The polemics of antidualist writers and speakers have made a great deal out of the fact, observed above, that the terms *nephesh* and *ruach*, "soul" and "spirit," do not really denote personal immaterial entities which survive death. The "spirit" which returns to God is not a person but a power. Although this may not even be true of *nephesh*, let's grant the claim for now. My point here is that even if true, it

2. H. Wheeler Robinson, *The Christian Doctrine of Man* (Edinburgh: Clark, 1911), p. 92.

3. Cf. the remarks of Otto Kaiser, *Death and Life* (Nashville: Abingdon, 1981), p. 34: ". . . it would be mistaken to conclude . . . that according to the Israelite belief man was utterly annihilated upon his death." "What survived down there below therefore was not simply nothing, but a shadowy, ghostly double of the living, his *'soul'* . . ." (emphasis mine). We will consider the debate over the word *nephesh* later in the chapter.

is irrelevant to the debate. It simply does not follow from the proposition that *nephesh* and *ruach* never refer to the discarnate dead that the dead were thought not to exist. The only knowledge we gain from that proposition concerns the meanings of *nephesh* and *ruach*. We learn nothing about Israelite eschatology. For in reality the Israelites did affirm the existence of the departed. As indicated by Robinson above, they simply had another term for them — *rephaim*. To draw the conclusion that the Hebrews were nondualists or annihilationists from the premise that they did not use *nephesh* and *ruach* to refer to existing dead persons is to commit the fallacy of non sequitur. The conclusion does not follow because the premise by itself is not relevant to the point at issue.

B. Sheol

Having focussed the disputed issues more finely, let's turn to the Old Testament treatment of the afterlife, beginning with *Sheol,* the realm of the dead.[4] It must be admitted at the outset that in some contexts *Sheol* might simply mean "the grave." When Jacob laments, "in mourning I will go down to Sheol to my son" (Gen. 37:35), he might just mean "I will die" or "I will go to my grave." But with much of the Old Testament, he might also understand Sheol much more literally and realistically. In terms of location, it is at the bottom or lowest level of Hebrew cosmology, down in or under the earth. It is "the Pit," reached by going into the earth, usually through the grave. It is the great subterranean chamber into which all graves eventually merge. Deep down, it is as far away as one can get in the Israelite world-picture from the heaven of heavens, the dwelling place of God. And it is hidden from the green earth, the realm of God's dealings with humankind. Not surprisingly, it is a place of deep darkness and gloom, cut off from the light. Its atmosphere is damp and dank, slimy and

---

4. Cf. Kaiser, pp. 43-45; Edmund Sutcliffe, S.J., *The Old Testament and the Future Life* (London: Burns, Oates, and Washbourne, 1946), Ch. VI, "Sheol and Its Inhabitants"; Eichrodt, *Theology of the Old Testament* (Philadelphia: Westminster, 1967), Vol. II, pp. 210-214; A. R. van de Walle, *From Darkness to the Dawn* (Mystic, CT: Twenty-third Publications, 1985), pp. 43-45; and especially Nicholas Tromp, *Primitive Conceptions of Death and the Nether World in the Old Testament* (Rome: Pontifical Biblical Institute, 1969), Part II, Ch. 1, "Localization and Scenery of Sheol," Ch. 2, "Structural Elements," and Ch. 5, "Inhabitants and Conditions."

foul. Sheol has gates and bars which prevent those who enter it from escaping. It is a prison with many rooms and beds. A number of scholars have pointed out its similarities with the Greek underworld, Hades.

Of course most of these characterizations are found in poetic and wisdom texts, so they must be carefully exegeted. But scholars seem to agree that such descriptions of Sheol, and Hebrew cosmology in general, should be taken neither as scientifically literal nor as purely symbolic. Rather they should be understood as imaginative and figurative accounts of the way the people actually pictured the structure of the universe.[5] The Israelites really did believe that Sheol exists beneath the ground.

Perhaps most interesting for traditional Christians to note is the fact that it is the resting place of the dead irrespective of their religion during life. Sheol is not the "hell" to which the wicked are condemned and from which the Lord's faithful are spared in glory. Although the Old Testament has a few hints that even in death the Lord spares and communes with his righteous ones, as we shall see, there is no doubt that believers and unbelievers all were thought to go to Sheol when they died. Job asserts repeatedly that this is where he is headed. So some form of existence in Sheol is the common lot of humanity in the Old Testament, with the notable exceptions of Elijah and Enoch, who were taken by God.

C. Existence in Sheol

But what is existence in Sheol like? Is it enjoyable or horrible? Does it involve any awareness and activity at all? Or is it more like sleep, a mere existence with no consciousness or activity whatsoever?

The general picture which emerges from the Old Testament is that there is overpowering lethargy and inactivity in Sheol, a lack of all the usual modes of existence on earth, although there may be echoes of earthly existence such as being with one's family group. However, occasional emergence from this generally comatose condition was still thought possible for the *rephaim*.

Numerous texts suggest that inactivity and perhaps even unconsciousness are the lot of the departed. Job (3:13) laments his miserable life by noting that in Sheol, ". . . I would be lying down in peace; I would be asleep

5. Cf. Kaiser, p. 44.

and at rest. . . ." The Preacher is even more explicit, apparently ruling out the whole roster of distinctively human capacities and achievements: ". . . in Sheol, where you are going, there is neither working nor planning nor knowledge nor wisdom" (Eccl. 9:10). Without these abilities there is little left of human life as we know it on earth. But even more crucial to existence is a positive subjective relation with the God who "dwells in the praises of his people." Even that seems forfeited in the underworld. Facing death, Hezekiah bargains with the Lord, reminding him that ". . . the grave *(Sheol)* cannot praise you, death cannot sing your praise; those who go down to the pit cannot hope for your faithfulness" (Isa. 38:18). The Psalmist expresses similar sentiment: "It is not the dead who praise the LORD, those who go down to silence; it is we who extol the LORD both now and forevermore" (Ps. 115:17-18). More extensive still is Psalm 88:10-12:

> Do you show your wonders to the dead *(rephaim)?* Do those who are dead rise up and praise you? Is your love declared in the grave *(Sheol)*, your faithfulness in Destruction *(Abaddon)?* Are your wonders known in the place of darkness, or your righteous deeds in the land of oblivion?

Reading all the passages of this sort together certainly leaves the impression that in the Old Testament perspective the dead possess nothing more than sheer unconscious existence.

But there are also texts which suggest that at least on occasion the inhabitants of the underworld are conscious and active. Consider Isaiah 14:9-10, where the king of Babylon is taunted by a prediction of his downfall:

> The grave *(Sheol)* below is all astir to meet you at your coming; it rouses the spirits of the departed *(rephaim)* to greet you — all those who were leaders in the world; it makes them rise from their thrones — all those who were kings over the nations. They will respond, they will say to you, "You also have become weak, as we are; you have become like us."

This is an unusual occurrence in Sheol. But it certainly does represent the dead as able to remember and recognize the Babylonian king, speak to him, and compare their former situations with the present. They admit that they are weak, having lost their political and perhaps also their personal power. But even in death they retain something of their former status. They are still identifiable as former rulers and they sit on thrones. Admittedly unusual, a great deal more than mere comatose existence is attributed to the dead in this passage. It seems to indicate that occasional activity was at least in principle possible in the Hebrew view of the deceased.

But an obvious objection to this conclusion is the fact that this is a poetic passage, a prophecy couched in highly figurative language.[6] Perhaps Isaiah had no intention of saying anything at all about Sheol or its inhabitants. Perhaps this is just an imaginative way of depicting the demise of a self-exalted tyrant. After all, twentieth-century people employ ghosts and goblins as metaphors without believing that they exist. And since it is difficult to sort out the literal from the figurative in Hebrew modes of expression, perhaps we have no warrant in this text for drawing any conclusion about what the Israelites might have thought possible for the dead. It should be noted, however, that this objection cuts both ways. It is also a problem for those who argue from Job, Psalms, and Ecclesiastes that pure unconsciousness is the literal Hebrew belief about the dead. Those texts cannot be taken at face value either. Invoking the indeterminacy of poetic language is a strategy which puts the whole issue beyond discussion.

Fortunately for our purposes there are nonpoetic legal and narrative texts which also address the possible conscious existence of the deceased. These pertain to necromancy — communication with the dead. Isaiah admonishes the people of Judah: "When men tell you to consult mediums and spiritists, who whisper and mutter, should not a people inquire of their God? Why consult the dead on behalf of the living?" (8:19). Here he is holding the people to the law of the Lord which several times explicitly forbids consulting the dead (Lev. 19:31; 20:6; Deut. 18:11). The cult of the dead and the practice of spiritism were widespread among Israel's neighbors, and the Lord's prohibition of such occult activities was of a piece with his general proscription of false Canaanite religion.[7] But surely if the Israelites did not believe that the dead existed or that they could be consulted, there would have been no need to warn them against such practices. As Ringgren concludes, "belief in an afterlife is also indicated by the practice of necromancy. . . ."[8]

---

6. Cf. Tromp's caution about Isaiah 14: "it is hard to tell how far the poet took this as literal truth himself" (p. 186). However, Tromp certainly does not take it as purely poetic and nonreferential.

7. Hans Walter Wolff, *Anthropology of the Old Testament* (Philadelphia: Fortress, 1974), pp. 102-105.

8. Helmer Ringgren, *Israelite Religion* (London: SPCK, 1966), p. 242.

The most graphic example of necromancy in the Old Testament is the story of Saul and the Witch of Endor in I Samuel 28. The prophet Samuel had died and the Lord had rejected Saul, who now was utterly alone and in despair. Although he had expelled all the spiritists from Israel, he nevertheless goes to consult one himself and requests her to "bring up Samuel" (v. 11). "The woman said, 'I see a spirit coming up out of the ground.' 'What does he look like?' he asked. 'An old man wearing a robe is coming up,' she said. Then Saul knew it was Samuel . . ." (vv. 13b-14b).

Of course it is possible to attempt explaining the story away. Perhaps it is intended to highlight Saul's desperation, not to tell us about the dead. Or possibly what appeared was not Samuel but a hallucination of the medium which both she and Saul took to be real. Yet most interpreters stand with Wolff: "The Old Testament itself is able to report a successful case of conjuring up the dead. . . . Samuel does actually rise up in ghost-like form."[9] Saul not only correctly concludes that it is Samuel from the medium's description of him, he actually has a conversation with Samuel. No mere phantom or passive apparition, Samuel recognizes Saul, chides him for the disturbance, and once more prophesies for the Lord against Saul. Grimly Samuel foretells Saul's doom: "Tomorrow you and your sons will be with me" (v. 19).

Treating this text as historical narrative, we can observe a number of things about Israelite views of the dead. First, it is clear that there is continuity of personal identity between the living and the dead. In other words, dead Samuel is still Samuel, not someone or something else. He is the very person who was once alive, and not a mere ghostly copy of him, recognizably similar but numerically distinct.[10] Second, although this is a highly unusual occurrence, Samuel is nonetheless a typical resident of Sheol. For he expects Saul and his sons to be joining him. That would not be true if he

---

9. Wolff, p. 104; cf. Kaiser, p. 35.

10. Some may object to my use of the term "person" to refer to the dead on the ground that persons are essentially active agents and relational beings, properties which the dead in Sheol may well lack. In this sense they deny that the Old Testament envisions personal existence even though the ghost survives death. I use "person" to refer to the self-identical individuality of the human being which perdures even through periods of non-relating and inactivity. On my view, if the being can appropriately be referred to by the proper personal name, it is the person herself, active or inactive. The inhabitants of Sheol can be so referred to by name in a way which their corpses or pictures of them could not be. Hence they are the self-identical persons as lived on earth.

were in some special state of suspended animation provided by God for this unique occasion. Third, although he implies he was resting, it was still possible for him to "wake up" and engage in a number of acts of conscious communication. Activity is still in principle possible for the dead even if they are usually "asleep." Fourth, Samuel is a "ghost" or "shade," not a Platonic soul or Cartesian mind. For Plato and Descartes the soul is immaterial, nonspatial, and imperceptible by the human senses. Samuel, in contrast, puts in a visual appearance, is recognized by his form, and is even wearing a white robe. In addition, he speaks with a voice that can be heard. No purely immaterial substance is he, but rather a ghost or spirit as conceived by the animistic peoples of the world — a quasi-bodily being. His corpse was buried at Ramah (v. 3), yet he was in Sheol and appeared at Endor in bodily form. Whether visibility is an occasional or constant property of the deceased is unclear. But bodiliness in some ethereal mode or other is a constant. The ghost retains the form of the earthly body.

We will reflect more fully on the significance of these observations in the philosophical section below. For now it seems warranted to conclude the following. Old Testament people believed that the dead continue to exist in a ghostly form in an underworld location called Sheol. Although their general condition might have been considered inactive and even unconscious, it was certainly thought possible that on occasion they could become conscious and active.

D. Terminology for the Dead

It is interesting to consider the term *rephaim* itself. Although a scholarly tradition has plausibly associated it with the root *raphah*,[11] "to be weak," a number of recent challenges to that hypothesis have been offered. Tromp, for example, has charged that many scholars have concluded that the *rephaim* are weak and lethargic simply because the term supposedly comes from *raphah*. To the contrary, he asserts that "the conception of a shadowy, flaccid existence of the dead cannot be associated with the title Rephaim."[12] First he reminds us of James Barr's exposure of the etymolog-

---

11. Cf. Brown, Driver, and Briggs, *A Hebrew and English Lexicon of the Old Testament* (Oxford: Clarendon, 1953, 1977), p. 952.
12. Tromp, p. 180; cf. also Eichrodt, II, p. 214 n. 1.

ical fallacy — meaning is not simply determined by derivation, but by use. Then he carefully proposes an alternative analysis. The fact is that this term also refers a number of times to giants who inhabited the land of Canaan.[13] Among Israel's neighbors these people seem to have taken on superhuman proportions and become mythologized in connection with the afterlife. In Ugaritic texts "the Rephaim appear to be helping and healing ancestral spirits. And thus the name very well may have remained in the Hebrew language. . . ."[14] So the word may actually be related to *rapha'*, "to heal or mend." Animistic mythology is also apparent in the fact that Ugaritic texts sometimes treat *rephaim* and *elohim* ("god" or "gods") as parallel terms or synonyms. The dead actually take on a semidivine status and thus must be reckoned with by the living.[15] Against this background it is most interesting to observe that the term the Witch of Endor uses for Samuel is *elohim:* "I see *elohim* coming out of the ground!" Perhaps she is a Canaanite. In any case here is an Old Testament usage of *elohim* which parallels *rephaim.* It would be foolish to draw any conclusions about Israelite beliefs from such meager linguistic data. But I will note in passing that the connotation of greatness or superhuman proportion is preserved even in the Septuagint. For it translates the dead *rephaim* in Proverbs 21:6 and in Isaiah 14 (considered above) as *hoi gigantes,* "the giants" or "the great ones." At the very least we may say that etymological data do not establish the view that existence in Sheol was considered virtual nothingness. There may very well be hints in the opposite direction.

Are *rephaim* and *elohim* the only terms used for those in Sheol? That depends on whether *nephesh* ever has this meaning, which is a matter of scholarly debate. The fact is that several times the Old Testament does speak of a *nephesh* departing at death or being in Sheol. The only dispute concerns what that means. According to Wolff:

> When there is a mention of the "departing" (Gen. 35:18) of the *nephesh* from a man, or of its "return" (Lam. 1:1), the basic idea . . . is the concrete notion of the ceasing and restoration of the breathing. When Yahweh leads up the *nephesh* from the underworld (Ps. 30:3; 86:13), the idea is the

13. Cf., e.g., Deut. 2:11; 3:11; II Sam. 21:16f. Cf. also Gesenius's *Hebrew-Chaldee Lexicon to the Old Testament* (Grand Rapids: Eerdmans, 1949, 1980), p. 776.

14. Kaiser, p. 42.

15. Tromp, Ch. 5.1, "The Rephaim and Elohim"; Kaiser, p. 42.

return to healthy life of the whole man who has, through his illness, already been exposed to the power of death.[16]

So talk of *nephesh* departing at death or being located in Sheol is not to be taken as literally about something which exists in the afterlife, at least according to Wolff.[17]

But does this really account for Psalms 16:10, 139:8, and especially 49:15, the latter unquestionably about the literal end of life? "But God will redeem my *nephesh* from Sheol; he will surely take me to himself" (NIV). Perhaps the term *nephesh* is not technically intended to denote persons in distinction from their flesh and bones, but just to mean "myself" or "my life." Any Israelite would agree nevertheless that the "self" or "life" in Sheol lacks flesh and bones. So *nephesh* would connote discarnate persons even if it did not denote them. These considerations have led some scholars to conclude that *nephesh* is occasionally used to refer to a personal being which survives physical death and remains in existence. Kaiser, for example, holds that this is the case for the Psalms mentioned as well as the souls of Rachel (Gen. 35) and the widow of Serapta's son (I Kings 17). The *nephesh* which left them at death was not merely a last breath, but their personal being — a substantial, separable soul or self. "The Hebrew could indeed actually understand the 'soul' *(nephesh)* to mean the soul of the deceased, and at least later did understand it this way."[18]

Holding that *nephesh* occasionally refers to human beings who have died is certainly possible, if not demonstrable, on the basis of Old Testament scholarship. It cannot be certified, but neither can it be discounted. And apart from the Old Testament itself, neither among Israel's neighbors nor among "primitive" peoples worldwide is there an antithesis between "life-breath" and "separable soul." For many of these people, all of whom have "holistic" anthropologies, it is not a matter of either breath or soul, but both/and.[19] Whether

16. Wolff, p. 20; cf. also p. 13.

17. Cf. also Eichrodt, II, p. 214.

18. Kaiser, p. 40.

19. Cf. Mircea Eliade, *From the Primitives to Zen* (San Francisco: Harper and Row, 1977), pp. 177-178. He draws material from E. B. Tylor's *Theory of Animism*, which gives examples from several diverse cultures in which one word means both "breath" and "soul" and in which the soul, the continuing locus of personal identity, departs as the last breath at death. Cf. also John Hick, *Death and Eternal Life* (San Francisco: Harper and Row, 1976), pp. 56, 422 n. 12. Eichrodt, II, p. 140, however, does not think that parallels can be drawn between Israel and other peoples on this point.

the Hebrews actually held this view or not, it cannot be ruled out simply by an a priori appeal to some "Semitic totality concept."

In summary, although there is some basis for affirming this view, it does not finally matter whether *nephesh* is used to refer to persons who have died. For *rephaim* clearly has that role. There can be no doubt that the Israelites believed them to exist.

E. Hope Beyond the Grave; Resurrection

Thus far in our survey of the evidence for dualism we have considered the existence of the *rephaim* in Sheol. Before moving to systematic conclusions there remains one topic of crucial importance: expressions of hope beyond the grave, including the anticipation of resurrection.

As numerous scholars have pointed out, the dreariness of existence in Sheol is not all the Old Testament emphasizes. Just as it speaks of both rest and activity among the dead, so it affirms the transcendence of death as intensely as it shrinks from the finality of the grave. The two need not be mutually exclusive in the Hebrew world-picture.[20]

First let's consider a few texts which strongly express this ultimate hope. Several Psalms read most naturally as confessing a steadfast if unspecified trust in God beyond death. We have already mentioned Psalm 49. The whole context is about human mortality. Then verse 15 says: "But God will ransom my soul from the power of the underworld; for he will release me" (RSV). Kaiser points out that the verb of the last clause is *laqach*, and means "take me out of Sheol."[21] The NIV reads, ". . . and he will take me to himself." Thus the expression signifies res-

---

20. Thus I am not persuaded that it is necessary to postulate an evolution of religious consciousness in order to account for the presence of both in the Old Testament. Cf. Kaiser, Chs. IV and VI; Wolff, pp. 107-110. The strategy of many scholars is to suggest that the ancient Hebrews viewed Yahweh as the God of the living only; his presence and power ceased at the borders of Sheol. But later Hebrews expanded his sphere of influence to include Sheol and thus began to hope beyond death. This provided a theodicy for the justice of God in the face of undeserved suffering in life. I am not an Old Testament scholar, but I do not see why the Hebrews could not have held both beliefs all along, sometimes stressing death as the horrible termination of earthly life and at others emphasizing trust in God even beyond the borders of life. Exclusive disjunction does not always function strongly in Hebrew thought and writing, as most scholars will readily admit.

21. Kaiser, p. 80.

cue from out of the realm of death, not mere restoration to health during life. The same is true of Psalm 73:26: "My flesh and my heart may fail, but God is the strength of my heart and my portion forever." The writer has hope beyond death which the wicked do not have. And Psalm 16:10 confesses, "you will not abandon me to the grave, nor will you let your Holy One see decay." Peter applies that verse to the resurrection of Jesus Christ in Acts 2. But even for the Psalmist himself it is a clear expression of hope beyond the grave. Summarizing a number of these passages, Wolff concludes: "Before Yahweh . . . there is not only the alternative between this life and the shadow existence in the world of the dead; there is a third possibility — a permanent, living fellowship with him."[22] The locus and mode of this fellowship are not indicated by these texts, however.

Adding some detail about this hope are the resurrection texts in the Old Testament. Due caution must be exercised, of course, for not every passage which tradition has taken as a prooftext for resurrection will stand up to scrutiny. Ezekiel 37, for example, the vision of the dry bones, must not be taken as a prophecy of personal resurrection but as a figure referring to the renewal of the covenant people of God. It should not be dismissed altogether, on the other hand, for it does use the imagery of personal resurrection even if it does not teach it. We know exactly how Ezekiel, and probably most Israelites of that time, would imagine a resurrection taking place. The Lord would bring the bones, muscles, sinews, and skin together out of the dust to form a human body. Then he would impart the *ruach* to give it life. It would parallel the original creation of humankind.

Another difficult example is Job 19:25-27: "I know that my Redeemer lives, and that in the end he will stand upon the earth. And after my skin has been destroyed, yet in my flesh I will see God; I myself will see him with my own eyes — I and not another." Suffice it to say that this is a very difficult text, especially in Hebrew. Some scholars read "without my flesh" instead of "in my flesh" in verse 26. And some take the destruction of the skin to indicate Job's terrible sickness rather than decomposition after death. So Job's vindication by his Redeemer may suggest his return to health in this life or to victory beyond the grave. If the latter, it might be either with a body or without one. Thus the traditional resur-

---

22. Wolff, p. 109.

rection interpretation may well be correct, but it is impossible to be certain.[23]

At least two resurrection passages are undisputed, however. Consider first Daniel 12:2: "Multitudes who sleep in the dust of the earth will awake: some to everlasting life, others to shame and everlasting contempt." This verse is significant because it connects resurrection, judgment, and two eternal destinies. Some will rise to eternal blessedness and others to the opposite fate. Such a direct and explicit reference to final separation is not obvious earlier in the Old Testament. At most there are hints of differences within Sheol. What is missing from the Daniel text, however, is an unambiguous designation of the status and location of the dead. They are "asleep in the dust of the earth" and shall "awake." But what do these metaphors mean? Though compatible with the Sheol view of the rest of the Old Testament, Daniel's figures of speech might also be interpreted as implying the nonexistence of the dead between death and resurrection. Perhaps during the interim they are nothing but dust. Strictly speaking, it is not clear whether affirmation of the resurrection here replaces or merely adds to belief in Sheol.

All such ambiguity is eliminated in Isaiah 26:19, however. Part of an apocalyptic vision of the future coming of the Lord, it reads as follows: "But your dead will live; their bodies will rise. You who dwell in the dust, wake up and shout for joy. Your dew is like the dew of the morning; the earth will give birth to her dead." That this speaks of actual resurrection and not merely national renewal is evident from verse 14: "They are now dead, they live no more; those departed spirits do not rise." But in verse 19 they do rise and live again. Highly significant for our inquiry is the fact that the term for the deceased both in v. 14b and v. 19d is *rephaim,* the word used in Isaiah 14 and throughout the Old Testament to designate the dwellers in Sheol. So here we have an unequivocal link between the future bodily resurrection and the inhabitants of the underworld realm of the dead. On the great day of the Lord, the *rephaim* will be reunited with their bodies, reconstituted from the dust, and they will live as the Lord's people again.

Thus we definitely do have Old Testament "prooftexts" for the resurrection. I claim no more than a whisper of the resurrection in the Old Testament. But it is a clear and distinctly audible whisper. This is enough to

23. Cf. E. S. P. Heavenor in *The New Bible Commentary: Revised* (Grand Rapids: Eerdmans, 1970), p. 432.

refute those who hold that in the Old Testament as a whole human existence ceases at death. And one need not think of resurrection as a foreign import from Persian religion, no matter when one dates Daniel and Isaiah 24–27. The logic of resurrection is contained within the Old Testament itself. For if the Lord is in control of everything, then he is Lord of death too and there is hope beyond the grave. And given the holistic emphasis on bodily, earthly existence considered above, the only way the Israelite could meaningfully think of future existence with the Lord was in bodily terms. Hence the resurrection.

But there is more in view. The time-line of personal eschatology inherent in Isaiah 26 is in embryonic form the time-line of the New Testament (we shall argue) and traditional Christian faith. At death the person becomes one of the shades and remains for a time in Sheol. Then at the Lord's coming she will return to resurrected bodily life. This implies that there is an intermediate state between death and resurrection in which the person exists, but not in an active, bodily way. This belief undergoes modifications and elaborations during the intertestamental period on the way to the New Testament, as we shall see. But its essential outline is present already in Isaiah. And once again it is unnecessary to suppose that this notion has been imported from Greece or Persia. For belief in Sheol was part of the Old Testament from earliest times. It could have been augmented quite naturally by the hope of resurrection through progressive revelation. That the intermediate state is natural to Hebrew thought is also Kaiser's conclusion:

> [I]t must be maintained that the conception of an intermediate state after death could develop organically on the basis of the Old Testament belief about death and the soul, whatever outside influences may have contributed to this development.[24]

This concludes our survey of the Old Testament view of what happens when people die. On the one hand, the completed picture forms an organic unity with our previous study of Hebrew anthropological terms and the holism which they strongly imply. On the other hand, the fact that something of personal existence not only survives biological death but comes to be thought of as returning to bodily life seems to entail an

---

24. Kaiser, p. 41. On the same page Kaiser denies that he personally believes in an intermediate state. So he cannot be accused of grinding his own ax in coming to this conclusion about the Old Testament.

ontological duality or dualism of some sort. What that amounts to remains to be seen.

II. Philosophical Reflection: Holistic Dualism

A. Clarifying the Anthropological Image

At the end of the previous chapter, it was very tentatively suggested that had Solomon been a prescient borrower of Greek philosophy, he would have had to modify the views of Aristotle less than those of Plato or the materialists to construct a theoretical anthropology. For Aristotle proposes a two-principle ontological holism in which the soul activates the whole entity. The Hebrew picture contains the parallel suggestion that humans are single beings comprised of inputs from two mutually irreducible sources, *ruach* providing the animating power. These similarities can be appreciated provided the essential differences between Aristotle and the Old Testament are borne in mind. We also noted, however, that ontological holism (Aristotelian or otherwise) would not allow for continued personal existence after death in any sense whatever. For neither element constitutive of a human being can be an individual substantial entity on its own. Now that the Old Testament data have stipulated some form of postmortem existence, we must modify our speculation about Solomon's preferred anthropologist.

In order to proceed we must get clear on the picture-image of human nature we are dealing with. Only then will accurate conceptualization be possible.

It seems that the postmortem appearance of Samuel is the clearest example we have of what the dead were thought to be like. We noted above that he did not have the characteristics of a wholly immaterial being — utterly devoid of shape and spatial location, and in principle imperceptible to the normal senses. Thus he was neither a Platonic soul nor a Cartesian mind. For he was recognized by his visible gestalt, was wearing a robe, and spoke audible sentences. In other words, Samuel was still an ethereal bodily being of some sort. He lacked the material substantiality of a fleshly body but was not wholly incorporeal.

John Hick describes this sort of ghostly being as "a double or shade or image of the bodily individual. That which survives death was not at this stage thought of as mind in distinction from body but rather as a shadowy and insubstantial counterpart of the body."[25] The philosopher Peter Geach likewise distinguishes this commonsense animistic view, still held by educated spiritists in the modern world, from the soul-body dualism of Plato and Descartes. The latter present a more philosophical view of the soul, defining it as wholly incorporeal. The spiritist belief "is that man has a subtle, ordinarily invisible body which survives the death of the ordinarily gross body."[26] So the dead are thought of as ethereal bodily beings whereas the living are fleshly bodily beings. The contrast is between fleshly and non-fleshly, not between bodily and nonbodily.[27]

What sort of relationship obtains between the fleshly and nonfleshly modes of existence and how do they relate to dust and life-principle — the two constitutive elements of human life discussed above? Is the ghost in the earthly body all along, as Geach suggests? If so, is it the same as the *nephesh* or *ruach* after all? Or is the ghost all that remains of the living creature once *ruach* is withdrawn and the flesh returns to dust? Or is it perhaps the case that the ghost has no directly continuous identity at all with the living person but is just an image, picture, representation, or apparition of a being which no longer exists? Those are the alternatives.

Let's consider the last possibility first, that the ghost is distinct from but similar to a person who formerly existed. A shadow, after all, is completely distinct from the body which casts it. However, recall the point made above in connection with Samuel, that the persons existing in Sheol are identical with those who lived on earth even if some of their properties

---

25. Hick, p. 56.

26. Peter Geach, "Immortality," in *Immortality*, ed. T. Penelhum (Belmont, CA: Wadsworth, 1973), pp. 11-12. It is interesting to notice here that the distinction between these views does not pit the Greeks against the Hebrews but philosophers against nonphilosophers. Belief in quasi-bodily ghosts or spirits is common among primitive people in general, including both Hebrews and Greeks, and is still held by those in England, for example, who subscribe to the reality of the "paranormal," as Geach points out. Both Plato and Descartes thought they were giving a philosophical account of the possibility of such "disembodied" entities. Perhaps they were off the mark. Philosophers often claim to be representing the views of the person-on-the-street, with mixed results.

27. This conclusion results from an analysis of Israelite beliefs about death, not from mere consideration of anthropological terms such as *basar* (flesh). Thus it stands even if *basar* never has this meaning. *Nebalah* is the word for "corpse," the lifeless mass of flesh, bones, and organs. The Hebrews certainly thought that the *rephaim* exist separate from their corpses. So the departed are corporeal in form, but lack flesh in the sense of muscles, bones, and organs.

have changed. It was Samuel himself and not a mere ghostly copy who spoke with Saul. The kings of the earth and not their look-alike representatives are the ones who rose up in Isaiah 14. The Psalmist hopes that he will be rescued from Sheol. So although treating ghosts as surrogate beings would greatly aid a monistic account of this material — one body-mind monad ceases to exist and is replaced by another monad — it simply will not stand up to scrutiny. The absolute continuity of personal identity beyond death is essential to the Old Testament picture.

So we are left with two options. Either the ghostly person is some third thing distinct from flesh and life-force or else it is identical with the life-force *(nephesh* or *ruach)* after all. In the first case the picture would look like this. A person comes into existence when God puts together the dust of the ground and the life-force; he or she is then a *nephesh chayah,* a living being. At death the life-force is removed and the flesh returns to dust. But we are not left with nothing — the person as ethereal body remains. Perhaps it is ghostly and lethargic precisely because it lacks the energy of heart and life and the substantiality of flesh and bones. Here the personal whole is more than the sum of the constitutive parts. And it can exist, occasionally even functioning, without them. But the person is distinct from *ruach* and *nephesh* in the sense of life-principle. Neither *nephesh* nor *ruach* becomes a substantial entity on this interpretation.

The only other option is that the ghostly person is what the *nephesh* and/or *ruach* becomes once it is withdrawn from the fleshly body.[28] If this is correct, the soul is the nonfleshly person who survives organic death. We have already noticed above that this view of *nephesh* is defended by at least one Old Testament scholar, Otto Kaiser, and that the identification of ghostly persons with the soul-breath by Semitic and non-Semitic peoples alike is widely recognized by cultural anthropologists. In the next chapter we will see that later Judaism did in fact use *nephesh* and *ruach* to refer to disembodied persons. This meaning is very possibly implicit in Old Testament usage as well. Of course the embarrassing implication of this inter-

---

28. I am distinguishing the two terms in case Eichrodt is correct that *ruach* is general life-force and *nephesh* is individuated life-force. Kaiser argues only that *nephesh* is used to refer to deceased persons; he does not include *ruach.* However, since both *nephesh* and *ruach* can stand for the person or self in Old Testament writings, either could stand for the self as it exists after death. There is nothing odd about this. In any case, I am not as interested in the terms as in their referent: the life-principle as identified with the subsistent person. For the argument it matters little whether it translates as "soul" or "spirit" or both.

pretation is that traditional Christian Platonists were tracking the right view all along, even if they favored it for the wrong reason — philosophical prejudice rather than Old Testament erudition. *Nephesh* and/or *ruach*, if this option is correct, are sometimes meant to refer to deceased persons after separation from their fleshly, earthly bodies and thus can sometimes be understood as "subsistent soul."

When all the evidence is weighed, the only responsible conclusion is that it is finally impossible to determine which of the last two options is correct. We do not know whether the ghost is the remainder when flesh, bones, and life-force are subtracted or whether the ghost is the life-force (*nephesh/ruach*) itself after bodily death, that is, a subsistent soul. Perhaps the Israelites themselves had no clear view of the matter.

B. Dualism: The Inescapable Implication of Existence in Sheol

This ambiguous outcome does not impede our investigation, however. For either way you cut it — whether with Kaiser you hold that the deceased person is the "soul" or with Eichrodt and Wolff that the ghostly person is distinct from the "soul" — you have some sort of ontological duality, that is, a dualism.[29] That conclusion is inescapable. For either way, persons are not merely distinguishable from their earthly bodies, they are separable from them and can continue to exist without them. At death there is a dichotomy of fleshly and personal existence. A person need not be a purely nonbodily substance as in Plato or Descartes for dualism to result. Being an ethereal or quasi-bodily entity will do just as well. The logic is just as inexorable.[30] Dualism is entailed and ontological holism is ruled out.

Eichrodt is one scholar who struggles mightily to dodge the dualist bullet and preserve the "whole man": "what survives, therefore, is not a part of

29. More precisely, we have at least a dualism. For if the first option is correct, we end up with three terms: dust, life-force, and person. Those who wish to defend a trichotomistic anthropology of body, soul, and spirit might appreciate this result. Subsequent chapters will indicate why the case for trichotomy is weak. Although I am not considering it as an option, I count defenders of this position as allies in the debate with monists.

30. Geach, p. 11, demonstrates that the so-called mind-body problem arises for the commonsense dualist as inevitably as it does for the Platonist. I would rather speak of the person-fleshly body problem in this context.

the living man but a shadowy image of the whole man." And again: "That, however, which lives on in the grave is not a soul which once had been present in the living person but the whole man."[31] Eichrodt is correct if he means that the ghost is not wholly incorporeal but retains bodily form. He is playing games with the term "whole man," however. The "shadowy image" is not the "whole man." For either flesh and bones are constitutive of the whole man during life or they are not. If they are, and if the *rephaim* have no flesh and bones, which they do not, then we do not have the "whole man" in Sheol. If, on the other hand, these "parts" are not constitutive of the whole man during life, then we do not even have holism in the first place, but a radical dualism. Logically speaking, therefore, the only possible choice is between kinds of dualism, not between dualism and nondualism.

C. Holistic Dualism: Philosophical Implication of Old Testament Anthropology

So the final result of our inquiry into Old Testament anthropology yields both functional holism and dualism. Holism is the conclusion of the previous chapter. We saw that the Hebrews certainly emphasized the goodness and desirability of an earthly, bodily existence lived richly in terms of all the relationships God created for human life. They prized food, family, friends, and a faithful walk with the Lord in the community of his people. That is what life was created to be. They viewed a human being as an integrated whole, using no dichotomous categories which compartmentalize body, mind, emotions, and will. Biological processes are not just functions of the body as distinct from the soul or spirit, and mental and spiritual capacities are not seated exclusively in the soul or spirit. All capacities and functions belong to the human being as a whole, a fleshly-spiritual totality. Surely the Old Testament people of God viewed human beings holistically as single entities which are psychosomatic unities.

At the same time they believed that human persons continue to exist after death, though in a state far less desirable than earthly life. While it is not clear whether the dead were thought to be totally unconscious or merely lethargic, they do lack the vitality of life in this world. Someday the righteous will return to bodily life on earth by the miraculous power of

31. Eichrodt, II, p. 214.

70

God. This view is unquestionably dualistic and yet it is fully compatible with Hebrew holism, even by the standards of Western or Aristotelian logic. More precisely, it is compatible with existential-functional holism but rules out ontological holism. For the former but not the latter is compatible with the claim that the personal part, dimension, or aspect of the human being can survive her physical death.

Returning to our speculations about the hypothetical Hebrew philosopher, Solomon, we must therefore modify our modest proposal. The two-principle ontology of Aristotle will not do, for although it yields holism, it does not allow for personal existence after death. But Platonism has not seemed adequate either, for Plato stressed the immaterial nature of the soul so strongly that after death it could not possibly be the quasi-bodily entity of the Old Testament. Further, he strongly held to the functional difference between soul and body even during this life. While he taught that the soul imparts life to the body and even that it is the seat of bodily appetites, he could never speak of the body as the seat of spiritual capacities as the Hebrew could. In Plato's defense it must be recognized that his definition of soul was in part an attempt to state philosophically what some nonphilosophical Greeks of his day believed about the soul as life-force and about ghosts and spirits, ideas in some ways similar to those of the Hebrews.[32] But Plato's definition does not fully square with those beliefs. For he prized the substantial soul as the real person and the body as an external encumbrance which hinders perfect existence rather than being essential to it. Such a view is faithful neither to the Greek picture of souls in Hades nor compatible with the Hebrew image of the *rephaim* in Sheol, much less of *nephesh* during life.[33]

32. Cf. the comments in note 26 above which distinguish Plato from non-philosophical Greeks and Hebrews alike. Notice also the similarities to the Old Testament in the following account of Homeric anthropology: "The *psyche*, which held the position of greatest importance from the time of Pythagoras, was merely a life-soul in Homer; it played no part in the thoughts, emotions, and actions of the living man. The *psyche* survived after death; it did not, however, retain the complete moral personality, as in the Platonic eschatology, but was a bloodless, helpless shadow. The thoughts and feelings of the living man were attributed to the *phrenes* (roughly speaking, the organs of the chest . . .), the heart, and the *thymos* (a mysterious entity probably connected, like *psyche*, with breath)." David Furley, "Homer," *The Encyclopedia of Philosophy*, 8 vols., ed. Paul Edwards (New York: Macmillan and Free Press, 1967, 1972), Vol. IV, p. 62.

33. An excellent introduction to Plato's idea of the soul is Diogenes Allen's "Plato: This World Is Not Our Home," the second chapter of his *Philosophy for Understanding Theology* (Atlanta: John Knox, 1985). Allen points out the important differences between Plato's views

What we need for Solomon then is something between Plato and Aristotle or perhaps some combination of the two. But that of course is precisely what was effected in later Christian thought by Thomas Aquinas, among others. He used Aristotle's hylemorphism to construct an anthropology which was holistic, avoiding both the implication that a living person consists of two distinct entities and any antipathy between matter and form. He thought of the human form or soul as organizing, energizing, and directing the entirety of human life, from biological processes to religious devotion. He insisted that the body-soul unity is the subject of all human functions and actions. But Thomas also synthesized Aristotle with Augustinian Platonism, for one reason because he could then account for the survival of the person between death and the resurrection of the body. The soul can survive physical death as a conscious subsistent being. But according to its created nature it needs a body and is limited without one. Thomas's synthesis, not Descartes's dualism, was in the main followed by most orthodox Christian theologians, Catholic and Protestant alike. In my own Dutch Reformed tradition Abraham Kuyper, Herman Bavinck, and even Herman Dooyeweerd are heirs of this legacy in spite of their important criticisms of aspects of it. My hunch is that if Solomon were philosophically minded and if he had to choose from among classical Western philosophies, Christian Aristotelian Platonism is what he would have found least incompatible with the holistic dualism of his own Old Testament anthropology.[34] But that, after all, is just speculation.

---

and those of the Greek myths of Hades. He also sets straight some Christian caricatures of Plato. His mature views, those of *Timaeus* and *Phaedrus,* do not represent the soul merely as pure mind, but also as will and emotions, i.e., a genuine person. Further, the older Plato no longer held a completely antithetical, proto-gnostic view of the body and its needs. He did not change his mind about the immortality of the soul and the ultimate necessity of transcending the body, however.

34. I do not imply by this judgment that the meanings assigned to various anthropological terms in this tradition are either explicitly derived from the Old Testament or that they fully coincide with Old Testament terminology. There are significant differences, for example, between *nephesh, ruach,* and Thomas's notion of the soul as the form of the body. For one thing, *nephesh* and *ruach* do not seem to give the body its form. But there are striking similarities as well. What I am asserting is that this philosophical tradition articulates a holistic-dualistic anthropology, the same general sort of anthropology implied by the non-philosophical picture of human nature presented in the Old Testament. Thus it is more compatible with Hebrew anthropology than any other classical Western philosophical tradition.

Chapter Four

The Anthropology of
Intertestamental Eschatology

I. Introduction

Many Scripture readers unwittingly assume that the whole Bible presents the same ideas about God, humanity, and salvation and that the Old and New Testaments mean pretty much the same things by the words they use. But theologians have traditionally pointed out that revelation is "progressive." The trinitarian character of God and the identity of the Messiah are clear examples of doctrines which highlight differences between the Testaments as well as their continuity. Developments in anthropology and eschatology are also cases of progressive revelation. There are differences between the Testaments which, if ignored, will hamper understanding what they actually say about human nature and its future.

In the debate between monists and dualists about biblical anthropology, there are those on both sides who seem to ignore these progressions. Traditional dualists, as we have seen, too easily read later Christian ideas of "body," "soul," and "spirit" into the Old Testament. Sometimes they have attempted to find New Testament teachings about heaven and hell in the Hebrew descriptions of Sheol. But modern monists also have their ways of glossing over the differences between the Testaments. They interpret the anthropology of the Old Testament monistically and minimize its view of the afterlife. They then proceed to read the New Testament as though its anthropology were identical with the Old Testament view. As regards personal eschatology, the only difference they recognize is that the New Testament has added a doctrine of resurrection to what would otherwise amount to nonexistence

73

after biological death. The New Testament, it is alleged, fully adheres to what the monist understands as the "Hebrew mind." At least some participants on both sides of the monism-dualism debate have assumed a kind of timelessness of meanings and ideas spanning the Testaments.

If a careful reading of the Old and New Testaments themselves does not reveal their striking differences as well as their basic continuity on matters of anthropology and eschatology, studying them in comparison with the literature of intertestamental Judaism surely will. For the vocabulary of human nature and the doctrine of death and the afterlife developed in important and unmistakable ways between the third century B.C. and the first century A.D.

In this chapter, therefore, we will consider the material which forms a bridge between the Testaments in order to achieve a finer focus in the subsequent discussion of the New Testament.[1] It will be interesting to begin by surveying the wide range of directions in which the Old Testament position was developed. But particular attention will be devoted to the themes which carry through to Palestinian Judaism and appear in the New Testament itself. Our survey will concentrate on questions about the nature and time of the resurrection, the affirmation and description of an intermediate state, and the various accounts of the location of the dead. The underlying purpose of the chapter will be to determine whether the holistic dualism of Hebrew anthropology was abandoned, modified, or reinforced during the intertestamental period.

II. Intertestamental Views of the Afterlife

A. Old Testament Background

The Israelites believed that identifiable though truncated human persons continue to exist after death. True to their holism, they thought of the dead

---

1. Consideration of the intertestamental material is necessary even for those like myself who do not consider the apocryphal and pseudepigraphal books to have the same divinely inspired and authoritative status as the canonical books. Even the most conservative principles of grammatical-historical exegesis mandate taking account of relevant nonbiblical data in the responsible interpretation of Scripture. In this spirit I will consider the intertestamental literature in an attempt to determine more clearly what certain New Testament passages are intended to say.

as ethereal bodily beings who remain in Sheol. Whether they are in any sense conscious and active is unclear. Although Sheol is the gathering place of all human dead, there are hints that the lot of the faithful and the wicked is not the same. Hope is expressed that the Lord will rescue his beloved from death itself. At least two texts clearly refer to bodily resurrection. But the predominant picture is of the *rephaim* in Sheol.

This scenario is the common point of departure for all the views expressed in the subsequent centuries. What is so striking about this period is the radical difference in conclusions reached from the same basic premise. Some Jewish writings seem to remain quite close to the idea of Sheol. Others move very far toward what looks like Greek idealism. Most seem to settle somewhere in the middle, affirming the resurrection and implying some sort of intermediate state. But even in the median there is a surprising variety of views on particular issues.[2]

2. The most systematic and comprehensive survey of this material is by H. C. C. Cavallin, *Life After Death: Paul's Argument for the Resurrection of the Dead in I Corinthians; Part I: An Enquiry into the Jewish Background* (Lund: Gleerup, 1974). He considers the Apocrypha, Pseudepigrapha, writings from the diaspora, Rabbinica, Targums, and tomb inscriptions. Another scholarly study is by George Nickelsburg, Jr., *Resurrection, Immortality, and Eternal Life in Intertestamentary Judaism* (Cambridge: Harvard University Press, 1972). A more popular summary is found in Donald Gowan, *Bridge Between the Testaments* (Pittsburgh: Pickwick Press, 1976), Ch. 26, "New Beliefs: Resurrection and Messiah." The most readable summary is still D. S. Russell, *Between the Testaments* (Philadelphia: Fortress Press, 1960, 1965), Ch. 7, "The Resurrection and the Life Beyond." However, the Russell book was written before more recent studies, which argue later dates for some of this literature and thus would complicate the picture of what was believed by most Jews during the lifetime of Jesus.

In my discussion I have considered the dates given in *The Old Testament Pseudepigrapha,* ed. James Charlesworth (Garden City, NY: Doubleday, 1983), but have generally accepted the judgments of George Nickelsburg, *Jewish Literature Between the Bible and the Mishnah* (Philadelphia: Fortress, 1981). I will use only that material which was likely extant before 100 A.D. even if redacted at a later time. My argument does not turn on showing the direct dependence of the New Testament on these texts but only that probably such ideas were "in the air" during the lives of Jesus and Paul and the composition of the New Testament. In a later chapter it will be my responsibility to show that these ideas are in fact present in the New Testament and not merely "in the air" at that time.

B. Sheol and the Sadducees

Consider first the most austere view, that even the believing dead remain forever in the silence of Sheol. Like the Psalmist and the Preacher, Sirach laments: "Who will sing praises to the Most High in Hades, as do those who are alive and give thanks? From the dead, as from one who does not exist, thanksgiving has ceased . . ." (Sir. 17:27-28a, RSV).[3] Even if strict nonexistence is not what is envisioned here, those who inhabit Sheol are so cut off from life and from God that they might as well be extinct.

This is most likely also the position of the Sadducees, whom we meet in the New Testament. There they are best known for their denial of the resurrection. But they are also supposed to have affirmed annihilation or ontological nothingness after death. This interpretation is confirmed by Josephus, who likens the Sadducees to Epicurean materialists in denying existence after death.[4] The claim that they adopted materialist Greek philosophy is certainly consistent with their reputation as promoters of Greco-Roman political and cultural values.[5] But Russell considers them to be faithful adherents of the Old Testament conception of Sheol, which does not include annihilation, strictly speaking.[6] Perhaps there were Sadducees of both sorts, Hebrew and Greek, or a synthesis of traditions.

In any case, here is as close as we get during this period to the idea that biological death results in immediate extinction or nonexistence. (Extinction is occasionally said to be the lot of the wicked after the final judgment.) In the next chapter we will encounter scholars who argue that nonexistence until the resurrection is the teaching of the New Testament. If they are correct, then either the New Testament writers were teaching something radically new or else they cast their lot with the Greek Sadducees, merely adding the resurrection to extinction. The Greek Sadducees, if there were any, would provide the only precedent for the extinction view during the entire intertestamental period.[7]

3. Cf. also Sir. 14:16-19; Gowan, p. 478.
4. Josephus, *The Jewish Wars*, II,8,2ff. and *Antiquities*, XVIII,1,2. Cf. also R. Meyer, "Sadducees," *Theological Dictionary of the New Testament*, trans. G. W. Bromiley (Grand Rapids: Eerdmans, 1974), Vol. VII, pp. 46-47.
5. Helmer Ringgren, *Israelite Religion* (London: SPCK, 1966), p. 343.
6. D. S. Russell, *The Message and Method of Jewish Apocalyptic* (Philadelphia: Westminster, 1964), p. 357. I am indebted to a former student, John Medendorp, for this reference.
7. Cf. Gowan, p. 481. The only mention of annihilation is as final judgment for the wicked.

For if they were faithful to the Old Testament, the Sadducees would not have been strict annihilationists.

C. The Immortality of the Soul

On the opposite end of the spectrum are those who strongly resemble Greek idealists. Here we have clear reference to the immortality of the soul without mention of bodily resurrection. Disembodied existence seems to be the eternal destiny of the believing dead. In the Wisdom of Solomon, for example, we read: "But the souls of the righteous are in the hand of God, and no torment will ever touch them . . . they are at peace . . . their hope is full of immortality" (3:1, 3b, 4b). This appears to be their final state. And the last word in the book of Jubilees is that "their bones shall rest in the earth and their spirits shall have much joy" (23:31). I Enoch 102–104 and IV Maccabees also apparently affirm the permanent separation of body and soul.[8]

Although this view parallels the idealism of Plato and the Orphic cults, except for Philo it is not known whether there is any actual dependence upon Greek sources. It is conceivable that such a view could have developed from a notion of the ghosts in Sheol which simply did not include resurrection as part of God's final redemption from death. We shall examine the question of Hellenistic influence more fully below. In any case, omission of the resurrection is the exception rather than the rule during this period.[9]

---

8. Cf. Nickelsburg, *Resurrection and Immortality,* p. 175; Gowan, p. 481; Russell, *Between the Testaments,* pp. 24, 84, 148. (All future references to Nickelsburg and Russell are to these works.)

9. Russell, p. 148, considers the immortal soul eschatology as "a breakaway from the firm conviction of the apocalyptic tradition." However, Cavallin, who considers a wider range of data, asserts: "Statements on an immortality of the soul which exclude the resurrection of the body are almost as common as those which explicitly state the resurrection of the body . . ." (p. 200). For our purposes it is important to note another of his conclusions: "the emphasis on the immortality of the soul, *excluding* the body, is not found in the Palestinian sources . . ." (*ibid.*). Resurrection, in other words, was taken for granted in Palestinian Judaism.

D. Varieties of Resurrection

Hope for the resurrection is a common theme among most of the eschatological visions developed between the Testaments. But although many
texts speak of "rising again," there is quite a variety of opinions about the
nature of resurrection and, occasionally, when it takes place.

In the first place, resurrection is not always an event which involves
the body. New life may be given to the spirit only. Jubilees 23:30 prophesies
that the righteous "will rise," but verse 31 makes it clear that their bones
will remain in the earth and only their spirits will ascend to God.[10] While
this use of the language of resurrection is rare, it does provide precedent
for those who claim that this is the New Testament understanding of resurrection.

The standard meaning of resurrection in emerging Jewish orthodoxy,
however, is the revivification and transformation of bodily existence. For
bodiliness is crucial to the holism of Jewish anthropology. As Davies explains: "Death, i.e. the separation of body and soul, for Judaism was not
natural to man but the consequence of sin, and this implied that the reunion of soul and body in resurrection was involved in any doctrine of
survival."[11]

But what sort of resurrection body? Even here there is great diversity.
Some texts suggest that the righteous dead are to receive "astral" or heavenly bodies which are located in the heavens like the stars. Daniel 12:3 says
they "will shine like the brightness of the heavens . . . like the stars for ever
and ever." This image is present in I Enoch 104, II Esdras 7, and II Baruch
51 as well.[12] Becoming like a star certainly would count as a transformed
mode of bodily existence, for the stars were considered heavenly bodies.
Most likely, however, such apocalyptic expressions ought not to be taken as
stating literal beliefs but as pointing metaphorically to a glorious and
highly exalted form of heavenly existence with God. For heaven was imagined to have several levels, as evident in II Enoch, for example. The stars
occupy the first level but the saints dwell in an upper story, closer to God.

10. Nickelsburg, pp. 174-175, suggests that I Enoch 102–104 might also respresent this
position. While this text does speak of the spirit alone, it does not explicitly mention "rising"
or "resurrection."

11. W. D. Davies, *Paul and Rabbinic Judaism,* 2nd ed. (London: SPCK, 1955), p. 299.

12. Cavallin, p. 203; cf. also Martin Hengel, *Judaism and Hellenism* (London: SCM,
1974), Vol. I, pp. 196-197.

The elect are not literally like stars or planets. But resurrection does involve a total transformation of the body's essence and appearance into a heavenly or spiritual being.

A certain range of opinion must be recognized even where the resurrection body clearly retains the form of the earthly body. While some writers stressed the identity of the resurrection body with the material earthly body, others saw the relationship as a significant transformation. The Old Testament resurrection text Isaiah 26:19 suggests the revivification of the same earthly body from the very dust into which it had decomposed. This notion is also found in Sibylline Oracles, Bk. IV,181-182: "Then God himself shall fashion again the bones and ashes of men, and shall raise up mortals once more as they were before."[13] Identity is likewise suggested in II Maccabees 7:11 and 14:46, where the dying faithful explicitly express the expectation of regaining the very bodies they are about to lose. There is evidence that many Pharisees and Rabbis held this opinion as well.

Thus far we have encountered a heavenly-spiritualistic view of the resurrection on one hand and an almost materialistic earthly version on the other. Not surprisingly, there are median accounts which combine elements of the two extremes. The depiction of the resurrection found throughout II Enoch and II Baruch 49–51, for example, includes continuity between the earthly and resurrection bodies and their similarity of appearance, but also suggests a transformation of the nature, needs, and capacities of the resurrection body. Continuity is insured by the fact that the very bodies buried are the ones which will be raised on the day of resurrection.[14] Such bodies will have the same visible appearance as their earthly predecessors, making recognition by the living possible, as in II Enoch 64. But they will not have the same nature. They will not require food, according to II Enoch 56, or have physical needs and desires. Interestingly, II Baruch 51 envisions the further transformation of these bodies after the resurrection until they become like the stars or the angels, that is, spiritual bodies.[15]

To summarize, we see that "resurrection" could mean a number of things in intertestamental Judaism. It could happen to the spirit or the

13. Cf. Russell, p. 159.

14. Russell, p. 160, sees in these texts a "spiritual body," a "glorious body" similar to Paul's in I Corinthians 15. Paul's view of resurrection may fall into this category, but I find the language in the texts Russell cites too general to warrant any identification.

15. Russell, pp. 160-161; Gowan, p. 486.

body; and if the latter, it could produce the identical physical body, a spiritually transformed yet visibly similar earthly body, or a physical body transformed into a literal heavenly body. The image of a heavenly or spiritual body merges with the idea of an everlastingly disembodied soul in a couple of texts. The diversity of views which emerged during this relatively short period of time is a bit dizzying.

Important to realize in this connection is the fact that beliefs about individual resurrection were not isolated developments but were directly correlated with cosmic eschatology. Individuals do not merely exist; they always exist someplace. In this life, individual and environment share some commonness of nature. We are "of the dust of the earth." By the same logic, if our eternal dwelling place is the future earth, our bodies will be earthly bodies. If our everlasting home is a purely spiritual realm — the environs of God and the angels — the body will likewise become spiritual. If we are destined for a renewed or transformed earth, then we will have renewed or transformed earthly bodies. The correlation between mode of existence and location of existence is a highly regular pattern in intertestamental literature.[16]

But when does the resurrection take place? If it is a spiritual resurrection and if our eternal home is in a spiritual realm which already exists, then an immediate assumption or instantaneous resurrection to a spiritual nature is possible. We have already encountered belief in the immediate assumption of the soul, but not in conjunction with the language of resurrection. Wherever that language is employed, the resurrection is considered to be a future historical event, something which will take place on the coming "day of the Lord."[17] That is even the case for the spiritual resurrection of Jubilees 23 and the eventual spiritual transformation of II Baruch.

---

16. Cf. Russell, "The Resurrection and the Messianic Kingdom," pp. 149-151; Gowan, pp. 485-486; and A. R. van de Walle, *From Darkness to the Dawn* (Mystic, CT: Twenty-third Publications, 1985), pp. 84-85. The same point is made about New Testament eschatology by Murray Harris in "Resurrection and Creation" in *Raised Immortal: Resurrection and Immortality in the New Testament* (Grand Rapids: Eerdmans, 1985), pp. 165-171.

17. Van de Walle, pp. 79-80, summarizes: "The resurrection event is looked on quite generally as something which takes place at the end of time, except in some texts which . . . can be interpreted in terms of a resurrection at death. We should also remember the exaltation model" (elevation of the soul at death). I agree that some texts could be interpreted as envisioning resurrection at death. My point is that they lack the explicit vocabulary of resurrection, e.g., the words "rise" or "receive new life." Such resurrection would be of the soul, not the body.

The idea of an immediate bodily resurrection, which some scholars find in II Corinthians 5, does not seem to occur in intertestamental Judaism.

E. The Intermediate State

Assuming a future resurrection of course raises questions about what takes place in the meantime. What is the state of the dead between their decease and the resurrection? Do they exist? If so, where are they and what is it like? The topic of the intermediate state cannot be avoided.

We have already encountered the embryonic form of the intermediate state in Isaiah 26:19: on the day of the Lord the *rephaim* in Sheol will awake and return to life in their revivified fleshly bodies. The intermediate state would thus consist in temporary existence in the underworld, whether or not it is conscious and active. During the intertestamental period this notion was developed in several significant ways. First, the dead are unmistakably referred to as "souls" and "spirits." Second, a number of texts picture them as conscious and in some ways active. These two claims will be documented in this section. A third fascinating development is the topography of the afterlife — the realm of the dead is imaginatively explored and mapped. That will be the topic of a section below.

To begin the analysis of the intermediate state, consider two interesting texts, one an early document and the other from the first century A.D. Dating from around 200 B.C. is I Enoch 22:

> At that moment, Rufael, one of the holy angels, who was with me, responded to me; and he said to me, "These beautiful corners (are here) in order that the spirits of [*sic*] the souls of the dead should assemble into them — they are created so that the souls of the children of the people should gather here." . . . I saw the spirits of the children of the people who were dead, and their voices were reaching into heaven until this very moment [and making suit]. . . . And he replied and said to me: "These three have been made in order that the spirits of the dead might be separated. And . . . the souls of the righteous have been separated . . ." (vv. 3, 5, 9).[18]

An even more graphic example is found in II Esdras, which dates from the late first century A.D. The seventh chapter is one of the most elaborate

18. Translation by E. Isaac in Charlesworth, ed., *The Old Testament Pseudepigrapha.*

accounts of death, the intermediate state, and the final judgment in intertestamental literature. Ezra asks the Lord "whether after death, as soon as every one of us yields up his soul, we shall be kept in rest until those times come when thou wilt renew the creation, or whether we shall be tormented at once?" (v. 75). The Lord answers him:

> Now, concerning death, the teaching is: When the decisive decree has gone forth from the Most High that a man shall die, as the spirit leaves the body to return again to him who gave it, first of all it adores the glory of the Most High. And if it is one of those who have shown scorn and have not kept the way of the Most High, and who have hated those who fear God — such spirits shall not enter into habitations, but shall immediately wander about in torments, ever grieving and sad, in seven ways (vv. 78-80, RSV).

Then follows an account of the seven ways in which the wicked will be tormented and seven ways in which the righteous will be comforted, all of this prior to the final judgment.

In approaching the subject of the intermediate state, we first focus on the terminology used to refer to the dead. Recall that an unresolved dispute divides Old Testament scholars. Some, like H. W. Robinson, Eichrodt, and Wolff, insist that the words *nephesh* and *ruach* are never used to refer to persons apart from living bodies, whereas others — Otto Kaiser, for example — argue that at least *nephesh* is occasionally used this way. For our purposes it does not really matter which party is correct. For in intertestamental literature both *nephesh* and *ruach* with their Greek counterparts *psychē* and *pneuma* are repeatedly and unambiguously employed to refer to the disembodied dead either in the intermediate or final state. The passages quoted above are only two of numerous examples.[19] In fact these terms are used both in parallel and interchangeably in connection with the afterlife. In this context they are therefore synonyms.[20] That is

19. Russell, p. 151, lists Similitudes of Enoch, Psalms of Solomon, II Enoch, Testament of Abraham, and II Baruch as other loci where "soul" is used this way; and Noachic Fragments of Enoch, I Enoch 108, Assumption of Moses, and III Baruch as other loci of this meaning of "spirit." This list is not exhaustive. In addition we have already encountered places in Wisdom of Solomon, Jubilees, and I Enoch 102–104 where these terms refer to the dead in their final state.

20. This fact seems to weaken the case for trichotomy, which affirms a metaphysical distinction between soul and spirit.

certainly a development beyond the Old Testament usage. *Nephesh* and *ruach* have unquestionably picked up a dualistic or dichotomous denotation. They refer to existent individuals who lack flesh and bones. As Russell observes: "We here pass from a conception of personality *wholly* dependent on body (as had been the case in Hebrew thought) to one in terms of soul or spirit which, whatever degree of physicality it carries with it, is different."[21]

Russell's remark about the soul's "physicality" deserves attention. For intertestamental imagery continues the Old Testament idea that the dead remain quasi-bodily beings even though they lack flesh and bones. As Russell observes: "Even when the apocalyptists thought of the spirit or soul of the departed, they still had to think in terms of body, for this discarnate spirit or soul was believed to possess form or appearance."[22] So the deceased are depicted in spatial and bodily terms. They seem to have spatial location and, in II Esdras, to travel cosmic distances. According to I Enoch 22, those who are awaiting divine punishment apparently suffer from the absence of water, a distinctly bodily affliction.[23] The bodily form of the spirits is an indication both of the holism of Jewish anthropology and of universal common sense. All people imagine the dead as they appeared in life, with faces and bodily form.

Not only can souls and spirits exist in separation from their physical bodies but they are also conscious and reactive as well, not merely asleep or inert — at least in some accounts. In I Enoch 22 they have voices which cry out, complaining to God about injustice. According to II Esdras 7, they are aware of God and of his just expectations. They foresee their own eternal destinies as well as the fate of others, already enjoying the anticipation of full blessedness or suffering the certainty of future torment. So these souls or spirits do have religious, moral, cognitive, and emotional capacities. As Russell observes: "So far as their emotions or mental processes are concerned, there would seem to be very little difference between their capabilities in the life after death and those which they possessed during their life upon earth."[24]

21. Russell, p. 151. Russell thinks of personhood as requiring conscious activity. Thus he cannot confirm that there are "persons" thought to be in Sheol. However, he does not dispute Old Testament belief in the existence of the ghosts of persons in Sheol.
22. Russell, p. 151 n. 2.
23. Recall the thirst of the rich man in Hades in Luke 16.
24. Russell, p. 152.

To be sure, the evidence about belief in activity and consciousness during the intermediate state is not entirely univocal. There are texts which simply posit the existence of the dead but do not specify whether they are conscious or not.[25] And many passages metaphorically refer to these souls as "resting" or "sleeping," an image which certainly does not suggest an active interim existence.

The texts which contain the sleep metaphor deserve closer attention, however, for the intriguing fact is that a number of them also express the language of conscious activity in virtually the same breath. I Enoch 100:5 speaks of the righteous as having "a long sleep," but 102:4-5 refers to the souls of the righteous as hopeful instead of sad and fearful. Jubilees 23:31 makes it clear that "their bones will rest in the earth, and their spirits will have great joy." And II Esdras 7, as we have seen, presents an active intermediate state. But the final resurrection is described as follows: "The earth shall give up those who are asleep in it, and the dust those who dwell silently in it; and the chambers shall give up the souls which have been committed to them" (v. 32). Sleep metaphors are used throughout II Baruch, but consider 36:11: "And now sleep in distress and rest in pain until your last time comes in which you will return to be tormented even more." The wicked in the intermediate state both sleep and experience suffering. It seems evident, then, that reference to the dead as asleep does not necessarily indicate belief in literal unconsciousness or nonexistence, nor is it incompatible with belief in a conscious and active intermediate state. Perhaps bodies sleep whereas souls do not. Or perhaps the interim condition is imagined as dreamlike, for dreaming conjoins both sleep and consciousness.[26] Ancient peoples often thought of dreams as ecstatic experiences and as occasions of commerce with the divine or spiritual realm. Whatever the explanation, it is much too hasty to leap from the mention of death as "sleep" to the conclusion that the deceased were thought to be utterly unconscious or literally nonexistent.

To sum up, then, in addition to those texts which are silent on the mat-

---

25. Cf. Cavallin, pp. 198-199.

26. Oscar Cullmann, who finally endorses a "soul-sleep" view as the teaching of the New Testament, at one point mentions dreaming in connection with sleep. Cf. "Immortality of the Soul or Resurrection of the Dead?", in K. Stendahl, ed., *Immortality and Resurrection* (New York: Macmillan, 1965), p. 57.

ter, there is plenty of incontrovertible evidence for belief in a conscious intermediate state throughout the four centuries of this period.[27]

F. Hellenistic Dualism?

It is sometimes alleged that the idea of souls and spirits conscious during the
intermediate state is not representative of genuine Jewish thought but be-
trays the distorting influence of Hellenistic dualism.[28] The situation is not
quite that simple, however. For one thing, it is no longer unproblematic to
posit a clean identification of dualism with Greek thought and holism with
the Hebrew-Jewish mind. For there were holists and monists among the
Greeks as well. And all parties within Jewish society and religion were influenced by the power of Hellenistic culture, not only anthropological dualists.
It is as easy to find Stoicism in Ben Sirach and materialism among the Sadducees as it is to find Platonism or Orphic anthropology among Jewish believers in the soul.[29]

Second, it is not clear that the idea of a surviving soul or spirit must be
understood exclusively as a Greek import. As Russell reminds us: "According to Hebrew psychology consciousness is a function not only of the body
but also of the *nephesh* which the apocalyptists came to think of in terms
of 'soul.'"[30] This notion could have developed from the Psalmist's reference
to the *nephesh* in Sheol without external cultural influence. Or perhaps

---

27. Cavallin, pp. 199-201, finds the intermediate state less widely held than Russell
does. He thinks that some texts merely juxtapose the ideas of immortal souls and future resurrection without thereby implying an intermediate state. It must be said in response, however, that such texts do *logically* imply an intermediate state even if that is not explicitly recognized by their authors, which is a speculative judgment at best. Cavallin does not dispute
that a number of writings do explicitly posit the interim existence of the soul. It is just that
he does not think the doctrine is pervasive or existentially important. He may be correct. For
our anthropological purposes, however, the issue is not whether it is important, but merely
whether it is affirmed.

28. Even Cullmann (*op. cit.*) suggests that a conscious soul is a Greek notion and endorses "soul-sleep" as the New Testament view. Cf. Nickelsburg, pp. 177-180, for a critical
evaluation of Cullmann's assumptions in light of intertestamental literature.

29. Cf. Hengel, "Summary and Conclusion," *Judaism and Hellenism*, Vol. I, pp. 310-
314.

30. Russell, p. 152. He explicitly warns against overhasty conclusions about the role of
Hellenistic influence in this whole development of individual eschatology.

Greek ideas were merely the stimulus for explicating a notion of the soul already implicit in ancient Hebrew anthropology.[31] The very same point could be made regarding *ruach*.

Furthermore, Hellenistic dualism emphasized the antipathy between soul and body. It exalted the idea of a disembodied soul as a superior form of human existence. In direct contrast, most Jews continued to think of the soul as retaining bodily form after death and included the notion of bodily resurrection in their eschatologies. Bodiliness remained essential to mainstream Jewish anthropology, for that is how God created humanity. Without the body, the soul's condition, though one of joy and hope, is seriously deficient. As Russell summarizes:

> The souls of the departed, deprived of their bodies, were at best only "truncated personalities" who must await the resurrection for their fullest expression. . . . The Greek doctrine of immortality . . . was utterly foreign to their Hebrew mentality. . . . Not the immortality of the soul but the union of soul and body in resurrection, that alone could ultimately express the survival of men's personalities in the life beyond.[32]

Although the influence of Hellenism is difficult to deny, it does not appear to have radically redirected or transformed the ethos of most Jewish anthropology. Affirming a dichotomy of body and soul at death does not necessarily contradict its holistic emphasis on human life and seems wholly compatible with Old Testament anthropology.

G. Where Are the Dead? A Topography of the Afterlife

A final source of background light for reading the New Testament is the topography of the afterlife. A great deal of imaginative exploration and mapping of the realm of death was done in intertestamental Judaism. This put some conceptual distance between Old Testament accounts of Sheol and the later depictions of paradise, heaven, and hell. On this topic, too, consideration of the intertestamental material will clarify a great deal.

31. Otto Kaiser, *Death and Life* (Nashville: Abingdon, 1981), pp. 86-91, pursues the question of Jewish dependence on Greek and Persian influences and reaches a similar conclusion.

32. Russell, p. 157.

In the Greek translation of the Old Testament, *Sheol* became *Hades.*
Similarities between Greek and Hebrew notions of the underworld have
already been noted. Sheol/Hades continues to feature prominently in
many of the intertestamental texts. In several books it retains its subterranean location. I Enoch 22, however, finds it in a far western mountain.[33]
And sometimes its location is simply not specified, allowing it to stand for
the generic realm of the dead.

An interesting development is the consolidation of Old Testament
hints that there are divisions within Sheol itself. I Enoch 22 refers to four
"chambers" or "corners" or "hollow places." Again in II Esdras the term
"chambers" or "habitations" is used. "In Hades the chambers of the souls
are like the womb" (4:41).[34] II Baruch 21:23 and 30:2 speak of "store-
houses" or "treasuries." The language of "many mansions" found in the
King James New Testament also occurs in Jewish apocalyptic. Clearly the
notion of dwelling places within Sheol or Hades has crystallized.[35]

These residences are not merely neutral environments for people of
equal eschatological standing. For the blessed and the damned are sorted
at death and wait for final disposition in different places within Hades. In
I Enoch 22, for example, three of the four hollow places are for the unfaith-
ful. These places are dark and lack water, which is part of why their inhabitants suffer. The fourth is for the blessed. It is brightly lit and features a
fountain of water. According to II Esdras 7, the blessed find rest in "habitations" but the cursed must roam about. Thus the Old Testament suggestions that the lot of all the dead is not the same are now explicitly spelled
out and associated with the architecture of Sheol.

But the picture is even more complex, since some texts begin to relo-
cate the place of the dead away from Sheol. The image of a garden where
the elect and righteous dwell is found in I Enoch 60:8. This immediately
suggests the term "paradise," a loan-word from Persia which is associated
in the Septuagint with the original Garden of Eden. In apocalyptic literature it refers to the home of the blessed dead, both during the intermediate
state and more frequently as their final abode.[36] The Rabbis, on the other

33. My Old Testament colleague, Prof. John Stek, pointed out to me that the far west is
considered a gate to the underworld. It is where the sun goes beneath the horizon at night,
for example.

34. Cf. also 4:35 and 7:32.

35. Cf. Gowan, p. 484; and van de Walle, pp. 80-81.

36. Cf. Russell, pp. 152-154.

hand, stressed the intermediate rather than the final character of paradise.[37] There are various accounts of its location. Strikingly, the Rabbis at times describe paradise as contained in Sheol.[38] It is sometimes linked with the New Jerusalem and the New Earth. In II Enoch 8 and 65 paradise is a mixture of the earthly and the heavenly, located in the final kingdom of God. In the Apocalypse of Moses the body of Adam is buried in the earthly paradise (38:5), but God tells the archangel to find it "in paradise in the third heaven" (40:2).[39] The central idea that paradise is where the blessed dwell with the Lord underlies the various accounts of its location.

It is not surprising to most Christians that paradise is frequently associated with heaven in these writings. Quite startling, however, is the fact that the third heaven can also be the place of eternal punishment, at least according to II Enoch 10 and III Baruch 4:4-5.[40] These texts depict two places, one of reward and one of retribution, both located in heaven. More often, however, the place of eternal punishment is a direct extension of the preliminary suffering which takes place in some sections of Sheol. Sometimes eternal punishment consists in outright annihilation or else being abandoned in Sheol. In other representations there is a transfer, with or without resurrection, to a place called "Gehenna."

Originally the Valley of Hinnom, where the Israelites burned their children to Moloch, Gehenna became the literal garbage dump of Jerusalem and the figurative designation for the place of eternal fiery torment of the damned.[41] This is what the New Testament means by "hell" as a place of punishment. It is not necessarily the same as Hades, the realm of the

---

37. Samuel Sandmel, *Judaism and Christian Beginnings* (New York: Oxford, 1978), p. 202. He writes, "It is clear, however, that both paradise and hell were not usually conceived of as being eternal, but rather only places of sojourn between death and the future Great Judgment. It is to be noted that in the Rabbinic literature the view of hell is relatively undeveloped, but that of paradise, the heavenly Eden, very much elaborated."

38. E. O. James, *The Tree of Life* (Leiden: Brill, 1966), p. 79. I owe this reference to W. John Holwerda, a Calvin Seminary student, Winter Quarter 1987. The conjunction of paradise and Sheol in rabbinic thought will help solve the puzzle about the location of Jesus Christ between his death and resurrection.

39. Russell, p. 160. It is interesting to note here that Paul also locates paradise in the third heaven; cf. II Cor. 12:2-4.

40. Gowan, p. 486.

41. Cf. Russell, pp. 153-154; Gowan, p. 485; and van de Walle, pp. 81-82, where the following references are given: I Enoch 90:26ff.; II Esdr. 7:36; II Bar. 59:10 and 85:13; "and above all in rabbinic literature."

dead. Although in some contexts Hades might refer exclusively to the place of punishment, in others it may simply signify the morally neutral dimension entered by all the dead.

From all of this a general, though not wholly consistent, map of the postmortem environment emerges. There is a definite sorting of people at death into the blessed and the cursed. This may be the final separation in a few cases, but most frequently it is a provisional division in anticipation of final judgment. The temporary location of the dead may be Sheol/Hades or, less frequently, heaven. Both paradise and Gehenna, what most Christians think of as heaven and hell, are thought of mainly as final destinations. But some, especially the Rabbis, feature them most prominently in connection with the intermediate state. Thus we simply cannot arrive at a single picture or univocal use of terminology. Within the plurality of visions, it is paradoxically possible, for example, to say both that one is in paradise and in Sheol/Hades at the same time, or conversely, that one must enter heaven to go to hell. Despite the varieties of eschatological imagery, however, familiarity with this material will be invaluable in interpreting the New Testament.

H. The Pharisees

In order to consolidate the material of this chapter and deposit it in the immediate vicinity of the New Testament, we will consider the beliefs of the Pharisees, who are prominent in the Gospels and in the education of Paul. The Pharisees represent all the central themes of intertestamental eschatology.[42] They held that at death, souls depart from bodies and continue to exist in an intermediate state, already enjoying or lamenting the anticipated consequences of God's judgment. The Pharisees awaited the coming Messiah, who would effect a resurrection of the dead and initiate his kingdom. That they affirmed the resurrection is clear from the New Testament itself, Acts 23:8 for example. That verse also implies that they held to the intermediate state,[43] a fact which is attested by Josephus, him-

---

42. Cf. Lester Whitelocke, "Pharisaic Ideas of Judgment, Resurrection, and the World to Come," in *The Development of Jewish Religious Thought in the Inter-Testamental Period* (New York: Vantage, 1976), pp. 99-116.

43. This claim will be defended in Chapter Seven.

self a Pharisee. In both *The Jewish Wars* (II,8,2ff.) and *Antiquities* (XVIII,1,2), Josephus outlines the views of the Pharisees along with those of the Sadducees and Essenes. The Sadducees are likened to the Epicurean materialists in denying the afterlife. The Essenes are said to believe in the immortality of the soul without his mentioning, as Hippolytus later does, their affirmation of the resurrection of the flesh *(sarx)*.[44] In contrast, the Pharisees held both the immortality and power *(athanaton te ischon)* of the soul *(psychē)* and the resurrection *(anabiosis)* of the body.

Of course some would argue that Josephus has read Greek philosophical concepts into these doctrines of Judaism, thereby misrepresenting them. But it is more likely that he is simply using Greek vocabulary to describe common first-century teachings of Judaism, a practice by now familiar to us from this period.[45] The accuracy of his account is corroborated by other sources. Consider the saying attributed to the great Pharisee Hillel, the grandfather of Gamaliel, the teacher of Paul: "Is not then my poor soul a guest in the body? Today it is here and tomorrow it is not here."[46] Admittedly, however, recent scholarship has questioned the reliability of rabbinic tradition about Hillel. But there is also the testimony of Luke in Acts 23:8: "The Sadducees say that there is no resurrection, and that there are neither angels nor spirits, but the Pharisees acknowledge them all." Though less than absolutely conclusive, without exception the evidence we have supports the judgment that the Pharisees not only affirmed the resurrection of the body but the temporary separation of the soul as well. Many scholars suppose that during the first century A.D. these beliefs were found among the common people as well.[47]

---

44. Cf. Nickelsburg, p. 167.

45. Nickelsburg, p. 167, argues for the reliability of Josephus against his detractors. There is no evidence that Josephus distorted the picture; the detractors usually assume that the Pharisees, being faithful Jews, could not have imagined a separated soul and thus that Josephus was misrepresenting them as Greek dualists. But we have demonstrated the falsehood of that assumption.

46. *Leviticus Rabba*, 34,3 on 25:25, in H. Freeman and M. Simon, eds., *Midrash Rabba*, Vol. IV (London: Soncino, 1939), pp. 428-429. I owe this reference to the 1984 paper by Joe S. Anderson, Grand Rapids Baptist Seminary, entitled "Teaching Anthropology to the Church: Some Suggestions for Translating Nephesh." Prof. Steve Spencer of GRBS pointed it out to me.

47. Cavallin, p. 194; Joseph Bonsirven, S.J., *Palestinian Judaism in the Time of Jesus Christ*, trans. W. Wolf (New York: Holt, Rinehart, and Winston, 1964), p. 163.

III. Summary and Conclusions

Now that we have completed our travelogue of the eschatological landscapes of intertestamental Judaism, what are the results for our attempt to understand Jewish anthropology philosophically? Does the variety of eschatologies entail a variety of anthropologies? Or does the diversity proceed from commonly held beliefs about human nature, a general affirmation of holistic dualism, for example?

Let's begin where we started the survey. The Sadducees denied the resurrection and any meaningful afterlife whatsoever. If they believed in literal annihilation at death, then they were probably monists or ontological holists. When the body dies, the whole person ceases to exist. Perhaps they adopted Hellenistic materialism, as Josephus suggests. However, if they were simply faithful to the Old Testament notion of Sheol, as they claimed, they would be minimal dualists of some sort. For the *rephaim* continue to survive biological death, even if they are comatose and eventually fade away.

On the other side of the spectrum are those whose vision of future human existence is purely spiritual. Most in this group are straightforwardly dualistic. Some hold that at death the body returns to dust and the soul receives eternal life. Others claim that the soul alone ascends to God at the resurrection whereas the bones remain in the earth. The dichotomy of substantial soul and body is unmistakable in either case.

However, what of those, if any, who believe that persons at death are immediately transformed into heavenly beings or instantly receive resurrection bodies? They could be monists, for in these cases one could theorize that the substantial unity of earthly life is transformed into the substantial unity of eternal life. But this would be monism only if the earthly body were included in the transformation. As in the cases of Enoch and Elijah, whole persons would have to be taken by the Lord. There could be no corpse left over. For if the flesh decomposes rather than undergoes immediate glorification, some part of the previous whole has apparently been left out. If it is only the soul which has been translated into glory or has instantly received a new body, then we do not have monism but only another version of dualism. The soul continues to exist separated from the earthly body. The only clear example of whole person transformation in the literature as far as I know is II Baruch 51, where the person is resurrected and then as a body-soul unity is transformed into a spiritual being.

91

Admittedly this final metamorphosis could be construed as a process of spiritualizing the entire person — possibly a form of monistic transubstantiation. But II Baruch also posits a body-soul separation during the intermediate state before the final resurrection — a clear case of dualism. Our conclusion with respect to the several spiritualistic eschatologies is that they entail dualism, not idealistic monism. All of them envision the soul or self as existing separate from the earthly body at one point or another. And the separability of the self from the earthly body is a sufficient condition for diagnosing dualism.

There ought to be no debate at all over the dualistic implication of the intermediate state–resurrection view. Whether conscious or not, the existence of the self-identical person as soul, spirit, or some other designation apart from the fleshly, earthly body entails dualism and excludes every form of monism.

With the possible exception of the Sadducees, therefore, all the varieties of intertestamental personal eschatology appear to entail a dualism of some sort, a dualism often more pronounced than that associated with the Old Testament conception of Sheol.

But what about the holistic emphasis so strong in Hebrew anthropology? Has that been given up? I do not believe so. A quick scan will reveal that the intertestamental writings continue to operate with the anthropological vocabulary of the Old Testament in a very Old Testament manner. *Nephesh, ruach, leb,* and *basar* and their Greek counterparts all continue to exhibit the variety of nuances they did in the Hebrew canon. It is just that they have gained additional meanings. Soul and spirit, for example, could now refer to the discarnate dead as well as to the whole person, the life-force, and the breath. The functional holism of the Old Testament has not at all been displaced.

There are discernible shifts in emphasis. Intertestamental writers are far more interested in the afterlife than the Old Testament is. In addition, the future life of God's people is no longer visualized in exclusively this-worldly terms. Heaven rather than earth may be the final home of the righteous. But even these developments do not necessarily negate a holistic view of earthly life, for even among Hellenistic Jews who affirmed the immortality of the soul there is little evidence of the principial anti-bodily, antimaterial bias of Greek idealism or Gnosticism. Rather, their belief was that although God created bodily existence good for this life, in his unfathomable wisdom he ordained a purely spiritual form of future existence. In this way it is perfectly consistent to hold a holistic view of this life and a spiritualistic view of the life to come.

The majority, at least among Palestinian Jews, envision the future life in terms of bodily resurrection. The psychosomatic unity of this life is retained or resumed in the life to come, even if it has been transformed in some way. The intermediate state is always an anthropologically deficient mode of existence because souls need bodies. Surely this reflects the heritage of Hebrew holism.

By factoring through the multiplicity of views, therefore, we have demonstrated that holistic dualism is the common denominator of almost all of them.

In concluding let me once again stress that the Jewish people, excepting a few such as Philo and Josephus, were not philosophically minded. So I am not claiming that they were articulate, self-conscious holistic dualists. I am merely insisting that if we unpack the implicit structure of their anthropological images and beliefs into more technical categories, holistic dualism is the general philosophical position which results. That is the underlying assumption of most of the startling variety of intertestamental visions we have considered. And it was held as well by many of the leaders and common people who were committed to Judaism at the time of Jesus. With this in mind we are now ready to approach the New Testament.

Chapter Five

The Monism-Dualism Debate about
New Testament Anthropology

I. Introduction

If traditional Christian dualists have come under attack for their uncritical
Platonistic interpretation of the Old Testament, they have suffered no less
reproof for their reading of the New. That a large portion of the tradition
is uncritically Platonistic is beyond dispute. One need only return to the
relevant passages in Calvin's *Institutes* for a classic example. Not only does
he interpret dualistically such texts as Matthew 10:28 and Luke 23:46,
which do seem to imply the separation of soul or spirit and body at death;
he also sees metaphysical dualism in numerous verses which merely use
the terms "body," "soul," and "spirit." Paul, says Calvin, would not mention
the defilement of both flesh and spirit in II Corinthians 7:1 or Peter speak
about "the salvation of . . . souls" in I Peter 1:9 "unless the soul were something essential, separate from the body. . . ."[1] Calvin appears unaware of
the many nonmetaphysical nuances of the anthropological terminology of
Scripture highlighted by subsequent scholarship. He does not consider the
possibility that such texts might employ stock expressions and figures of
speech from ordinary language which are wholly lacking in anthropologically dualistic implications. It does not occur to him that such words
might refer to inseparable aspects or capacities rather than separable substances. He simply finds confirmation for his own selfconsciously

---

1. Calvin, *Institutes*, I,xv,2, trans. F. L. Battles (Philadelphia: Westminster, 1960), pp.
185-186.

Platonistic categories. Thus he is a legitimate target for the charge that his philosophical prejudice caused him to misconstrue the biblical text.

There is little dispute among contemporary biblical scholars of all backgrounds that the anthropological terminology of the New Testament is as complex and pluriform as that of the Old. In most cases it simply cannot be read as suggesting metaphysical categories, much less those of substance dualism. As George Eldon Ladd observes: "Recent scholarship has recognized that such terms as body, soul, and spirit are not different, separable faculties of man but different ways of viewing the whole man."[2] Apparently, then, traditional dualistic anthropology is less easy to document with New Testament prooftexts than was previously assumed.

But some scholars have gone beyond recognizing the complexity, pluriformity, and nonphilosophical nature of New Testament anthropology. They have come to the conclusion that the New Testament positively rules out the separability of the soul, spirit, or person from the body. According to Bruce Reichenbach, a Christian philosopher, soul and body "are not different elements of man capable of separate existence." Thus he concludes that the Bible does imply a specific anthropology — monism. "A monistic anthropology also has the general support of both the Old Testament and the New. . . . Despite a few exceptions, then, Pauline anthropology, and the New Testament anthropology in general, is monistic."[3]

So the lines of debate are drawn again, this time around the New Testament. The tradition has generally assumed that the New Testament implies, if not teaches, a dualistic anthropology. But a number of modern scholars hold that monism is what it endorses. So there is reason to take another look at the evidence and arguments adduced by each side in favor of its position. Perhaps the whole matter is just too complex and ambiguous to allow for a final judgment. But perhaps not. It is worth another look.

2. George Ladd, *A Theology of the New Testament* (Grand Rapids: Eerdmans, 1974), p. 457.

3. Bruce Reichenbach, *Is Man the Phoenix? A Study of Immortality* (Grand Rapids: Eerdmans, 1983 reprint of 1978 edition), p. 180. This is an excellent, balanced introduction to the body-mind question in philosophy. My criticisms are aimed at the chapter devoted to biblical anthropology, not the book as a whole.

Cf. also A. R. van de Walle, *From Darkness to the Dawn* (Mystic, CT: Twenty-Third Publications, 1985), p. 152, who judges that the Bible is Semitic and therefore "anachronistically" monistic.

II. A Preliminary Assessment of the Case for Dualism

For the sake of advancing the debate I will not contest that much of the traditional argumentation which has been offered in favor of a dualistic interpretation of the New Testament fails to make the case. A number of points deserve explicit attention.

In the first place, the New Testament neither implicitly contains nor explicitly teaches a philosophical anthropology as such or any theoretically precise or systematically consistent definitions of body, mind, soul, or spirit.[4] Its use of anthropological terminology is extremely complex and diverse. Particular words such as *sarx, sōma, psychē, pneuma,* and *kardia* have a variety of meanings which can vary from one New Testament book to another.[5] Scholars cannot even achieve consensus in mapping the diversity of nuances and connotations. The only agreement is that there is no simple way to move directly from Scripture to philosophical anthropology, psychology, biology, or sociology. The Bible is neither theoretically clear in its mode of expression nor is it interested in addressing such philosophical issues as the number of substances of which human beings are composed. Since this is so, one cannot simply base one's case for a dualistic anthropology on the many texts which employ "body," "soul," or "spirit" — words which some philosophers use to articulate dualism. Those words might not signify philosophical categories at all. Simple occurrence of the words "body" and "soul" does not necessarily imply a Platonistic definition of body and soul. If the New Testament sets forth no philosophical anthropology at all, it cannot be teaching philosophical dualism. It must be granted that traditional dualists have often erred in this regard.

The next several points identify the appropriate ways of reading New

---

4. Cf. G. C. Berkouwer, *Man: The Image of God* (Grand Rapids: Eerdmans, 1962), pp. 194-195, and A. A. Hoekema, *Created in God's Image* (Grand Rapids: Eerdmans, 1986), pp. 204-205, for statements of this common theme.

5. The argument does not require that I engage in a detailed analysis of the various uses of these anthropological terms. Much more competent and exhaustive studies have been done elsewhere. Cf. the entries in Bauer, Arndt, and Gingrich, *A Greek-English Lexicon of the New Testament and Other Early Christian Literature* (University of Chicago, 1957) or *Theological Dictionary of the New Testament,* trans. G. W. Bromiley. Cf. also Rudolf Bultmann, *Theology of the New Testament,* trans. K. Grobel (New York: Scribner's, 1951), Vol. I, pp. 191-239; Berkouwer, Ch. 6, "The Whole Man"; Hoekema, pp. 213-216, "New Testament Words"; Ladd, Ch. 33, "The Pauline Psychology"; and most exhaustive of all, Robert Jewett, *Paul's Anthropological Terms* (Leiden: Brill, 1971).

Testament anthropological expressions, assuming they ought not to be interpreted philosophically.

Synecdoche is a common occurrence in the New Testament, as it is in the Old. Often anthropological part-terms are plausibly interpreted as referring to the person as a whole.[6] They might even be translated properly as personal pronouns. Consider Luke 12:19, where the foolish rich man schemes: "I will say to my *psychē*, '*Psychē*, you have plenty of good things stored up. . . .'" In all likelihood the man is simply speaking to himself rather than to his life-principle or spiritual substance. Similarly, Paul's injunction to love one's spouse as one's *body* (Eph. 5:28-29) can only mean loving her as one*self*, as the rest of the passage makes clear. Jesus' summary of the law might also be an instance of synecdoche: "You shall love the Lord your God with all your heart, soul, mind, and strength."[7] The terms here do not necessarily refer to different parts, faculties, or capacities within a person. Each on its own could refer to the person as such and collectively they would strongly emphasize the totality of life: "you shall love the Lord with your total being." Consider also Paul's benediction in I Thessalonians 5:23 that "your whole spirit, soul, and body be kept blameless." He might simply be blessing whole people in three different ways rather than three distinct parts of persons. In sum, many anthropological texts may be cases of synecdoche and as such stress the wholeness and totality of human existence, not its metaphysical divisibility. There is no sure foothold here for dualism.

Adding to the holistic impression are all the cases in which anthropological terms are used as synonyms or parallels and thus share meanings. Hebrews 8:10 quotes Jeremiah 31:33: "I will put my laws in their minds *(dianoia)* and write them on their hearts *(kardia)*." Hebrews 10:16 is identical except that mind and heart have changed places. They therefore seem to be synonyms, not picking out distinct organs or faculties. Numerous examples could be given demonstrating that heart, soul, spirit, and mind are each used to refer to the seat of the emotions, the source of thoughts and actions, and the deep self which knows and is known by God. This intersection of meaning simply continues Old Testament ways of speaking,

6. Cf. Ladd's observation in note 2 above; also Ray Anderson, *On Being Human* (Grand Rapids: Eerdmans, 1982), p. 207.

7. Based on Deut. 6:5, this saying of Jesus is recorded in Mt. 22:37, Mk. 12:30, and Lk. 10:27, each varying the anthropological terms.

considered above. What it suggests is the spiritual-ethical centeredness of personal existence in its totality rather than a list of discrete faculties which humans possess. Thus it points toward holism and provides no evidence for dualism at all.

What about cases where significant distinctions are apparently being made? Do they support dualism? Consider how Paul describes praying in tongues (I Cor. 14:14f.): "my spirit *(pneuma)* prays, but my mind *(nous)* is unfruitful." Hebrews 4:12 is even more interesting because it is sometimes used to prooftext trichotomy:[8] "the Word of God . . . penetrates even to dividing soul and spirit, joints and marrow; it judges the thoughts and attitudes of the heart." The different terms in these texts do suggest a separability of referents. But in neither text is the suggestion strong enough to justify the claim that one member of the pair could survive separation from the other at death or that they refer to different substances. When Paul mentions "spirit" and "mind," he might not mean to pick out distinct "organs" or "faculties" as such, but merely to suggest striking differences between ordinary prayer and charismatic prayer. Mental prayer is intentional and propositional, whereas spiritual prayer is involuntary and ineffable. And turning to the Hebrews text, we may actually find it suggesting holism. One could argue that bones and marrow are not normally separable but are organically bound together. The same might therefore be true for soul and spirit. But the Word of God permeates and scrutinizes the entirety of human existence. Plausibly interpreted, the distinctions and separations which are suggested in these verses once again turn up nothing which clearly indicates anthropological dualism or trichotomy.

That conclusion might even be argued for those passages in which body and soul or spirit are explicitly said to separate at death. Matthew 10:28 suggests that body and soul *(sōma* and *psychē)* are separable at death. Matthew, Luke, and John state that when Jesus died he gave up his spirit *(pneuma).* And all four Gospels use the term *sōma* to refer to his dead body. But numerous scholars have argued that soul and spirit merely indicate the breath or life-principle which ceases to exist and function at death, not an immaterial entity or person which survives death.[9] In support of this they claim continuity with the Old Testament meanings of *nephesh* and *ruach.* If this interpretation is correct, then even texts which mention

8. Cf. Hoekema, p. 208.
9. Cf. Reichenbach, p. 180.

separation of body and soul do not vindicate dualism. For the soul might not survive the separation. Thus the dualist must demonstrate that "soul" and "spirit" do mean "surviving person" in these cases. Otherwise dualism remains without foundation.

A final point against a facile Platonistic interpretation of the New Testament is the fact that Paul's well-known opposition between the flesh *(sarx)* and the spirit *(pneuma)* is not a body-soul dichotomy or duality of metaphysical substances, but an ethical-religious antithesis.[10] Whether "spirit" in these texts is divine or human, it is clear that this distinction pertains to regenerate and unregenerate people as whole beings. It refers to the "old nature" and the "new nature," to loving God with all of life or rebelling against him. Thus it in no way resembles the matter-spirit antithesis of Gnosticism or the body-soul distinction of Platonism.

Summing up our survey of the New Testament material thus far, it is evident that the case for dualism is pretty slim. Not only does the New Testament fail to endorse a dualistic philosophical anthropology directly; much of the textual data traditionally used to establish dualism indirectly turns out to do no such thing. In fact much of it suggests the integration and wholeness of human life before God. The burden of proof remains on the dualists. They will have to work much harder than Calvin did to vindicate their claim to truth.

But what follows from the weakness of the dualist case? Does it mean that the monists have won the debate? Are they even ahead? Does the New Testament clearly imply monism just because it does not, on the basis of what we have seen so far, imply dualism?

III. A Preliminary Assessment of the Case for Monism

These are crucial questions, for some scholars have apparently inferred the truth of monism from the vulnerability of the traditional case for dualism. Fairness dictates that the monist claim be assessed just as critically as its opponent.

To begin, let's consider the following paragraph by Bruce Reichenbach:

---

10. Cf. Ladd, pp. 469-474.

It is true that Paul's terminology might not be as clearly and uniformly monistic as generally thought. The analogy of the tent in II Cor. 5:1-10 is disconcertingly dualistic, as is I Cor. 7:34. However, not only are these exceptions to Paul's general train of thought, but they can best be explained, not on the grounds that he is dualistically inclined, but on the grounds that his anthropology is not developed philosophically. His concern was not to present a coherent anthropology in consonance with or contrast to Hellenistic thought, but to develop a theology in relation to the redemption of man. Despite a few exceptions, then, Pauline anthropology, and New Testament anthropology in general, is monistic.[11]

Here we see an argument for monism based on premises which include most of the points raised against dualism in the preceding section. At first glance there is "disconcertingly dualistic" material in the New Testament, Reichenbach admits. But since its author's interest is kerygmatic and not philosophical, these data do not imply dualism. To the contrary, the "general train of thought" is monistic, a conclusion Reichenbach reaches in this essay by appeal to many of the linguistic phenomena which, as shown above, do not necessarily bear the dualistic interpretation. So Reichenbach's argument for the truth of monism is based in part on the weakness of the case for dualism.[12] He is not alone in using this strategy. But how compelling is this argument?

Let's consider first the claim that dualism is not implied by the New Testament because its message is neither philosophically sophisticated nor intentioned. Several points must be made in response. The first has to do with simple consistency. If the Bible contains no philosophy, it not only fails to teach dualism; it cannot be teaching monism either. For monism is just as much a philosophical theory as dualism is. What's sauce for the goose is sauce for the gander. If the New Testament writers are interested solely in proclaiming the gospel and for that reason are philosophically inarticulate, then they are neutral toward all theories of human composition alike. It is utterly arbitrary and inconsistent to operate with the double standard this antidualist polemic employs.

Second, the use of the double standard creates a question-begging ap-

---

11. Reichenbach, p. 180.

12. In fairness to Reichenbach it must be stated that his conclusion is also based on the premise that there is no intermediate state, a position for which he argues vigorously. That issue will be treated below and thus is not considered here.

proach to the textual data. Reichenbach admits the presence of "disconcertingly dualistic" material in the New Testament. But this can best be explained, he says, not by taking it at face value and seriously considering whether Paul might be a dualist, but by dismissing it on the grounds that Paul is neither philosophically interested nor astute. The material which appears "disconcertingly dualistic" is summarily dismissed as an irrelevant exception to the issue of New Testament anthropology. Not so with the evidence for monism, however. Word studies, uses of synecdoche and synonymity, and parallels with the Old Testament are all offered as sufficient evidence of monistic anthropology. So we have here an analysis in which the material supporting one position is taken seriously whereas data which would favor the opposite viewpoint are dismissed as inconsequential. That seems to lack methodological integrity. A sounder approach would insure that all the data are given equal treatment and a conclusion reached which does justice to all.

A final point with respect to the presence or absence of philosophy in the New Testament: perhaps it is wiser to recognize a certain complexity of the question than to demand a simple yes or no. I certainly agree with Reichenbach that the New Testament writers are primarily interested in the proclamation of the gospel and not in promoting a particular theoretical anthropology. But it might nonetheless be true that they express the gospel in terms of a worldview, including a view of human nature, which at least in general presupposes or implies positions on philosophical issues. Although worldviews are typically nontheoretical — more pictographical than conceptually precise — they can be rendered conceptually, suggesting some formulations and ruling others out. As we saw in the Old Testament and intertestamental literature, the authors' nonphilosophical assumptions about the human constitution do imply some generic philosophical positions and exclude others. Disembodied survival of death does entail some sort of dualism, for example. This is perfectly compatible with the claim that the Bible does not contain or teach a theoretical anthropology or psychology. Thus it does not follow from the fact that biblical texts are neither philosophically interested nor explicit that they have no philosophical implications.[13] If the

---

13. An illuminating exploration of the relation between Scripture and philosophy on another question is by C. F. D. Moule, "The Borderlands of Ontology in the New Testament," in Brian Hebblethwaite and Stewart Sutherland, eds., *The Philosophical Frontiers of Christian Theology* (Cambridge University Press, 1982), pp. 1-11.

intentions of the New Testament authors in the relevant texts can be determined with some degree of assurance, it might very well be possible to identify some kind of implied anthropology. So I do not question the methodological legitimacy of the claim that biblical texts imply monism. In
principle that is possible. I only insist that the alleged evidence for monism
be scrutinized as critically as that brought forward for dualism and that the
"disconcertingly dualistic" material be taken as seriously as the apparently
monistic data. Of course it might also be true, as argued above, that many of
the anthropological texts in the New Testament are philosophically neutral
in that they imply neither monism nor dualism in spite of their use of words
like "body," "soul," and "spirit."

The possible neutrality of some texts raises a point of logic. If there are
indeed New Testament texts which use anthropological terms without automatically implying either monism or dualism, then monism and dualism are
not the only possibilities. They do not constitute an exclusive disjunction for
exegesis. There is a third option, a reading entailing neither monism nor dualism. But if there is a third option, then it does not automatically follow
from a text's failure to endorse dualism that it endorses monism. It might
also be neutral both to monism and dualism, compatible with either. Put
more succinctly, if the only options are d(ualism) or m(onism), then if *not d,
m*. But if the options are *d* or *m* or *(neither d nor m)*, then it is simply falla-
cious to conclude *m* from *not d*. Nevertheless, much of the case for monism
appears to rely on this simple mistake. Often scholars seem to draw the conclusion that because the nonphilosophical nature of New Testament terminology or its complexity or parallelism or synonymity or its use of
synecdoche fails to establish dualism, monism is thereby established. But
this is much too hasty. As a matter of logic, it is perfectly possible that a text
which uses anthropological language nonphilosophically was authored by a
dualist. That would follow from the fact that the third option is philosophically neutral, thus compatible with either monism or dualism. So Paul could
be a dualist even if, for example, his use of *sarx* and *pneuma* in Romans 8 indicates religious and ethical commitments rather than the structure of human nature.

The possible nondualistic use of language by a dualist deserves elaboration. It was readily admitted above that the dualist tradition has sometimes naively and mistakenly believed its case could be established simply
by pointing to the words "body," "soul," and "spirit" in the New Testament.
We acknowledged the complexity and pluriformity of their meanings and

uses. We recognized not only that different terms are often used as synonyms, but also that they are meant to refer to whole human beings, not just their parts, dimensions, or spiritual orientations. We agreed that when such terms are used in opposition, as flesh against spirit, they do not necessarily indicate different substances or structural constituents of humankind. All of this, we admitted, provides no incontrovertible evidence for dualism whatsoever. But now I wish to subject the monist argument to the same scrutiny. Does the textual material imply monism? Does it even rule out dualism?

Not obviously. Consider the command to love the Lord with one's whole heart, soul, mind, and strength. At face value we have here an address to us humans to love God with our whole beings, with all the capacities he has given us. Heart, soul, mind, and strength might be different ways of referring to the whole person, each by way of a different aspect or dimension — an instance of multiple synecdoche. But absolutely nothing is implied as to whether persons and some of their capacities, including some referred to by these terms, might survive biological death or whether human beings consist of one substance or two. The text is completely silent on such matters. So while it is no proof for ontological dualism, neither does it justify monism or ontological holism. It is philosophically indeterminate. In fact it is hard to see just what would clinch the monist-holist position short of some explicit statement such as "body, soul, and spirit are inseparable" or "humans consist of only one substance." For synecdoche and parallelism are as logically compatible with dualism as with monism. Thus it could very well be that the Gospel writers are typically Jewish holistic dualists, as I shall argue below. At most it can be said that the phraseology of Jesus' love command suggests functional holism, the view that the various capacities, aspects, and dimensions of earthly human life constitute an integrated totality which either responds to God in obedience and love or does not.[14]

The same analysis applies to frequently quoted Pauline passages. In I Thessalonians 5:23 Paul writes of our "whole spirit, soul, and body." While this, too, may be a simple case of synecdoche or perhaps refers to

---

14. Recall the distinction between functional and ontological holism, spelled out below in connection with the Old Testament. Both consider humans to be single, functionally integrated entities. But ontological holism adds the implication that persons cannot exist apart from the whole psychophysical complex.

distinct but inseparable aspects of human existence, it might also be consistent with a trichotomist anthropology. There is nothing in this passage either to prove trichotomy or to rule it out. My point is that, strictly speaking, no clear and distinct philosophical implications follow from this text. It is consistent with trichotomy, but no prooftext for trichotomy. It is compatible with monism, but certainly does not suggest it. The same holds for dualism. Paul's mode of expression underdetermines all philosophical theories alike. But of course it then supplies no ammunition for monism against dualism. Considering everything up to this point, therefore, the monist's case is just as weak as the dualist's.

I am willing to admit that if all occurrences of anthropological terms in the New Testament were cases of synecdoche, parallelism, and synonymity in contexts where the wholeness of human life is being stressed, then ontological holism or perhaps some sort of monism would be a reasonable guess about the implicit anthropology of the New Testament in spite of the strict philosophical indeterminateness of the texts. The picture might look more like monism or ontological holism than dualism simply because of the lack of implied separability. But that would hold only in the absence of any cases which seem to imply dualism. If there are such cases, they should be carefully examined to discover whether the implication stands up. If it does, then the most reasonable conclusion to draw is that the New Testament implies an anthropology which is both holistic and dualistic — the conclusion we have already drawn after careful study of the Old Testament and intertestamental literature.

In the next chapter, therefore, I will explore a number of texts which do seem to suggest dualism. If they fail to stand up, I will yield the New Testament to the monists. If they withstand scrutiny, the stakes should be the same.

IV. The Key Issue: What Happens When We Die?

A. An Intermediate State Presupposes Dualism

There is more at stake in this debate than merely a philosophical position, for if the dualistic reading is incorrect, then the beliefs of most Christians down through the ages about what would happen to them at death are simply mistaken. Most traditional Christians would affirm something like Answer 57 of the *Heidelberg Catechism:*

> Not only my soul will be taken immediately after this life to Christ its head, but even my flesh, raised by the power of Christ, will be reunited with my soul and made like Christ's glorious body.[15]

This confession implies a period of time — an interim or intermediate state — between death and the resurrection during which the soul will exist with Christ apart from the body. But if it is false that the soul — the essential person or self — can survive separation from the body, if human beings are monistic or ontologically holistic entities, then this eschatological scenario is a flat impossibility. Traditional views of the afterlife necessarily assume a dualistic anthropology. The essential person is distinct from and can exist apart from the earthly organism. If dualism is mistaken, then so is the belief that we exist with Christ between death and resurrection.

This implication is not lost on contemporary scholars.[16] According to George Carey, ". . . it is a false trail to look within the human body for an immortal 'soul,' mind, or residual self which *somehow* survives the destruction of the flesh."[17] And Reichenbach, opting for the resurrection of the whole person, boldly asserts: "[T]here is no continuously existing inner self or soul."[18] Thus he concludes that "there is no New Testament warrant for holding that there is an interim existence between death and re-creation."[19]

But if the traditional belief in temporary personal existence apart from the earthly body is false, what then is the proper New Testament doctrine of individual eschatology? What does happen when we die? Here contemporary Bible scholars radically part ways. Broadly speaking, there are two possible strategies for viewing death and resurrection which avoid the intermediate state and its commitment to dualism. One is to affirm an

---

15. *The Heidelberg Catechism,* the 1975 translation of the Christian Reformed Church.

16. I know of a few pastors and college teachers who both deny dualism and affirm the intermediate state, which is to hold a logically incoherent position. But scholars generally understand the implications of denying dualism.

17. George Carey, *I Believe in Man* (Grand Rapids: Eerdmans, 1977), pp. 171-172.

18. Reichenbach, p. 181.

19. Reichenbach, p. 186.

immediate or instantaneous resurrection. The other is to hold that humans pass out of existence at death and remain nonexistent until the resurrection, when they are completely re-created by God. A number of scholars, including evangelical Christians, have opted for one or the other of these alternatives to the intermediate state.

Since our inquiry regarding anthropology depends on determining whether the New Testament does clearly speak to the issue of individual eschatology, it will be useful to describe the alternatives a bit more fully.

B. Alternative One: Immediate Resurrection

The immediate resurrection option is a general position which has gained in popularity during this century.[20] It includes a variety of specific formulations which differ according to how each defines the term "resurrection" — whether receipt of a renewed body, transformation into a spiritual mode of existence, or simple union with God. But whatever the final resurrection amounts to, it is said to occur for the individual at the instant of death. That might involve passing into another dimension of time beyond earthly time. Or it might mean transcending time altogether. In any case, this view holds that there is no temporary mode of existence or period of nonexistence between individuals' deaths and their final resurrections. The transition is instantaneous. The New Testament depiction of a general resurrection of all people at a future time — at the second coming of Christ — cannot be taken literally. The final resurrection occurs for each person at the instant of his or her death. Thus there is no time at which persons exist without bodies. In this way the dualism entailed by alleging the separation of persons (or souls) and bodies is thought to be avoided.

20. Murray Harris, *Raised Immortal*, p. 98 n. 2, provides a long list of scholars who take this position, which is based on II Corinthians 5. The most prominent evangelical among them is F. F. Bruce. In different forms it is the position of Karl Barth, Wolfhart Pannenberg, and Eberhard Juengel. Among Roman Catholics it is held by Hans Kueng and A. R. van de Walle, a student of Schillebeeckx; cf. *Darkness to Dawn*, pp. 129-130.

C. Alternative Two: Extinction–Re-creation

The extinction–re-creation view is the other nondualist strategy.[21] Since the soul or conscious ego is considered an inseparable aspect of the whole psychophysical human being, when the body dies, the whole person ceases to be. It is not merely that the soul continues to exist although unconscious or "asleep." There is no self, ego, soul, mind, or spirit which survives biological death and continues to exist. In fact the human being as a whole has been annihilated by death and is extinct. But at the future time of the general resurrection, God will re-create, that is, bring again into existence, the very same human beings who had previously existed, perhaps in some altered or glorified form. So resurrection really amounts to re-creation after a period of nonexistence. This is not as horrible as it initially sounds, according to its proponents. A moment's reflection will show that from the first-person point of view there is no awareness of the possibly lengthy temporal interval between death and resurrection. Just as eight hours may seem to elapse in a moment to one who is asleep, so millennia could pass between death and re-creation in what would seem to be the twinkling of an eye. In fact the New Testament writers are interpreted as taking the first-person subjective point of view when they imply continuous existence after death, as Paul does in Philippians 1 and II Corinthians 5. When he states that absence from the body means presence with the Lord, he does not intend to suggest uninterrupted objective personal existence, but merely implies the continuity of subjective awareness.[22] Although

21. Cf. John Hick, *Death and Eternal Life* (San Francisco: Harper and Row, 1976), Ch. 15, "The Resurrection of the Person." His view is the same as what he takes Paul's to be. "When someone has died he is, apart from any special divine action, extinct. But in fact God, by an act of sovereign power, either sometimes or always resurrects or reconstitutes or recreates him . . ." (p. 279). It should be noted, however, that Hick's formulation is compatible with both immediate and future resurrection. Reichenbach, p. 176, holds that "according to the New Testament, resurrection (re-creation) is of persons, not of bodies alone, and that it sees no existent in objective time between one's death and his re-creation." This position is also implied by Donald MacKay, *Brains, Machines, and Persons* (Grand Rapids: Eerdmans, 1980), pp. 100-102. It is suggested, though not clearly stated, by George Carey, "The Destiny of Man," in *I Believe in Man*. It is endorsed by Otto Kaiser and Eduard Lohse, *Death and Life* (Nashville: Abingdon, 1981), p. 139. And it was the view of the phenomenologist of religion, Gerardus van der Leeuw; cf. Berkouwer, *Man*, pp. 251-252.

22. Cf. Reichenbach, p. 185. Technically, Paul is supposed to be speaking phenomenologically, not ontologically — i.e., describing how things appear to us, not necessarily how they really (objectively) are.

the continuity of objective existence cannot be admitted by the extinction–re-creation position, it does acknowledge the future temporality of the general resurrection and consistently avoids any dualistic separation of persons and their bodies.

In summary, there are three main competitors which claim to represent the New Testament doctrine of the afterlife: the intermediate state–resurrection view, the immediate resurrection view, and the extinction–re-creation view. A final judgment about the monism-dualism debate will depend heavily on whether it is possible to decide which of these positions is correct.

V. The Strategy for Concluding the Debate

Since the monism-dualism debate is closely tied to the doctrine of personal eschatology, the first order of business is to get clear on just how the New Testament depicts what happens when we die. This will determine whether in its use of anthropological terminology there is any hard evidence for dualism after all. That project will occupy the next two chapters.

Having gotten as clear as possible on the relevant New Testament material, it will be necessary to probe the results philosophically to see precisely what they entail and also to evaluate more carefully the implications of the alternative theories of the afterlife. Some may contain less than meets the eye. For there may be philosophical as well as exegetical reasons for avoiding a position. Most of the philosophical analysis will be handled in Chapter Eight.

It will come as no surprise that I intend to defend holistic dualism as the anthropology implicit in the New Testament. I have already argued that the anthropological terminology of the New Testament continues to suggest the functional integrity and phenomenological wholeness of human existence much as the Old Testament did. But it also seems to assert that persons can exist without earthly bodies and do exist between physical death and future resurrection. That impression is created by a straightforward reading of the New Testament text itself, and it is strongly corroborated when the text is considered in terms of its historical context, first-century Judaism and to some extent Hellenism. Thus it continues the line we have traced to this point from the Old Testament through the intertestamental period.[23]

23. Special care will be taken to establish that the New Testament indeed incorporates the implicit dualism of its theological environment. For it does not simply follow from the fact that orthodox Judaism is dualistic that the New Testament is. To be decisive, the evidence must be direct and not merely circumstantial. For there are scholars such as Kaiser and Lohse who recognize the animistic dualism of the Old Testament and intertestamental period and who nevertheless interpret Paul, for example, as holding the implicitly monistic extinction–re-creation position. Cf. *Death and Life,* pp. 41 and 139.

Chapter Six

Anthropology and Personal Eschatology in the New Testament: The Non-Pauline Writings

I. Introduction: Refining the Terms of the Debate

Adjudicating the monism-dualism debate among biblical anthropologists will depend upon determining which personal eschatology, if any, is taught by the New Testament. If a view of the afterlife is presented which does not entail the separation of the person from the earthly body, the case for dualism will be lacking. The monists could then claim victory by default, although this would not actually demonstrate the truth of their position. But if New Testament eschatology does imply the survival of persons apart from earthly organisms, if such anthropological terms as "soul" and "spirit" are used in contexts which imply their existence without the body, then we must conclude that dualism has been established beyond a reasonable doubt as the operative anthropology of the New Testament.

In order to make a proper determination of what the New Testament authors meant to teach, we must consider their writings in historical context. For they used the language and religious terminology familiar to their intended audiences. Admittedly, they often criticized and reshaped the beliefs of their readers. But to do so they had to begin from a common frame of reference. Parts of the framework in which they worked are the eschatology and anthropology of orthodox Judaism. As seen above, a common core of anthropological themes undergirds the diversity of most groups and parties within Judaism. That core, we have argued, is best described as holistic dualism.

Scholars are fairly confident of the common currency of these teachings. According to Cavallin, "[I]t seems likely that a belief in life after death was shared by rather wide circles among Jews both in Palestine and the diaspora . . . in the latter half of the first century A.D."[1] The French authority Joseph Bonsirven puts these ideas even closer to the lifetime of Jesus: ". . . at the beginning of the first Christian century, many Jewish circles believed that at the time of death, souls are separated from their bodies and brought to judgment."[2] This is consistent with our own study of intertestamental eschatology.

So New Testament anthropological texts, at least those aimed at Jewish audiences, cannot be read apart from the holistic dualism of their historical context. Caution, however, must be exercised, for it does not follow automatically from the fact that New Testament authors employed current Jewish terms and categories that they endorsed them. It could be that they were actually polemicizing against these ideas. Or it might be that this terminology was simply part of the means employed to teach another point. Jewish eschatology might have been used, for example, as a vehicle for illustrating an ethical precept and thus would not itself be the intended teaching of the author. Use of dualistic body-soul language or reference to the intermediate state might not constitute endorsement. But then again it might.

On the other hand, if Jewish anthropological and eschatological ideas are used to describe or affirm something about death or the afterlife, that would reasonably count as evidence that the New Testament author does endorse those ideas. They are thereby taken up as part of the framework in terms of which the Christian gospel is to be understood and proclaimed. They are integral to what the Bible means to teach. Unless we have good reason from elsewhere in Scripture not to accept these pieces of framework, they are part of what Bible-believing Christians ought to affirm. Or at least the burden of proof falls heavily on those who wish to maintain that such beliefs are not essential to the faith, but are merely incidental pieces of cultural baggage which can be abandoned by modern Christians.

At this point, therefore, we turn to the project of determining whether the case for dualism in the New Testament does stand up, all things consid-

---

1. H. C. C. Cavallin, *Life after Death* (Lund: Gleerup, 1974), p. 194. Here he is summarizing the variety of views we encountered in intertestamental Judaism, virtually all of which entail a dualism of some sort.

2. Joseph Bonsirven, S.J., *Palestinian Judaism in the Time of Jesus Christ* (New York: Holt, Rinehart, and Winston, 1964), p. 163.

ered. In this chapter we will consider the relevant texts in the non-Pauline writings, and in the next chapter we will focus on the epistles of Paul.

II. Dualism in the Anthropological Terminology

Crucial to the monist's case is the claim that there are no instances in the New Testament where anthropological terms are employed in ways which suggest the truth of dualism. Never are words such as *psychē* and *pneuma* meant to suggest that there are existing human persons who lack earthly or resurrection bodies. The dualist counters that there are such examples. Let's first consider the most frequently mentioned occurrences of "spirit." In the next section we will look at the word "soul."

A. "Spirit"

1. I Peter 3:19-20

A very difficult text is I Peter 3:19-20, in which Christ is said to have "preached to the spirits in prison who disobeyed long ago when God waited patiently in the days of Noah while the ark was being built."[3] Are these the spirits of humans during the intermediate state? That is a live possibility, defended by a number of scholars. Between his death and resurrection (cf. v. 18), Christ went to the realm of the dead to preach to Noah's wicked contemporaries. This interpretation is fully consistent with current Jewish eschatology in using *pneuma* to refer to the preresurrection dead. But it cannot be defended conclusively. There are other possible explanations. One less favored is that the preincarnate Christ preached to Noah's wicked neighbors before the flood. Another is that the spirits mentioned are not humans but angels. Although the nod might finally go toward those who favor the disembodied humans view, this is an extremely obscure passage and provides no firm foundation for inferences about the intermediate state.[4]

3. Cf. John Feinberg, "I Peter 3:18-20: Ancient Mythology and the Intermediate State," *Westminster Theological Journal*, Vol. 48 (October 1986), pp. 303-336, for an excellent recent analysis of this text and the history of its interpretation.

4. Feinberg both favors this interpretation and sounds this note of caution; cf. pp. 321, 336.

2. Hebrews 12:23

Much less ambiguous is Hebrews 12:23. Its context is a vision of the heavenly Jerusalem, the city of God. Among Zion's inhabitants are angels and "the *pneumatais* of righteous men made perfect." There is no question here that the spirits are human spirits. The only issues are whether they are persons or merely the impersonal life-principles some take Old Testament *ruach* to signify; and if persons, whether they are in the intermediate or final state.

With respect to the first question, it is most improbable that these spirits are merely life-principles. For in the first place, when *ruach* separated at death according to the Old Testament, it did not remain an individuated entity. But Hebrews mentions a plural number of individuals. Second, these spirits have been made righteous, a status which is predicable of persons, but not of mere life-principles, except metaphorically. But the mention of God and the angels is not intended metaphorically in this context. So probably neither is reference to these human spirits. Much more reasonable is the view that the author here is speaking of deceased but existent human beings. In addition, that was common in the Jewish eschatology of the time.[5]

As to the intermediate–final state question, this verse is silent. At bottom the question is moot. For in either case we have dualism. If it is the final state, then perpetual disembodiment is envisioned here: the saints are everlastingly spirits. In that case the book of Hebrews would contain not only dualistic anthropology, but the eschatology of Hellenistic Judaism. However, Hebrews 6:2 and 11:35 mention the resurrection. Although a couple of intertestamental texts envision resurrection as a spiritual transformation apparently compatible with permanent disembodiment, it is almost always bodily and viewed as future in Jewish eschatology. The viewpoint of this verse is present — what obtains right now in the heavenly Jerusalem. Most probably these spirits are awaiting the final resurrection, the "better resurrection" of 11:35.[6] Given both internal and external evidence, therefore, it is rather unlikely that the spirits of the righteous dead

5. The phrase "the spirits of righteous men made perfect" virtually paraphrases Wisd. 3:1 and I Enoch 22:9; cf. F. F. Bruce, *The Epistle to the Hebrews* (Grand Rapids: Eerdmans, 1964), p. 378.

6. The reference in 11:35 is to the Maccabaean martyrs, who clearly hoped for a future, not an immediate resurrection. Cf. Bruce, pp. 337-339.

in 12:23 are in their final state. So we have identified a case where the term "spirits" probably applies to human beings during the intermediate state.[7] But even if this is their final destiny, we have a dualistic use of *pneuma* nonetheless. The dead exist apart from their earthly bodies.

3. Death as "giving up the spirit"

What about the several verses in the New Testament which speak of death as "giving up the ghost *(pneuma)*," to quote the King James? Do these entail a dualistic anthropology? Or does *pneuma* merely mean "breath" or "life-force," as *ruach* did in the Old Testament? Consider the death of Jesus Christ. Matthew 27:50 and John 19:30 say, "he gave up his spirit." Luke 23:46 reports Jesus committing his spirit to his Father. But what does "spirit" denote? Mark 15:37 and Luke 23:46 use the verb *exepneusen*, which can simply mean "breathe out" or "expire." Is this clear evidence that *pneuma* ought to be translated merely as "breath?"

That conclusion would be overly hasty. First, it would make little sense for Jesus to commit his exhaled air to God. At the very least he must be yielding his life to his Father. Second, in Koine Greek as in many languages, the same word for exhaling is used for giving up the life-force or personal soul at death.[8] So appealing to *exepneusen* settles nothing. Third, we have seen that *ruach* and *pneuma* had multiple meanings for intertestamental Jews, including reference to the disembodied dead. It is therefore mistaken to assume that the term can have one meaning only: either breath or personal spirit. The phrase "giving up the spirit" commonly meant the cessation of breathing, the loss of life-force, and the departure of personal existence to another realm.

It might be objected, however, that this is all circumstantial evidence. Appealing to Jewish religion and even to the book of Hebrews does not prove what the Gospel writers had in mind when they used the word *pneuma*. Is there direct evidence in any of the Gospels for the claim that *pneuma* can mean "personal spirit without a fleshly body?"

Luke 24:37, just a chapter after the crucifixion, removes any reason-

7. Bruce, p. 378; B. F. Westcott, *The Epistle to the Hebrews* (Macmillan; reprinted by Eerdmans, 1980), p. 416.

8. Cf. *ekpneuō* in Bauer, Arndt, and Gingrich, *Greek-English Lexicon* (Chicago: University of Chicago, 1957), p. 243. Mircea Eliade, *From the Primitives to Zen* (San Francisco: Harper and Row, 1977), pp. 177-179.

able doubt. Jesus appears to his disciples in the upper room on Easter Sunday evening. "Peace be with you," he says. "They were startled and frightened, thinking they saw a ghost *(pneuma)*." Luke does not say whether they recognized the likeness of Jesus or were reacting to an unknown spirit. The point is that the sudden appearance of a visible human figure was immediately interpreted as the appearance of a ghost. So obviously Luke uses the word *pneuma* to signify deceased, nonfleshly, yet bodily formed human beings. This view of the dead can be traced back through the intertestamental literature to the Old Testament notion of the *rephaim* in Sheol. Jesus himself employs the word "spirit" in distinction from flesh and bones in attempting to reassure them: "a ghost does not have flesh and bones, as you see I have" (v. 39). There is no doubt that Luke uses "spirit" to mean "discarnate person."

Thus we understand that Jesus in committing his spirit to God yielded *himself* to God, not just his breath or life-force. Here is a case where synecdoche plays into the hands of the dualist. Just as in the Old Testament, here "spirit" can simply mean "person" or "self." So our Lord, about to lose his earthly life, entrusted *himself* to the care of his Father. Jesus' location between his death and resurrection will be treated below. For the present we can count another indisputable example of the use of "spirit" to refer to discarnate persons. And it might not be unwarranted to extend a dualistic reading to the other instances of "giving up the ghost" in the New Testament as well.[9]

B. "Soul"

1. Revelation 6:9-11

We turn now to *psychē*, the Greek word for "soul." One passage in which it is unambiguously used to refer to dead saints between death and resurrection is Revelation 6:9-11.[10] The souls of the martyrs are under the heavenly altar and cry out for the Lord to avenge their deaths. They are given white

9. In Acts 5:5, 5:10, and 12:23 Luke uses the verb *ekpsychō* (give up the soul) rather than *ekpneuō* (give up the spirit).

10. Cf. Robert Mounce, *The Book of Revelation* (Grand Rapids: Eerdmans, 1977), pp. 157-160; and George Ladd, *Revelation of John* (Grand Rapids: Eerdmans, 1977), pp. 102-106.

robes and told to be patient a little longer. That they are awaiting resurrection is clear from Revelation 20:5-6.[11] It has not taken place yet. They are portrayed as conscious of their condition and of redemptive history and are imagined as bodily enough to be given white robes.[12] Not surprisingly, this scene is highly reminiscent of intertestamental depictions of the afterlife. For it is of the same apocalyptic genre as they are and draws from the same stock of imagery. There can be no dispute about the fact that this is a case where, within its universe of discourse, "souls" refers to persons during the intermediate state.

The only question concerns the literal beliefs behind these figurative visions. How literally does the Holy Spirit want us to read apocalyptic? Does Revelation 6 at least teach an intermediate state for the martyrs? Does it also teach consciousness? Bodiliness? Location under an actual celestial altar in an actual heavenly temple? Or does "souls" simply refer metaphorically to the lives of the martyrs who for the time being do not exist but will eventually be vindicated by God?

The incredible richness of allusion to Old Testament and Judaistic symbolism cannot be explored here. But suppose the basic exegetical choices are three: strict representationism — picturing everything as literally as possible; pure symbolism — referring to no identifiable states of affairs whatsoever except that Jesus values martyrs; and a median position which sees here metaphorical references to existing realities and redemptive-historical epochs.[13] Surely the latter is the most responsible approach. Apocalyptic writers did take themselves to be describing actual states of affairs in highly imaginative ways. Our study of the intertestamental period has shown that people did believe in the conscious but not yet perfected existence of the righteous in heaven awaiting the resurrection. Certainly the Rabbis believed this. Apocalyptic was understood to symbolize actual states of affairs. So it is not wholly unwarranted to suppose that John

11. All three traditional interpretations of Revelation's eschatology — amillennialism, premillennialism, and postmillennialism — hold to the future time of the resurrection.

12. Cf. Mounce, p. 160, and Ladd, p. 106, on why the robes are not symbols of resurrection bodies. Receiving a resurrection body at the instant of death is crucial for the immediate resurrection theory. The book of Revelation does not support this view.

13. I appreciate Reichenbach's warning against literalism (*Is Man the Phoenix?* [Grand Rapids: Eerdmans, 1983], p. 186). But I cannot accept the rather minimal symbolic interpretation of Revelation 6 he gives (merely that martyrdom is a sacrifice to God) to avoid dualism as the only alternative.

meant to affirm the intermediate state, if not consciousness, of the martyrs in Revelation.

However, this is a difficult text and cannot bear much weight in the monism-dualism debate. Perhaps if we are reluctant to view Armageddon literalistically as a military conflict in the Middle East, we ought to be equally cautious about the souls under the altar. Although the battle of interpretations goes on, however, one thing is clear: *psychē* is used in the apocalyptic genre to refer to humans in the intermediate state. Whatever else may be concluded from this fact for theological anthropology, the semantic claim that the word "soul" is never used dualistically in the New Testament is contradicted by this text.

2. Matthew 10:28

Matthew 10:28 is another verse which receives regular mention in the debate. "Do not be afraid of those who kill the body *(sōma)* but cannot kill the soul *(psychē)*. Rather, be afraid of the One who can destroy both soul and body in hell." On first reading the dualistic implication of this verse is hard to miss: when people kill the body, the soul is still left.

But monists legitimately raise the question about the meaning of "soul." Is it the person in distinction from the body or only a symbol for "life?" Eduard Schweizer, for example, attempts to construe the text nondualistically by linking it with the Old Testament: "In the Old Testament, 'flesh' and 'soul' always designate man as a whole, but under different aspects." Then he asserts: "Probably Matthew, like the Old Testament and most of the New Testament, simply cannot conceive of life apart from the body."[14] His strategy is to consider Matthew's vocabulary as identical with the Old Testament's and to construe "body" and "soul" here as cases of synecdoche.

But this simply will not work. For starters, synecdoche can be ruled out; each term cannot stand for the whole bodily person in this text. For whatever soul is, it can exist before God without the body, whatever it is. "Body" and "soul" cannot both be referring to the same thing in different ways. A human without a body is not the same as a human with a body, no matter how these words are defined.

14. Eduard Schweizer, *The Good News According to Matthew*, trans. David Green (Atlanta: John Knox, 1975), pp. 247-248.

Furthermore, taking *sōma* and *psychē* as identical in meaning with *basar* and *nephesh* will not work. For if *psychē* is no more than the life-force or bodily-person in the Old Testament, it makes no sense to say that killing the body does not kill the soul. In the Hebrew mind, killing the body is killing the *nephesh*. Unless the Israelites were dualists, *nephesh* could not survive bodily death. But Matthew assumes it can. Besides, if most scholars are correct, the Israelites did not hold that *nephesh* actually goes to Sheol, nor does *basar* for that matter. The *rephaim* are neither soul nor flesh.[15] But Matthew speaks of both body and soul in Gehenna.[16] The more they are compared, the less Matthew sounds like the Old Testament.

Mention of Gehenna is a final reason why the attempt to treat them as identical fails. Gehenna is not part of Old Testament eschatology but a product of the intertestamental period, as we have seen. It is the place of final punishment whose tormented inhabitants are often said to be present in body and soul. Admittedly Matthew 10:28 does not explicitly define soul as "person" rather than mere "life-principle."[17] But it is much more likely that Matthew is using *sōma* and *psychē* in the way his own contemporaries did than that he is anachronistic by centuries. Most Jews who spoke of Gehenna were holistic dualists. They believed that souls — persons — exist temporarily without bodies but that both "parts" will be reunited for eternity.

All things considered, the evidence strongly favors reading Matthew as expressing Jewish dualism.[18] Although he is not intending to teach an an-

---

15. However, recall Otto Kaiser's defense of the view that *nephesh* does depart from the corpse and descend into Sheol. Of course if he is correct, Schweizer's argument can be turned against him. For then the Old Testament use of *nephesh* itself is dualistic and likewise Matthew, who allegedly follows it.

16. Cf. also Mt. 5:29-30.

17. Bruce Reichenbach admits that this text sounds dualistic but then attempts to avoid that conclusion by pointing to the various other meanings *psychē* has and the fact that Luke's account of this saying does not use *psychē*. But this strategy fails. For it does not follow from the fact that *psychē* has other meanings that it cannot sometimes also mean "fleshless person." We have shown that it does. And how does making an observation about Luke tell us anything at all about Matthew? Cf. *Phoenix*, pp. 180 and 187-188 n. 8.

18. Schweizer, p. 248, finally admits that the dualistic implication cannot be explained away: "it remains unclear how much Hellenistic Jewish notions may have influenced the language and possibly also the thought of this passage. . . ." But why suppose that dualistic language must be the result of Greek influence? We have shown above that the holistic dualism of Judaism is rooted in the Old Testament and in principle could have developed without Greek influence.

thropology in this passage, he appears to be using one. Is it assuming too much for us to infer from this verse that humans can in fact kill the body but not the soul? And is it improper to suppose that the anthropology he uses in chapter 10 is presupposed in his teachings on final judgment, reward, and punishment in chapters 24 and 25, for example? If it is presupposed, then his body-soul distinction would be included in what Matthew teaches. Or is his eschatological vision incidental cultural baggage as well?

C. Summary on "Soul" and "Spirit"

Discounting I Peter 3 because of obscurity, we have discovered substantial evidence against the claim that "soul" and "spirit" are never used dualistically to refer to deceased but existing humans. Hebrews 12 and Luke 23–24 almost certainly use *pneuma* that way. Far more probably than not, *psychē* has that meaning in Revelation 6 and Matthew 10. From a scholarly point of view, the dualist's case seems significantly more defensible than the monist's on this issue.

Thus far we are merely drawing a semantic conclusion, however. We are claiming something about the meaning of these words in the New Testament. To some extent that gives us an indication of the personal beliefs of the human authors and thus the framework in which they express the gospel. But a distinction must be maintained between the personal vocabularies and beliefs of New Testament authors on the one hand and the teachings of the New Testament on the other. Christians ought to believe what Scripture teaches. Thus we have not yet made the claim that modern biblical Christians are obligated to accept these meanings and beliefs as the teaching of the New Testament. We are not rushing to theological and philosophical conclusions on the basis of such problematic texts as Revelation 6. The debate as a whole has not yet been concluded. But the dualist has scored some points.

III. Is There a Non-Pauline Eschatology?

Resolution of the monism-dualism debate cannot be based on anthropological terminology alone, but requires determination of what the New Testament teaches about the afterlife. In what follows we will consider a number of issues and texts which have figured prominently in the debate to see whether they present a coherent picture and, if so, what that picture implies.

A. The Time of the Resurrection

Since one important theory of personal eschatology is the immediate resurrection view, we must consider whether any non-Pauline texts clearly address the time of the resurrection.

Consider first Jesus' exchange with the Sadducees about marriage "at the resurrection."[19] Luke 20:35 explicitly fixes the occurrence of the resurrection "in the age to come." It certainly sounds as though this refers to the historical future, and it was undoubtedly understood that way by the Pharisees in Jesus' audience. The age to come is interpreted as a future time in general salvation-history by almost all Lukan scholars.[20] However, immediate resurrectionists might nevertheless maintain that this future becomes present for each person at her death, death providing entrance to the new age, which already exists beyond earthly time. So by itself this verse is not absolutely conclusive.

Another relevant point is that Jesus grounds the reality of the resurrection in God's covenant with the patriarchs: "even Moses showed that the dead rise, for he calls the Lord 'the God of Abraham, and the God of Isaac, and the God of Jacob.' He is not the God of the dead, but of the living, for to him all are alive" (Lk. 20:37-38). Although this seems to rule out the possibility that the patriarchs are extinct, it does not specify whether their resurrection has already taken place or is still future. For the immediate resurrectionist could assert that the patriarchs are alive precisely because they have already been raised. However, it could just as well be claimed that they are now alive in the intermediate state and will be raised. But as a matter of fact, popular Jewish belief held that the patriarchs have a special role during the intermediate state.[21]

So Jesus' rebuttal of the Sadducees' position does not nail down the

19. Mt. 22:23-33; Mk. 12:18-27; Lk. 20:27-38.

20. Cf. A. J. Mattill, Jr., *Luke and the Last Things* (Dillsboro: Western North Carolina Press, 1979). I was introduced to this work by my New Testament colleague, Prof. Andrew Bandstra.

21. Cf. notes 26 and 37 below in connection with the parable of Dives and Lazarus.

time of the resurrection. The answer to that question depends on how Luke understands the time of the age to come and whether Jesus' view is similar to that of the Pharisees. The fact that Jesus wins the approval of the Pharisees (Lk. 20:39) suggests that he affirmed their position: the resurrection is a future historical event. Although most scholars favor this interpretation, however, immediate resurrection cannot absolutely be ruled out.[22]

More definite is the Gospel of John. In spite of the fact that John stresses the present possession of eternal life for believers, he twice locates the resurrection at a single future time: "[A] time is coming when all who are in their graves will hear his voice and come out — those who have done good will rise to live, and those who have done evil will rise to be condemned" (5:28-29).[23] And if that saying is alleged to be somehow ambiguous, nothing could be more plain than 11:23-24, just before Jesus raises Lazarus: "Jesus said to her, 'Your brother will rise again.' Martha answered, 'I know he will rise again in the resurrection at the last day.'" Then Jesus says, "I am the resurrection and the life. He who believes in me will live, even though he dies." Here Jesus is teaching Martha that he is the one who brings resurrection and eternal life. He is not telling Martha that her view of the future resurrection is mistaken, but grounding that view.[24] Jesus himself says that Lazarus will rise (future time), and Martha specifies "the last day." It is exceedingly difficult to make this text say that an immediate resurrection for individuals is envisioned. John's account of Jesus' words is clear. The only question is whether we are obliged to take them at face value in formulating our doctrines.

B. The God of the Living

Above we considered Jesus' reply to the Sadducees to determine whether it would support an eschatology of immediate or future resurrection. It strongly favored the latter, if it did not prove it. Since future resurrection is held both by the intermediate state and the extinction–re-creation

22. I. Howard Marshall, *Commentary on Luke* (Grand Rapids: Eerdmans, 1978), pp. 741-743.

23. Cf. Murray Harris, *Raised Immortal* (Grand Rapids: Eerdmans, 1985), pp. 150-152.

24. Harris, p. 152, concludes: "The distinctive element in the eschatology of the Fourth Gospel is not the eradication of the Jewish doctrines of future judgment, future resurrection, or future eternal life," but the addition of their presence already in the work of Jesus.

eschatologies, we now turn to Jesus' exchange with the Sadducees to see whether it helps us decide between these two.

The extinction–re-creation view holds that persons do not exist between death and resurrection. If that is true, then Abraham, Isaac, and Jacob do not now exist nor did they exist during the earthly life of Jesus. But Jesus implies that Abraham, Isaac, and Jacob are alive because God "is not the God of the dead, but of the living, for to him all are alive" (Lk. 20:38). Of course the extinction–re-creationist could interpret being "alive to God" as meaning that although people are nonexistent, they are remembered by God and thereby in line for resurrection in the future. But this would be a strained reading. Furthermore, as many commentators point out, Jesus and his disciples most likely operated with the Jewish notion of Sheol, which assumes the existence of the dead.[25] In much Jewish thought, there is a special place and status until the final resurrection for the patriarchs and other heroes of the faith from the Old Testament.[26] Almost surely, therefore, Jesus is saying that God will raise the patriarchs from the dead and implying that they exist in the meantime, present and "alive to God." Given the circumstantial and textual evidence, that is much more reasonable than trying to reconcile these words of Jesus with the extinction–re-creation theory.

C. The Transfiguration

Moses and Elijah appear with Jesus on the Mount of Transfiguration.[27] Where are they before and after this event? If the extinction–re-creation view is correct, then God would have had to re-create them for a little while and then "extinguish" them again until the next re-creation. That

25. Cf. Marshall, pp. 742-743, for a discussion of the anthropological and eschatological assumptions in this text.

26. Consider the role of Abraham in paradise in the parable of Lazarus and the rich man in Luke 16. Cf. the extensive discussion of this parable in relation to Jewish apocalyptic by Mattill, pp. 26-31. Cf. also A. Robertson and A. Plummer, *The International Critical Commentary on First Corinthians* (Edinburgh: Clark, 1911, 1961), p. 365. Referring to Jesus' exchange with the Sadducees in connection with I Corinthians 15, the authors quote from IV Maccabees that the godly do not die but "are alive to God" and conclude that Jesus intends to affirm the continued exalted existence of the patriarchs.

27. Mt. 17:1-13; Mk. 9:2-13; Lk. 9:28-36.

might even be a conceivable account of what happened to Moses, since he had died. But Elijah had not died. He "went up to heaven in a whirlwind" (II Kings 2:11). Apparently he had been there all along. Certainly the extinction–re-creation theory is false in his case. How likely is it that God sent Elijah back to earth but re-created Moses especially for this occasion? First-century readers would have found that a most puzzling suggestion.[28]

How do the other theories handle this event? Does the glorious appearance of Moses and Elijah suggest that they already have resurrection bodies? That is a plausible hypothesis, especially for Elijah, who had ascended bodily into heaven. It is not conclusive, however. Jesus also was gloriously transfigured, but only in anticipation of his resurrection body. So having a resurrection body was not necessary for Jesus' being transfigured; perhaps it was not so for Moses and Elijah either. How then did they appear, if they did not have resurrection bodies? The Jewish vision of the intermediate state, as we have seen, did not consider the dead to be purely incorporeal. The *rephaim* and the martyrs under the altar, for example, are typically represented as nonfleshly beings who nonetheless have bodily form. That would be sufficient even for Moses to make a glorious earthly appearance, visible to the eyes of the disciples. And if Elijah already had a resurrection body, it would only be due to the fact that he had not died. It would not be evidence that this was thought to happen to everyone at death.[29] Even if, hypothetically, Moses' and Elijah's ordinary condition were wholly incorporeal like the angels', God could still give them bodily form for an earthly appearance as he did for the angels. On the other hand, having already undergone resurrection would certainly explain the glorious appearance of Moses and Elijah.

We conclude that the Transfiguration counts against the extinction–re-creation view. When taken on its own, it favors neither the immediate resurrection nor intermediate state theory. But read in terms of Jewish es-

---

28. In Jewish apocalyptic thought, Moses is one of the patriarchs of Israel who not only exists between his death and the future resurrection, but has a special place of honor above and beyond the ordinary righteous dead. Of course it does not follow from the fact that Jews believed this that it is true. But it does illustrate how the readers of the Gospels and probably also their authors understood the event of the Transfiguration.

29. This judgment is supported by the books of Enoch. Enoch, too, had not died but had been taken by the Lord in Genesis 5. His tours through Sheol and heaven were bodily. But the dead whom he observed were souls before the resurrection.

chatology, it fits best with the intermediate state–future resurrection account.

D. The Rich Man and Lazarus

In Luke 16:19-31 we find a parable which is often taken to say something about the intermediate state. Lazarus and the rich man both die. Their situations in life are now reversed. For Lazarus is carried to the bosom of Abraham, whereas the rich man suffers in Hades. Although a great gulf separates them, the rich man futilely begs Abraham to send Lazarus on two errands. He wishes Lazarus to cool his tongue with water and to return from the dead to warn his family to repent lest they share his fate.[30]

What can be concluded from this about biblical eschatology? Taken at face value, the parable seems to be an imaginative representation of the intermediate state as visualized by the Pharisees and ordinary Jewish people in Jesus' audience.[31] But why is this a picture of the intermediate rather than the final state of the dead?

Several reasons can be given for this judgment. In the first place, it depicts the intermediate state because the final resurrection as Luke understands it has not taken place. The rich man's brothers are still alive on earth. Now although it is possible that they would still be on earth if their brother had been immediately resurrected to his final destination in hell, this is not how Luke views the last things. He links resurrection with future apocalypse.[32]

A second argument often given in support of the view that this depicts the intermediate state is that the rich man is said to be in Hades, not Ge-

30. Interesting to note is the fact that Lazarus' return is described as "arising from the dead" *(ek nekrōn anastēi)*, the verbal form of the word "resurrection." Extinction–re-creationists insist that "resurrection" really means "re-creation" in the New Testament. Here is one indisputable counter-example to that claim. Even if the parable teaches nothing about the intermediate state, we see that the word "resurrection" is sometimes used to mean "return to earthly existence after temporary nonearthly existence."

31. Cf. the excellent discussion of the background of this parable, replete with references to Jewish sources, by Marshall, *Luke*, pp. 632-639.

32. Mattill, pp. 28-29. Likewise Marshall, p. 636: "since the reference is to the state of the man immediately after his death, it is most likely that the intermediate abode of the dead before the final judgment is meant."

henna, the place of final punishment.[33] Against this argument some scholars simply dispute the claim that the New Testament never uses Hades to designate the ultimate destination of the damned.[34] Whatever the outcome of the debate in general, however, it is clear that Luke himself uses Hades to refer to an interim condition which does not hold the dead, Jesus Christ preeminent among them (Acts 2:27, 31).[35] Most likely, therefore, this parable imagines the intermediate state if anything at all.

Finally, the fact that the rich man suffers bodily torment and thirst does not count against this interpretation. It actually strengthens the case. For intertestamental depictions of the dead in the intermediate state frequently represent them as conscious, quasi-bodily beings. The striking parallels of phraseology and conception between this parable and the depiction of the intermediate state in I Enoch 22 have often been noted, including the great chasm and the thirst of the damned.[36] There is little footing here for the view that the characters have undergone immediate resurrection. References to Jewish eschatology consistently favor the intermediate state.

Intertestamental literature also helps us appreciate more fully the roles of Abraham and Lazarus. Jewish tradition accorded Abraham and the other patriarchs the honor of welcoming and comforting the righteous dead, who were "gathered to their fathers," according to the Old Testament.[37] The figure of Lazarus is likewise taken from popular lore, with a

33. Cf. J. Jeremias, "Hades," *TDNT,* I, pp. 146-149. Murray Harris, *Raised Immortal,* p. 134, argues in connection with this passage that Hades is always an interim location in the New Testament.

34. Cf. Karel Hanhart, *The Intermediate State in the New Testament* (Franeker: Wever, 1966), pp. 198-199.

35. Mattill, pp. 31-32.

36. Mattill, pp. 27-31. He concludes, p. 31: "it seems quite probable that Luke has handed down to us Enoch's popular conception of Hades as a divided intermediate state, with Lazarus in the happy side, which includes Abraham's bosom and the fountain of magical, living water, and Dives in the unhappy side, separated by a great chasm. Here Dives and Lazarus experience preliminary blessing and punishment and await the resurrection, when the souls in Hades will be united with their bodies to stand in the last judgment."

37. Cf. Gen. 15:15; 47:30; Judg. 2:10; I Kings 1:21. Marshall, p. 636, refers to IV Maccabees 12:17, where Abraham receives the martyrs; cf. also Alfred Plummer, *A Critical and Exegetical Commentary on the Gospel of Luke,* 5th ed. (Edinburgh: Clark, 1922), p. 393. Abraham's bosom "is not a synonym for paradise; but to repose on Abraham's bosom is to be in paradise, for Abraham is there."

surprising twist, however. He is not merely some fictional poor person. Very plausibly he is Eliezer (Greek: Lazarus), the servant of Abraham in Genesis 15, who according to tradition had been elevated to patriarchal status and in this parable had returned to earth to test the charity of the rich man.[38] (The context of the parable is the Pharisees' love of riches.) Thus although the parable may draw on popular views of the damned in the intermediate state, it may not explicitly portray the condition of the blessed dead in general. The bosom of Abraham may be a special place for the other patriarchs and the martyrs only. Although the story certainly draws from the beliefs of the Jewish people, it may not tell us about how they imagined the lot of the ordinary blessed dead awaiting resurrection.

A caution of a different and more serious nature must be sounded as well. This is a parable whose point is not to teach about death or the intermediate state, but to warn its hearers about the dangers of riches and the consequences of failing to love their neighbors.[39] Although it does corroborate what we know from other sources about popular eschatology, it does not necessarily tell us what Jesus or Luke believed about the afterlife, nor does it provide a firm basis for a doctrine of the intermediate state.[40] For it is possible that Jesus simply uses popular images in order to make his ethical point. He may not have been endorsing those images. He may not have believed them himself because he knew them to be false.

If we then return to the initial question — what does this passage tell us about the intermediate state? — the answer may be, "Nothing." The dualist case cannot lean on this text as a main support. And even if it does affirm the intermediate state, how are we to exegete the imagery in coming to ontological conclusions? Will we be bodily beings? Will the blessed and the damned be able to see each other? Surely these questions press the parable beyond its limits. On the other hand, the story cannot simply be dismissed on the ground that it is a parable and has

---

38. I am indebted to Rolf Bouma, a former student at Calvin Seminary, for pointing out this interpretation in an unpublished paper, "Dives, Lazarus, and the Afterlife" (1987). It is proposed by J. D. M. Derrett, *Law in the New Testament* (London, 1970), pp. 85-92.

39. Cf. Hanhart, pp. 193-199.

40. Nevertheless, competent scholars as diverse as Oscar Cullmann and Murray Harris conclude on the basis of Luke's theology in general that this parable does shed light on the issue of the afterlife. Cf. Cullmann, "Immortality of the Soul or Resurrection of the Dead?", in K. Stendahl, ed., *Immortality and Resurrection* (NewYork: Macmillan, 1965), p. 79; and Harris, *Raised Immortal*, pp. 134-135.

nonbiblical roots.[41] For if we find firm footing elsewhere for the claim that Jewish beliefs about the intermediate state are incorporated into Luke's Christian proclamation, then less self-sufficient texts such as Luke 16:19-31, properly exegeted, certainly corroborate those findings and thus add to the weight of evidence.

E. Jesus and the Thief on the Cross

A text which can carry great weight is Luke 23:42-43, Jesus' ministry to the dying thief. This man, unlike the other criminal and most of the crowd, did believe that Jesus is the Christ of God, the Chosen One, the King of the Jews.[42] "Then he said, 'Jesus, remember me when you come into your kingdom.' Jesus answered him, 'I tell you the truth, today you will be with me in paradise.'"

The penitent thief is appealing to Jesus in terms of his Jewish beliefs about eschatology. When the Messiah would come, he would set up his kingdom, the dead would be raised, and the blessed would dwell on the renewed earth. So he was asking Jesus to remember him when he came to establish his messianic rule at some future time.[43] Jesus' gracious response to this man's faith for the future is to grant him something even better: "today will you be with me in paradise." By "today" Jesus meant Friday, the day of the crucifixion.

In order to avoid that conclusion some scholars have attempted to understand "today" exclusively as "future eschatological age" or "epoch of salvation." According to them, Jesus did not mean to promise fellowship in paradise later that day, but that the thief would be included as a partaker in the age to come.[44] In response we must point out that it is a false dilemma

41. Reichenbach, p. 184, does dismiss it on these grounds.

42. Cf. vv. 35-39 for the titles mockingly attributed to Jesus by his detractors.

43. According to Marshall, p. 872, "the reference is to the parousia of Jesus as the Son of Man as a future event associated with the raising of the dead. The criminal thus regards Jesus as more than a mere martyr; he implicitly confesses his faith that Jesus is the Messiah or Son of Man."

44. Reichenbach, pp. 184-185, for example, denies that Jesus is speaking of objective time and asserts that he means subjective time. Thus even though it would really be in the future, it would seem like the same day. Hanhart, pp. 211-213, argues that "today" is not really about regular time, but about salvific time. But the very examples he gives undermine

to oppose the day of Jesus' death and the eschatological age of salvation. For Luke the crucifixion and resurrection are eschatological events. The new age significance of his promise to the thief is not excluded by the natural reading of "today" as "Friday." This reading embeds it all the more in salvation history. For grammatical, semantic, and historical-theological reasons, "today" ought to be read literally. As Marshall summarizes: "The criminal's petition expresses the hope that he will attain to life at the parousia; Jesus' reply assures him of immediate entry into paradise."[45]

The fact that Jesus uses the term "paradise" is highly significant.[46] In intertestamental Judaism we have seen that it denotes the Edenic abode of the Lord's saints, both the final kingdom and the intermediate resting place of the dead. Often it is located in heaven. It can also be in Hades. The New Testament treats it similarly. In Revelation 2:7 it refers to the present and future kingdom of God. And in II Corinthians 12:2-4 Paul considers it a present reality, located in the third heaven. All of this must be taken seriously in understanding what Jesus said to the thief. He promised this repentant sinner the fellowship of paradise, the dwelling place of the faithful dead even before the resurrection, that very day. The relevant data all point clearly in this direction.[47]

Most important of all for our study is the fact that this is not merely a parable intended to teach an ethical point, not just a highly imaginative piece of apocalyptic, but a straightforward teaching text. This is not just an interesting throwaway line, but one of Jesus' "truly" sayings: "*Amen*, I say to you. . . ." Luke clearly means for his readers to hear the same promise that Jesus made the thief: "If you confess Jesus as Christ, paradise is yours immediately upon your death." Luke is not merely reporting the words of

---

his case. When Jesus says to Zacchaeus, "today salvation has come to this house" (Lk. 19:5), he very likely meant "this calendar date" as well as something epochal and eschatological.

45. Marshall, p. 873, which also contains a fine discussion of the debate about the word *sēmeron*, "today." Grammatically, the word occurs at the beginning of the sentence for emphasis and contrast: "not the future, but today." Semantically it can function both as "Friday" and as "age of salvation." So it is false to infer from its eschatological significance that it does not mean ordinary time as well. Historically, taking it to mean what it literally says comports best with the Jewish beliefs likely held by the thief.

46. Cf. J. Jeremias, "Paradise," *TDNT*, V, pp. 765-773.

47. Cf. Mattill, pp. 33-34, where paradise is said to be "the happy side of Hades," not heaven itself. Hanhart, pp. 212-213, fails to consider its connection with the intermediate state in arguing that paradise is parallel to Jesus' final kingdom, which he was to assume immediately upon his death.

Jesus. Through them he is proclaiming the gospel. So here we have a virtually unambiguous case in which Jewish eschatology, with its anthropological implications, is appropriated as part of the Christian kerygma.[48]

Since we have established that most likely Jesus and Luke do endorse the general eschatology of their Jewish contemporaries, it seems as though a text like the parable of the rich man and Lazarus provides additional substance to that position. Luke does believe in conscious existence immediately after death and may very well accept the popular account in Luke 16, even if he does not intend to teach it there. Because of what Luke 23 teaches, the eschatological imagery of Luke 16 cannot be dismissed as wholly irrelevant to New Testament ideas about the afterlife.

F. Where Was Jesus between
Good Friday and Easter Sunday?

The words of Jesus to the thief seem to eliminate the extinction–re-creation view. Both persons would continue to exist. But does this promise favor either of the other two theories? Consider an immediate resurrection. It seems possible that the thief would not only enter paradise, but would do so with a resurrection body or immortalized spirit. Of course that is not likely what he would have expected, since he probably thought of the resurrection as a general future event. However, he might simply have been mistaken and thus was in for a pleasant surprise.

But there is no ambiguity about the time of Jesus' resurrection. He died on Friday and was raised early on Sunday morning. During that interval either he was extinct until re-created on Easter or he existed in a nonfleshly intermediate state. Immediate resurrection is absolutely ruled out. For it was the body in the tomb which was raised. However it happened, the tomb was empty.

If we are to take Luke 23:43 at face value, Jesus spent at least part of

---

48. Even Hanhart, p. 205, admits that this is the least difficult of the possible exegeses, although he defends another. Mattill, p. 40, summarizes Luke's eschatology: "Luke . . . finds the concepts of an intermediate state to be followed soon by all of the realistic end-time events to be an adequate framework for his eschatological hopes. Therefore Luke can allow for the death of individuals before the parousia, with preliminary blessing and punishment in the intermediate state, but also he can stress salvation in the kingdom of God and punishment in Gehenna at the end of the world for most of his readers."

that time in paradise, the interim residence of the blessed dead. But some will object that this conflicts with the view that Jesus "harrowed hell" during the interval, preaching to the spirits in prison (cf. I Peter 3). It certainly seems to contradict how many Christians understand the phrase "he descended into hell" in the Apostles' Creed.[49] And Scripture itself in Acts 2:27 seems to present a problem. For at least in some translations it seems to say that Jesus' soul was in "hell," not paradise.

The first thing which should be pointed out is that all of these possibilities presuppose the existence of Jesus between his death and resurrection. The only questions are where he was and what he was doing. So it is hard to see how these different views of Jesus' whereabouts would count against the intermediate state and for the extinction–re-creation theory unless the apparent contradiction entitled us to dismiss the whole topic as speculative fiction.

In the second place, a moment's recollection of the intertestamental topography of the afterlife will reveal that these various accounts of Jesus' whereabouts between Friday and Sunday are consistent with each other. Jesus could have been in paradise and "hell" at the same time. With respect to "hell," Acts 2:27 and 31 refer to Psalm 16:10 and actually say that Jesus went to Sheol or Hades, the realm of the dead. Nowhere does it say that he went to Gehenna, the "hell" of final punishment. Great confusion has been caused by the King James translation of both Hades and Gehenna as "hell." We have seen that intertestamental Judaism pictured Sheol/Hades as containing different locations or compartments in which the dead of different eternal destinies are quartered. Both believers and unbelievers populate the general realm of the dead. Further, we know that the Rabbis thought of paradise as located in Hades. So although the details and terminology of intertestamental eschatology are neither univocal nor consistent in all respects, it is possible to hold that Jesus entered the realm of the dead, Sheol/Hades, and there was in the company of the saints in paradise.[50] He might even have preached to the spirits in prison, whatever that means. In fact if communication across the great divide is possible, as in the parable of the

---

49. The Reformed tradition has not affirmed this interpretation but has viewed the descent into hell more symbolically as referring to the whole humiliation of Christ, especially his passion and death. Cf. Heidelberg Catechism, Q. & A. 44.

50. Mattill, pp. 33-34. If this conclusion is correct, the Reformed tradition could admit that Jesus literally went to the realm of the dead without endorsing traditional speculations about what he did there.

rich man and Lazarus, Jesus could have preached to the unbelieving dead in Hades from a "pulpit" on the paradise side of the chasm.

I do not mean to take all of this imagery literally. I am merely arguing that in terms of Jewish eschatology the allegedly contradictory New Testament and traditional accounts of how Jesus spent the intermediate state are not contradictory at all. The composite picture is a fully coherent one which necessarily presupposes the existence of the person Jesus Christ between his death and resurrection. Continued personal existence follows from the Old Testament notion of Sheol as well as from later Jewish eschatology. All the evidence appears to be against the extinction–re-creation view, at least as an account of what happened to Jesus.

In addition to the biblical material there is an important theological matter at stake here. Since the Council of Chalcedon the church has officially recognized what is taught in the New Testament and held by the early church: that because of the incarnation Jesus Christ is both truly God and truly human; that he is one person with two natures, one divine and one human; and that these natures are neither mixed together nor are they separable.[51]

Now if the extinction–re-creation account of Jesus' resurrection is true, then the teaching of Chalcedon is false. The two natures of Christ are separable and were in fact separated between Good Friday and Easter Sunday. The human being Jesus completely ceased to exist. For on the monist-holist view motivating the extinction–re-creation theory, persons are essentially linked to their organisms. Bodily death is complete death. Persons do not survive. So the divine-human person Jesus Christ did not exist for the interim. Only the nonincarnate Word, the wholly divine Son, the Second Person of the Trinity, existed during that time. What occurred on Easter is essentially the same as the miracle of Christmas. Once again the Word became flesh, this time resurrection flesh. We do not have an incarnation and something essentially different — a resurrection — in the life of Christ, but two incarnations. If the extinction–re-creationists are consistent, they seem closer to the heresies which Chalcedon rejected than to orthodox Christology itself. For either the human nature of the Son is incidental even after his incarnation and was nonexistent for three Jewish days; or else we have two persons in Jesus Christ, a divine person who con-

---

51. Cf. Louis Berkhof, *The History of Christian Doctrines* (Grand Rapids: Eerdmans, 1937; reprint, Baker, 1975), p. 107.

tinued to exist and a human person who did not. Neither option would have escaped condemnation at Chalcedon.[52] Admittedly Christians ought not to take the declarations of councils as seriously as they take Scripture. But the extinction–re-creation view does not stand up well in the light of Scripture or tradition.

The intermediate state account, entailing a dualistic anthropology, would generate no christological difficulty. In fact it would solve this problem. Since human nature is such that persons can exist temporarily without their bodies, Jesus Christ could have existed between Friday and Sunday without his body and yet have been one person with both a divine and a human nature. Lacking a body does not entail lacking human nature completely.

Once again the intermediate state doctrine seems most preferable, all things considered. The death and resurrection of Jesus rule out an immediate resurrection and strongly imply an intermediate state for him. The real question which remains at this point pertains to the uniqueness of Jesus. Is the way that he went from death to life an experience unique to himself? Or is he the firstfruit of all believers, having pioneered the route which all of his brothers and sisters who die before his return will follow? If the latter, then the question is settled.[53]

IV. Provisional Conclusion

By now we have moved beyond the merely semantic claim that "soul" and "spirit" are used in the New Testament to refer to persons in the intermediate state. We have come to the conclusion that Jesus, Luke, and John themselves embraced this position and that at least Jesus and Luke meant to have us embrace it. Armed with this conclusion, we notice that it is the same position which is suggested in all of the material we have considered. Matthew seems to assert the survival of the soul and a final resurrection to judgment. Likewise the book of Revelation and probably the book of Hebrews. It is consistent with Jesus' reply to the Sadducees and with the Transfiguration and

52. Cf. "The Christological Controversies" in Berkhof.

53. Cf. Harris's excellent study of the "firstfruit" metaphor and the relation between the resurrections of Christ and of believers in *Raised Immortal*, pp. 107-114. Unfortunately he does not address our specific question, perhaps because he endorses an immediate resurrection for believers.

probably with how observers understood these events. There does appear to be a consistent eschatological scheme in the New Testament even if details and vocabulary vary.

Least compatible with the data is the extinction–re-creation view. It seems to conflict with a number of texts which presuppose or affirm the existence of the dead. Furthermore, there is no evidence that anyone in the environment of the New Testament held this position. It looks like an anachronism which comports poorly with Scripture.

So we are down to the two eschatologies which affirm continuous existence after death. Although immediate resurrection is as consistent with some texts as temporary discarnate existence, other passages clearly state a general future resurrection. The facts that persons survive physical death and that they are resurrected in the future together entail an intermediate state. That conclusion is unavoidable. In addition, general future resurrection was far more widely held among Jewish believers of the time than immediate individual resurrection. Since the New Testament writers appear to have adopted the beliefs of their audience, neither endorsing immediate resurrection nor attacking the notion of a future resurrection, the fact of popular opinion adds circumstantial evidence for this conclusion. All things considered, therefore, the intermediate state theory and its implied anthropological dualism are the most reasonable positions to hold in interpreting the New Testament, unless of course they are contradicted by St. Paul.

Chapter Seven

Anthropology and Personal Eschatology in the New Testament: The Pauline Epistles

I. Introduction

More has been written on Paul's anthropology and personal eschatology than on those topics in the rest of the New Testament. Hefty tomes have explored his use of anthropological terms. Learned volumes have attempted to trace both his Hellenistic and his Jewish roots. Prominent scholars have defended a monistic interpretation; others have argued that Paul is a dualist.[1]

Obviously our present study cannot survey the entire field of arguments which have been deployed, nor can it advance the frontiers of Pauline scholarship. Instead we will compare the standard approaches to the exegesis of the most important texts within their historical settings to determine as clearly as possible what Paul meant to say. On that basis we can see whether any of the three theories of the afterlife can best account for the data. We will consider the epistles in chronological order,[2] since some

---

1. Robert Jewett, *Paul's Anthropological Terms* (Leiden: Brill, 1971), is an exhaustive historical and systematic analysis of its topic. W. D. Stacey, *The Pauline View of Man* (London: Macmillan, 1956), explores the Jewish and Hellenistic background. W. D. Davies, *Paul and Rabbinic Judaism* (London: SPCK, 1955), is a classic on its subject. M. E. Dahl, *The Resurrection of the Body* (London: SCM, 1962), and H. M. Shires, *The Eschatology of Paul in the Light of Modern Scholarship* (Philadelphia: Westminster, 1966), defend a monistic interpretation. Robert Gundry, *"Sōma"* in *Biblical Theology, with Emphasis on Pauline Anthropology* (Cambridge University Press, 1976), and L. Cerfaux, *The Christian in the Theology of St. Paul* (London: Chapman, 1967), argue for what must be termed dualism.

2. Of course this is a much debated topic. For our purposes, however, the sequence in-

134

scholars argue that Paul's views developed and changed as he gradually realized that the return of Christ was not imminent.[3] In that case, it would be mistaken to assume uncritically that his position in one epistle held for the rest. Even if he did believe an intermediate state at one time, according to this hypothesis, he may very well have abandoned that view. Our analysis must consider this possibility.

II. Relevant Pauline Texts

A. Acts 23:6-8

An interesting place to start our inquiry is not within the Pauline corpus, but in Luke's account of Paul's defense before the Sanhedrin.[4] Noticing that both Pharisees and Sadducees were present, Paul said, "I am a Pharisee, the son of a Pharisee. I stand on trial because of my hope in the resurrection of the dead." This declaration divided the house. In verse 8 Luke explains this reaction for his readers: "The Sadducees say that there is no resurrection, and that there are neither angels nor spirits, but the Pharisees acknowledge them all."

Here according to Luke we have Paul's own words identifying himself with the personal eschatology of the Pharisees. Though their doctrines were not fixed, most Pharisees believed in a conscious intermediate state until the general future resurrection. Certainly they were neither immediate resurrectionists nor extinction–re-creationists. We must be cautious, however, for Paul does not explicitly mention either the intermediate state

---

volves only I Thessalonians, I and II Corinthians, and Philippians. That order is generally accepted by scholars.

3. Cf. Murray Harris, *Raised Immortal* (Grand Rapids: Eerdmans, 1985), pp. 100-101, 137-138; and F. F. Bruce, *Paul: Apostle of the Heart Set Free* (Grand Rapids: Eerdmans, 1977), pp. 309-313.

4. I start from this point in order to raise the issue of Paul's education as a Pharisee, attempting to claim that he began as a Jewish holistic dualist. However, if the chronology of Paul's life held by many conservative scholars is accurate, then this event took place in A.D. 57 after Paul had written Thessalonians, Corinthians, and Romans. Cf. F. F. Bruce, *Paul*, p. 475. If it is probable that he is a dualist in Acts 23, that in itself makes it probable he was a dualist in all those letters. However, we will attempt to argue the case for each text on its own.

or the time of the resurrection. And perhaps his appeal to the Pharisees was simply a defense lawyer's ploy. So all three theories could initially claim to be consistent with Paul's affirmation of the resurrection.

There are several arguments in favor of the intermediate state view, however, whereas the other theories can only argue from silence. First, Paul actually had been a Pharisee, educated by Gamaliel, who was successor to and very likely the grandson of the great Hillel.[5] Almost certainly, therefore, Paul had at one time accepted the whole rabbinic view of the afterlife — the intermediate state as well as the resurrection. And Pharisees could become Christians without greatly modifying their theology. They merely had to accept Jesus as Messiah and righteousness as a gift of grace.[6] Paul need not have given up his personal eschatology when he was converted.

Second, the fact that Paul mentions only the resurrection in Acts 23 does not likely indicate that he ignored or rejected the intermediate state, but that "resurrection" was meant to include the entire Pharisaic eschatology. The Sadducees denied any meaningful afterlife whatsoever. Against this, the Pharisees' belief in the future resurrection included affirmation of the intermediate state. Individuals continue to exist after death and are eventually raised. That is what resurrection means to the Pharisees. Thus there is absolutely nothing in the fact that Paul mentions only the resurrection to imply that he had abandoned the intermediate state while retaining the resurrection. Without evidence to the contrary, we must assume that Paul affirms the whole scenario.

A third clue is Luke's statement that the Pharisees believed in angels and spirits *(pneumata)*. Some scholars argue that "spirits" here does not mean human spirits but nonhuman spiritual beings who can communicate with humans (v. 9).[7] No doubt the Pharisees believed in the existence of such beings. But they also believed that human spirits exist until the resurrection, which after all is what is being disputed here. In addition, we recall from Luke 24 that the author of Acts sometimes uses *pneuma* to refer to discarnate human persons. It is perfectly possible that this is its meaning here. Even if it is not, the other evidence is undiminished.

---

5. "Gamaliel," in *The New Bible Dictionary,* ed. J. D. Douglas (Grand Rapids: Eerdmans, 1962), p. 451.

6. F. F. Bruce, *The Book of the Acts* (Grand Rapids: Eerdmans, 1954), pp. 452-453.

7. Cf. Bruce, *Acts,* p. 453.

In conclusion, although we have less than absolute proof, there is strong circumstantial evidence in Acts 23 that Paul held the intermediate state–resurrection eschatology. There is nothing which favors either of the other views.

B. I Thessalonians 4:13-18

First Thessalonians is the earliest Pauline epistle in which the issue of the afterlife is addressed. Apparently the Thessalonians mistakenly believed that all Christians would live until the return of Christ. Thus they were confused because some of their group had died. They were worried that the deceased would not participate in the celebration of Christ's second coming. So Paul instructs and comforts them. "God will bring with Jesus those who have fallen asleep in him," he says (v. 14). "The dead in Christ will rise first" (v. 16). Those who are still alive will meet Christ and the resurrected dead in the air, and all will be with him forever.

Whatever one makes of the logistical details, the time of the resurrection is crystal clear. It is at the return of Christ. Individual Christians do not undergo resurrection immediately upon their deaths. Believers will all be raised at the same time — at the second coming. Scholars who claim that Paul and the New Testament teach immediate resurrection must hold that I Thessalonians is out of step, asserting a position later abandoned by Paul himself, and no longer a valid source of doctrine for the church.

But extinction–re-creationists reckon this passage in their support. For Paul refers to the dead as "asleep," "a metaphorically nice way of speaking of the dead," not an "ontological claim about their condition or status."[8] In literal ontological language, they do not exist.

In response it must be admitted that prima facie this is one plausible interpretation. It could be that the New Testament uses sleep as a metaphor for persons who do not exist but who will one day "awake," that is, be re-created. But it is even more plausible that Paul is speaking here of soul-sleep, a situation where persons continue to exist but lack consciousness. Furthermore, as we saw in intertestamental literature, it is not uncommon that metaphors of sleep and rest are used of persons in

8. Bruce Reichenbach, *Is Man the Phoenix?* (Grand Rapids: Eerdmans, 1983), pp. 185 and 188 n. 17.

the intermediate state who are conscious and active, but not in earthly, bodily ways.[9]

Since there are several plausible interpretations, extinction–re-creationists must do more than merely assert their position and demonstrate its consistency with the text. They must show why theirs is preferable. And that will be difficult indeed. For the only instances of sleep as a metaphor for nonexistence come from pagan sources.[10] Among Jewish believers it meant conscious or unconscious existence until the resurrection. That certainly is true of Paul's rabbinic heritage. Mere use of sleep imagery is no evidence at all of a shift in his position. Given the evidence we have about the historical context and Paul's own background, it is more likely that "those who have fallen asleep in Jesus" (4:13, 14, 15), "the dead in Christ" (16), are in an intermediate state with Christ awaiting the resurrection than that they are extinct.

The same is true for I Thessalonians 5:10, where Paul writes that our Lord Jesus Christ "died for us so that, whether we are awake or asleep, we may live together with him." While it is *prima facie* possible to assert that those who are "asleep" simply do not exist, background information makes it much more likely that Paul meant that they are already living with Christ, just as those who are still "awake" will live with him after his return. It is true that in verse 6 "asleep" does not describe the dead but those still alive who are unconcerned about Christ's coming. Could it mean that in verse 10 as well? Virtually all commentators take "asleep" in verse 10 to mean death, as it does in 4:13-15.[11] After all, it is nonsense to construe Paul as saying that those who do not care about his return will be "with Christ." His point is just the opposite. Thus it is more likely that those who have died are said to be alive with Christ in I Thessalonians 5:10. Paul's position at its writing is probably intermediate state–future resurrection, not immediate resurrection or extinction–re-creation.

9. This is Murray Harris's conclusion; cf. *Raised Immortal*, pp. 134-137, 142. Cf. also Karel Hanhart, "Not a Condition of Sleep," *The Intermediate State in the New Testament* (Franeker: Wever, 1966), pp. 106-114.

10. Cf. *New International Version Study Bible* (Grand Rapids: Zondervan, 1986), note on I Thess. 4:13, p. 1824.

11. Leon Morris, *The First and Second Epistles to the Thessalonians* (Grand Rapids: Eerdmans, 1959), p. 162. Cf. also James Frame, *A Critical and Exegetical Commentary on the Epistles of St. Paul to the Thesssalonians* (Edinburgh: Clark, 1911), pp. 189-190.

C. I Corinthians 15

This incredibly rich chapter, the most extensive discourse on the resurrection in the New Testament, seems to presuppose the same basic picture of the last things as I Thessalonians. For even its language is the same in proposing the sleep-resurrection sequence: "We will not all sleep, but we will all be changed — in a flash, in the twinkling of an eye, at the last trumpet. For the trumpet will sound, the dead will be raised imperishable, and we will be changed" (vv. 51-52). The occasion of the resurrection is unmistakable — at the last trumpet, a Jewish apocalyptic symbol adopted by the New Testament for the royal return of the Lord, the "end" mentioned in verse 24.[12] The resurrection is to be a future historical event, occurring after a time of "sleep." Furthermore, it is a corporate, not an individual event: all shall be changed at once, not each at the moment of her death. So here is another future general resurrection text — the most important in Scripture — which the immediate resurrectionist must regard as rescinded by other parts of the New Testament.

The extinction–re-creationist will argue that this whole chapter speaks about the resurrection of persons, not just bodies to which souls reattach. In fact the soul is not even mentioned. He will claim that there is nothing here to suggest an intermediate state or surviving soul.[13]

In response it must be admitted that there is no direct proof of the dualist view. But that fact by itself would not establish the monist view. For what Paul writes in I Corinthians 15 is just as compatible with dualism as it is with monism. Consider that he speaks not only of the resurrection of dead persons; he also wonders specifically about the nature of the resurrection body *(sōma)*, noting that God created different sorts of flesh *(sarx)*. The body that is sown is a natural body — literally a "soulish" *(psychikon)* body — and will be raised a spiritual *(pneumatikon)* body (v. 44). It is beyond the bounds of our inquiry at this point to entertain the fascinating question regarding the nature of the resurrection body.[14] But it

12. Cf. Leon Morris, *The First Epistle to the Corinthians* (Grand Rapids: Eerdmans, 1958), pp. 233-234.

13. Cf. George Carey, *I Believe in Man* (Grand Rapids: Eerdmans, 1977), pp. 171-172; Dahl, p. 72; Reichenbach, p. 181.

14. The topic will be considered below in connection with II Corinthians 5 and Philippians 1. An excellent discussion is found in Murray Harris, pp. 114-133.

It is interesting to note that Paul departs from the position of some of the Rabbis in

is necessary to point out that Paul might very well be speaking not about nonexistent persons, but only about their earthly and resurrection bodies. In saying "they will come with bodies" (v. 35), he could be distinguishing persons and their bodies, implying that they can be with or without them. In that case his mode of expression would be compatible with dualism.[15] However, it could also be the case that "bodies" and "flesh" are instances of synecdoche, both referring to persons as such. If so, the discussion would be consistent with monism. It turns out, then, that I Corinthians 15, important as it is, might just be indeterminate on the monism-dualism question, at least when taken on its own.

Does it become clearer when taken in historical context? Consider first Paul's personal views. One must not overlook the importance of the sleep metaphor in I Corinthians 15:18, 20, and 51. For in I Thessalonians this figure most likely refers to the dead "living together with Christ" in the intermediate state, and there is nothing to suggest that Paul had a change of mind between these epistles. The extinctionists can provide no evidence that Paul switched to their position. The evidence still favors the dualist position.[16]

But doesn't the seed metaphor favor the monist? In verses 36-38 Paul speaks of the body buried as the seed of the resurrection body. Isn't that proof that he locates the continuity of personal existence in the body? There is no mention of a soul which exists between death and resurrection. The only thing which exists is the decaying earthly body — the seed of the incorruptible resurrection body. Although the seed metaphor has been interpreted monistically, contextual evidence actually favors the dualist reading; we have examples from rabbinic literature in which the very same metaphor is used, and here it is not meant to deny the existence of the soul,

---

distinguishing the two kinds of body. For they held that the resurrection body would be an earthly body of the very same material particles. Paul seems to be saying that they may have similar properties, but not the same nature. Cf. Robertson and Plummer, *First Corinthians* (Edinburgh: Clark, 1961), p. 368. However, there was apparently room for the notion of a "spiritual body" among the Pharisees, as there was in Jewish eschatology in general. Cf. C. F. D. Moule, "St. Paul and Dualism: The Pauline Conception of Resurrection," *New Testament Studies*, Vol. 13, pp. 106-123, esp. 109-112. (My thanks to David Kromminga for the reference to Moule.)

15. Gundry, pp. 50, 80; Harris, p. 120.

16. Dahl, p. 72, argues that we should assume that Paul holds "the Semitic totality concept" in I Corinthians 15. He does so by identifying Paul with the Old Testament, however, not by appeal to the Pauline texts themselves or to contemporary Judaism.

which the Rabbis clearly affirmed. It is not given to account for the continuity of personal identity in the face of personal extinction but is merely intended to explain the continuity between the earthly and resurrection bodies.[17] Once again circumstantial evidence favors dualism.

A further appeal of the dualist might be the assumptions of the Corinthians, who were Greek. There were many Greeks who believed in the existence of the soul after death. The Corinthians themselves were inclined to this opinion, as Paul's reference to "nakedness," a metaphor for disembodied existence, in II Corinthians 5 implies. One could argue that he presupposes this position throughout his discussion of the resurrection. However, other Greeks were materialists who thought that death meant the end of everything. As Robertson and Plummer point out: "St. Paul shapes his argument to meet both classes, — those who denied the resurrection of the body, but allowed the survival of the soul, and those who denied both."[18] So appeal to Greek thought would not necessarily help settle the question.

Summarizing this all too brief discussion of I Corinthians 15, it is clear that an immediate resurrection is ruled out by Paul's assertion of a future resurrection at the parousia. That is admitted even by those who think Paul later became an immediate resurrectionist. Of the other two contenders, there is significant contextual evidence for the intermediate state interpretation and none which particularly favors extinction–re-creation.

D. II Corinthians 5:1-10

This is the passage in which some commentators see a change in Paul's view of what occurs at death.[19] According to F. F. Bruce, during the year's interval between the writing of I and II Corinthians, Paul had some close brushes with death which motivated a "change in perspective."[20] It struck him that he might actually die before the return of Christ. Where would he be in the meantime? On reflection he gave up his previous belief that the resurrection would occur at the second coming of Christ. By II Corinthi-

17. Cf. Davies, pp. 305-306, and Hanhart, pp. 101-103. The Rabbis located bodily continuity in the spine, which they believed was indestructible.

18. Robertson and Plummer, p. 365.

19. Cf. Harris, pp. 100-101 and 255-256 n. 5, for various theories which attempt to account for the change.

20. Bruce, *Paul*, p. 310.

ans 5:1-10 he has moved to immediate resurrection —believers have resurrection bodies from the moment of their death until the parousia of Jesus.

Bruce's psychobiographical speculations are interesting, but they presuppose that Paul has altered his position and attempt to explain it. They provide no evidence for the alleged change of mind itself. So one wonders what in II Corinthians 5 itself has convinced scholars of the shift.[21] To see that we must first consider the passage as a whole.

It is divided into two sections. The first five verses are highly figurative in expression, using images of buildings and tents, being clothed and being naked. Verses 6 through 10 more straightforwardly contrast being in the body and away from the Lord with being away from the body and at home with the Lord. What do the metaphors mean and how do the two sections modify one another? Is there a clear indication of the time of the resurrection?

There are two possible interpretations of section one which refer to the resurrection.[22] The first option is that Paul contrasts life in the earthly body, which all agree is symbolized by the "earthly tent" (vv. 1, 4), with immediate acquisition of the resurrection body — the "building from God, an eternal house in heaven" (v. 1), "being clothed with our heavenly dwelling" (vv. 2, 4). Thus Paul rejects altogether an intermediate condition of "being naked" (v. 3) or "unclothed" (v. 4), which scholars widely acknowledge to mean disembodied existence. According to the other possibility, Paul is saying that the period of disembodiment is only temporary and by no means as desirable as the resurrection body, perhaps a caution to those who long for disembodied existence.[23] So both immediate resurrectionists

21. Cf. Harris, pp. 98 and 255 n. 2, for an impressive list of scholars who have held this position.

22. Some scholars hold that resurrection is not addressed in this chapter. The "eternal dwelling" is not taken as referring to a resurrection body, but to the secure mode of existence with God in Christ. Similarly, "being naked" does not symbolize disembodiment, but being totally exposed by the penetrating gaze of God's judgment apart from the clothing of Christ's righteousness. If the resurrection is not addressed here, then either we are confronted with permanent disembodiment or the temporary disembodiment of the intermediate state, both implying dualism. For we must still reckon with being away from the earthly body in vv. 6-10. This approach to "being naked" and the "eternal dwelling" is therefore useless to monists. Cf. Hanhart, pp. 149-176, for a thorough discussion of the various approaches to this passage.

23. Even Harris, who favors the immediate resurrection interpretation, does not find a horror of disembodiment as the main issue here: "We shall defend the view that Paul is here expressing, not his fear of temporary physical disembodiment or permanent spiritual dis-

and intermediate statists can claim this text. Extinctionists cannot explain it; they can only explain it away. Nonexistence between embodiments is out of the question.

In truth it is extremely difficult to determine conclusively what Paul means here and thus whether the time of the resurrection is indicated. Each side raises numerous points which cannot all be analyzed in our study. The fact that Paul uses a present-tense verb in verse 1 — "we have a building from God" — settles nothing, for it refers to the promise of a future acquisition, but favors neither the future at death nor the future at the parousia.[24] "Being clothed, we shall not be found naked." But it does not explicitly say when this clothing will take place.

Immediate resurrectionists' strongest argument is Paul's use of the verb *ependyein* with "the heavenly dwelling" in verses 2 and 4. This, they say, does not mean "to put on" *(endyein)* as when a naked person gets dressed, but "to put on over" as when someone pulls on a sweater over his shirt.[25] Since Paul had used *endyein* in I Corinthians 15:53-54, the presence of *ependyein* in II Corinthians 5 is taken to indicate a major shift in perspective. In I Corinthians 15 Paul might very well have thought that the resurrection body would clothe the naked self at the parousia. But in II Corinthians 5 "the physical body was the undergarment over which the cloak of the resurrection body was cast."[26] There is no interval of nakedness. The resurrection body immediately covers over the earthly body which dies.

This is an interesting argument, but far from conclusive, as the intermediate statist will point out. First, there might be no major significance at all in Paul's switch from *endyein* to *ependyein*. For although the latter can mean something different from the former, it might also be a synonym. Second, if it does mean "put on over," it might mean "put on over the naked self" rather than "over the earthly body."

---

embodiment, but his assurance of spiritual embodiment and his rejection of any idealisation of disembodiment that may have been advocated by certain gnosticising Corinthians" (p. 139).

24. Contra Harris, pp. 98-99.

25. Harris, p. 99. Harris favors this interpretation (although he is not dogmatic about it) and is one of its leading exponents. F. F. Bruce in *Paul* relies heavily on Harris's unpublished Ph.D. thesis, *The Interpretation of II Corinthians 5:1-10 and its Place in Pauline Eschatology,* and his article, "II Corinthians 5:1-10: Watershed in Paul's Eschatology?", *Tyndale Bulletin,* Vol. 22 (1971), pp. 32-57.

26. Harris, *Raised Immortal,* p. 99.

Third, elsewhere in these verses Paul writes that the earthly tent is destroyed, not that it is retained while a heavenly dwelling is built around it.
That figure paints a different picture. Basing a technical distinction on a
metaphor is always risky. But here even the proposed interpretation of the
metaphors is inconsistent. Paul first seems to say that one dwelling (body)
is destroyed and a new one provided. Then he implies, if Harris is correct,
that one suit of clothes (body) is not completely destroyed, but a new suit
is put on over it. Is the specially chosen member of this apparently dissimi-
lar pair of metaphors by itself sufficient to substantiate the claim that Paul
had a significant change of mind? Or do both of them really just say that
the earthly body is destroyed and then, either immediately or later, a heavenly body is provided? If the latter, then *ependyein* has no special meaning,
or at least not a meaning which would eliminate the possibility of a temporal gap before putting on the new body.

Finally, this interpretation of *ependyein* is hard to square with experience. When we die, our bodies decay. They are not immediately clothed
upon with resurrection bodies. A corpse is left which is not apparently
swallowed by a resurrection body in an instant. Paul himself was gripped
by the fact that "outwardly we are wasting away, yet inwardly we are being
renewed" (II Cor. 4:16). If something new is already being put on, it is
more likely going on over the inner man than the decaying remnants of
outwardness. The heavenly garment, if anything, is being tailored inside
the old clothes, not over the top of them. Is Paul really committed to the
counterintuitive view that the earthly body is somehow retained as the
heavenly body is received? How then does one account for the dead earthly
body? The principle of *habeas corpus* is relevant here. Has Paul really left
common sense in thinking that the resurrection body is "put on over" the
earthly body? No matter how one approaches it, this explanation of
ependyein does not make sense.

If one were to affirm an immediate resurrection, other accounts would
be more reasonable than putting one body on over the other. One version
would be an instantaneous exchange of bodies. At death one would instantly pass from the mortal to the immortal body. The other would be
that the resurrection body, viewed as a spiritual reality, is part of the renewal of the inner self referred to in 4:16.[27] The resurrected spiritual person would remain after the death of the mortal body.

27. This view is held by many who believe that Paul here speaks of an immediate spiri-

Each of these options, of course, has its own problems. An instantaneous exchange of bodies would involve abandoning the continuity between the earthly and resurrection bodies which Paul insisted on in I Corinthians 15. One can imagine how an interred earthly body might count as the "seed" (I Cor. 15:37) of a future resurrection body. But where is the continuity between the two when there is an instantaneous exchange? The alternative, holding that resurrection transforms the inner self but does not entail a new body, directly contradicts Paul's notion of a spiritual *body* (*sōma pneumatikon*) in I Corinthians 15. It posits an immortal soul, not a resurrection body.[28] Either option implies that Paul has abandoned key themes which he stressed in I Corinthians 15. These implications are not fatal. Perhaps Paul did change his mind. But they are sobering.

So there are serious problems with the *ependyein* argument as well as with alternative ways of picturing an immediate resurrection in II Corinthians 5:1-5. Of course that does not prove the intermediate state position. I will not attempt to do so. Let's admit that we are actually left with a standoff — the intermediate state and several versions of instantaneous resurrection are all compatible with verses 1-5.

Does the rest of the passage shed any light on the issue? In verses 6-10 Paul repeatedly contrasts two conditions: being at home in the body and absent from the Lord; and being absent from the body and at home with the Lord. No third option is mentioned, such as nonexistence. So once again the extinction–re-creation view can do nothing but specially plead that Paul is speaking phenomenologically, not ontologically. And taken at face value, Paul's two options seem to cut against the immediate resurrection theory.[29] For being away from the body is the condition of being with

---

tual resurrection, taking the "spiritual body" of I Corinthians 15 in the sense of II Baruch 51, literal transformation of human existence into a spiritual reality. Cf. Paul Gooch, "On Disembodied Resurrected Persons: A Study in the Logic of Christian Eschatology," *Religious Studies*, Vol. 17, pp. 199-213.

28. Cf. Gooch's term "disembodied resurrected persons."

29. Even Bultmann, no friend of dualism, finds that "Paul comes very close to Hellenistic-Gnostic dualism . . . by speaking of the *soma* under the figure of the 'tent-dwelling' and 'garment.' . . . Here the *soma* appears as a shell for the self. . . . Here, quite dualistically, to be 'at home in the body' and its correlate to be 'away from the Lord, our home' confront their opposites . . ."; cf. R. Bultmann, *Theology of the New Testament* (New York: Scribner's, 1951), Vol. I, p. 202. I would suggest that Paul's dualism is not Gnostic, but Hebraic and thus holistic at the same time. There is no polemic here against bodiliness as such. The "heavenly dwelling" might very well be a resurrection body.

the Lord. The literal meaning clearly seems to imply disembodiment, either temporary or perhaps even permanent, as some have argued.[30] No resurrection embodiment is mentioned or hinted.

The immediate resurrectionist has a reply, however. He does not proceed from the clear language of verses 6-10 and then attempt to sort through the imagery of verses 1-5. He claims that verses 1-5 have established his case and therefore control the interpretation of verses 6-10. Although the Greek speaks of "the body," which certainly refers to the earthly body and seems to imply no heavenly body whatsoever, the apparent implication of incorporeal existence with the Lord is an illusion. For the article "the" is alleged not to be definite but anaphoric; thus it really means "this" body, thereby implying the resurrection body after all. "Therefore it is probable that the reference in verse 8 to 'taking up residence with the Lord,' so far from implying incorporeality, conceals a reference to investiture with the spiritual body," according to Harris.[31] Once their true meaning is revealed by the immediate resurrectionist, verses 6-10 turn out to assert the opposite of what they initially seem to say.

All things considered, this appears a bit strained. Moreover, even if it is a defensible interpretation, it is far from decisive. It is just as exegetically responsible to suppose that Paul envisions a sequence of death, immediate disembodied judgment (v. 10), fellowship with the Lord, and future resurrection of the body.[32] That, too, can account for all elements in II Corin-

---

30. C. F. D. Moule argues in "St. Paul and Dualism" that the instant resurrection of II Corinthians 5 is a transformation from flesh to spirit (I Cor. 15:50-52) and therefore a form of permanent disembodiment. To preserve the correlation of resurrection and parousia, however, he must also argue that this process is only completed at the return of Christ. Cf. also Gooch, "On Disembodied Resurrected Persons."

31. Harris, p. 99.

32. Cf. Joseph Bonsirven, *Palestinian Judaism in the Time of Jesus Christ* (New York: Holt, Rinehart, and Winston, 1964), p. 171: "It is evident that except for those terms which refer to Christ, this Pauline declaration . . . could very well have been repeated by a contemporary rabbi who believed in retribution for the righteous after death. It may have been difficult to define their state, but there was no doubt that it was quite different from resurrection."

Provided "Greek" notions of disembodiment are avoided, this is also the conclusion of Herman Ridderbos, *Paul: An Outline of his Theology* (Grand Rapids: Eerdmans, 1975), pp. 499-506.

George Ladd, *Theology of the New Testament* (Grand Rapids: Eerdmans, 1974), p. 552, writes: "Nevertheless, in spite of Paul's natural abhorrence of being disembodied, he finds courage in the fact that to be away from the body — a disembodied spirit — means to be at home with the Lord"; note 4 lists a number of others who take this position.

thians 5:1-10 without undue distortion. The tent and present clothing are earthly existence, being unclothed is dying, and nakedness is disembodied existence. The heavenly dwelling we have with God can mean either of two things. It can refer to the resurrection body which we will receive at the parousia, an inheritance which will be ours in the future. Or it can indicate the entirety of eternal life in general — being "with Christ" — without explicitly referring to the resurrection body which will be given at the parousia. An intermediate state–future resurrection interpretation of II Corinthians 5 is no less defensible than an immediate resurrection account.

In addition, it seems more coherent with Pauline thought and with the New Testament as a whole.[33] Virtually all who hold the instant resurrection view of II Corinthians are willing to admit that resurrection at the parousia was Paul's earlier belief. Is their confidence in their interpretation warranted enough to postulate a major shift in his thought? As we have seen, probably no other New Testament writers affirmed an instantaneous resurrection. If the immediate resurrection interpretation of II Corinthians 5 is correct, then Paul abandoned the view most likely embraced by the rest of the New Testament. Thus Christians must either follow the later Paul or the rest of the New Testament; or else they must hold that these positions cancel each other out and consequently that Scripture does not finally speak clearly to the issue. If overall coherence is a legitimate hermeneutical principle, then one ought to prefer the intermediate-state reading of this important text.

So why are some Pauline scholars so sure of the immediate resurrection interpretation? I would like to suggest that one reason for many is their acceptance of the dogma of anthropological monism in Paul. Many scholars who take this view of II Corinthians 5 also subscribe to Paul's monism and use monism as a premise in arguing that interpretation.

33. An honest scholar, Harris lists the objections to his view: "that 2 Cor 5:1-10 is prefaced by 'we know' (v. 1) which suggests that traditional teaching will follow; that the interval of time elapsing between the two Corinthian letters was too short to allow any modification in Paul's eschatological thought; that to place the resurrection of the body at death is to rob the Parousia of its temporal significance, do less than justice to the corporate emphases of Pauline eschatology, and remove the tension between the 'already' and the 'not yet' which characterises the entire period between the two events of Christ; that non-Pauline parallels to the idea of transformation at death seem to be lacking" (p. 255 n. 4).

F. F. Bruce simply asserts that Paul "could not conceive of conscious existence and communication with his environment in a disembodied state." And this functions as a premise for his conclusion that "some kind of embodiment is necessary at death."[34] H. M. Shires makes the same assumption: "As a Jew, Paul was unable to imagine personal existence except in terms of a body. . . ."[35] M. E. Dahl, whose monistic "Semitic totality concept" we have already encountered in connection with the Old Testament, writes: "it does not appear that any evidence has yet been adduced that St. Paul had abandoned this totality-concept when he wrote I Corinthians."[36]

This assumption of monism cannot stand unscrutinized. Many competent scholars have argued that since Paul's Judaism is from the diaspora — he was raised in Tarsus — his anthropology was dualistic even before he studied with Gamaliel.[37] This thesis need not appeal to Gnostic-Hellenistic dualism, but the solid holistic dualism of orthodox Judaism. The question of Paul's monism or dualism must remain open unless one side can marshall clearly stronger evidence than the other. We have made the case from Acts 23 that Paul began from an orthodox Jewish, specifically Pharisaic position, which is clearly dualistic according to our definition of the term. That claim is substantiated by I Thessalonians. Our arguments are grounded in the New Testament, not merely in historical context. What real evidence is there for monism?

Bruce recognizes Paul's Pharisaic origins, but is not willing to admit that the Pharisees were dualists in spite of intertestamental literature, Josephus, and the rabbinic writings.[38] Dahl and Shires interpret the Old Testament as monistic and then assume the identity of Paul's view with

---

34. Bruce, *Paul*, pp. 313 and 311 respectively.

35. Shires, *Eschatology of Paul*, p. 98.

36. Dahl, *Resurrection of the Body*, p. 72. Notice that Dahl affirms monism already in I Corinthians 15 and throughout Paul's life.

37. This is the approach of Rudolf Bultmann, for example.

38. Bruce, *Paul*, pp. 300-302. I have offered good reasons why the Pharisees were holistic dualists, a conclusion reached by many other scholars. I cannot refrain from wondering if Bruce's hesitation about that conclusion has to do with maintaining his theory about Paul's development. His position is much harder to hold if Paul was a dualist in Acts 23. For on Bruce's reckoning, by the time of his appearance before the Sanhedrin Paul had already written his epistles to the Thessalonians and Corinthians; cf. p. 475.

that of the Old Testament. The mistakenness of those moves has already been indicated.[39]

In conclusion, it is at least as likely that Paul was once a dualist than not. If so, his monism ought not to function as an unquestioned assumption in the interpretation of II Corinthians 5. And without that assumption, the immediate resurrection interpretation seems a lot less weighty, all things considered.[40] But the case against the assumption of Paul's monism does not finally rest on appeal to his youthful Judaism. It can be argued from II Corinthians itself.

E. II Corinthians 12:1-4

In this fascinating passage Paul recounts an ecstatic experience in which he had received visions and revelations from the Lord.[41] He was "caught up to the third heaven" (v. 2), that is, "caught up to paradise" (v. 4). "Whether in the body or out of the body" (v. 2), "in the body or apart from the body" (v. 3), he does not know.

Here Paul raises the possibility of temporary disembodied existence not only after death, but even during life. The option of personal separation from the body is beyond dispute. For the Greek prepositions employed, *ektos* (v. 2) and *chōris* (v. 3), denote distancing and local separation. The possible absence of the mystical subject from his body is thus emphasized in Greek. According to Bultmann, Paul "is clearly reckoning with the possibility that the self can separate from the *soma* even in this present life, and this *soma* can only be the physical body."[42] Barrett agrees: "he does not deny the possibility that the soul may leave the body and have

39. An excellent discussion of the difficulties of presenting Paul simply as monistic and Hebraistic is presented by S. Laeuchli, "Monism and Dualism in Pauline Anthropology," *Biblical Research* (Papers of the Chicago Society of Biblical Research), Vol. 3 (1958), pp. 15ff., and referred to by Moule, "St. Paul and Dualism," p. 116 n. 3.

40. Those who argue for an immediate disembodied spiritual resurrection acknowledge Paul's dualistic anthropology, thus making their case for immediate resurrection without assuming monism. Since the goal of this study is finally to get clear on New Testament anthropology by means of its individual eschatology, their recognition of Paul's dualism is gratefully noted.

41. Although he speaks in the third person, verse 7 makes it clear that this event is autobiographical. For our purposes, however, it makes no difference of whom he is speaking.

42. Bultmann, *Theology,* Vol. I, p. 202.

dealings with spiritual, non-corporeal beings."[43] Surprisingly, Bruce himself notes that ecstasy "usually involved temporary detachment from the body."[44]

But disembodied experience is only one option. The other is that Paul remained in the body. Modern readers will leap at this as the only real possibility. Paul did not actually think he left his body, they will say. He really just stayed where he was and had a trance-like experience in which he was unaware of his body and earthly surroundings. But it is quite unlikely that this is what Paul meant. He twice asserts that he was taken up to heaven or paradise. The only question is whether his body came along or remained behind. When Jewish people spoke of mystical experience, "ecstasy" — literally standing out of the body — was one possibility. But unlike the Greeks, they also thought it possible to be taken bodily up to heaven or paradise. In Jewish tradition, Enoch, whom the Lord took in Genesis 5, was said to have "paid a bodily visit to the celestial realms."[45] In fact II Enoch is one text where paradise is located in the third heaven, a striking parallel to what Paul says here. He entertains the possibility that he was taken into heaven bodily, not that he had a trance while at his kitchen table. Bultmann's linking Paul's dualism to Gnosticism is therefore unnecessary; both the embodied and disembodied possibilities of mystical experience are found in Jewish tradition, although Paul could also be accommodating the Greek dualism of his Corinthian friends. In any case, the modern interpretation — that Paul thought he remained on earth while receiving his revelation from the Lord —is most improbable. He thought of himself in heaven, with or without his body.

Caution must be exercised in drawing conclusions from this. For Paul does not assert that he was apart from his body, a claim which would clinch the case for dualism. He only says that it might have been so. But the mere fact that he would entertain this possibility raises problems for those who insist he is a monist. If Paul could not think of existence and fellowship with the Lord without a body, as Bruce claims, if he could not imagine the possibility, as Shires asserts, then how do we account for his entertain-

43. C. K. Barrett, *Commentary on the Second Epistle to the Corinthians* (New York: Harper and Row, 1973), pp. 308-309.
44. F. F. Bruce, *I and II Corinthians* (London: Oliphants, 1971), p. 247. It is surprising because Bruce elsewhere (*Paul*, p. 311) asserts that for Paul communion with Christ without a body is unthinkable.
45. Bruce, *I and II Corinthians*, pp. 246-247.

ing the possibility here? Is he merely using some Corinthian figure of speech which he does not endorse? Everything points to his seriously entertaining the out-of-the-body option, which entails dualism. If he were a monist, disembodiment would indeed be inconceivable. But if he were a dualist, remaining in the body would be just as possible as leaving it. Assuming that Paul is a dualist therefore explains the logic of this passage fully, whereas assuming he is a monist does not. In addition, there are the references to the third heaven and to paradise which, we have seen, are part of the general Jewish worldview, which includes holistic dualism. Once again both the textual and circumstantial evidence favors the dualist position.

Recall that we began to consider II Corinthians 12 in connection with the assumption that Paul is a monist in II Corinthians 5. We provided circumstantial arguments above to neutralize that assumption. But straightforward exegesis of II Corinthians 12 yields material from the book itself that monism ought not to be assumed as Paul's anthropology at the time of its writing. If chapter 12 does not prove Paul's dualism, its incompatibility with monism at least strengthens the cumulative case for dualism by undermining the claim that he had changed his earlier views by the writing of II Corinthians 5.

F. Philippians 1:21-24

This passage need not detain us long, for it parallels II Corinthians 5:6-10 in the anthropologically relevant details. Paul's views in the two books are therefore probably the same. What we find again here is the distinction between being in the body and being with Christ:

> For to me, to live is Christ and to die is gain. If I am to go on living in the body, this will mean fruitful labor for me. Yet what shall I choose? I do not know! I am torn between the two: I desire to depart and be with Christ, which is better by far. But it is more necessary for you that I remain in the body.

On the face of it there seems to be a simple contrast between living in the body and departing life in the body to be with Christ. There is no mention of a body with Christ. The options appear to be embodiment and disembodiment, either temporary or eternal. The fact that Paul speaks in verses 22 and 24 of *sarx* rather than *sōma* (v. 20) is interesting but probably insignificant, for they often function as synonyms. As with II Corinthians 5, there is no hint of the extinction–re-creation view, which seems to be ruled out. Immediate resurrection can likewise be argued only from silence.

But the immediate resurrectionist will respond that since II Corinthians 5 is on his side, as a parallel text, this is as well. Moreover, there is significance to the shift in terminology from *sōma* to *sarx*. Paul actually contrasts "being with Christ" with "living in the flesh," not with "living in the *body*." So he is not necessarily contrasting an earthly body with no body at all. He is contrasting being in the flesh with not being in the flesh. In other words, we have an immediate resurrection to a spiritualized body. Already in I Corinthians 15:50 Paul denied that flesh and blood could inherit the Kingdom of God. The resurrection body is a *sōma pneumatikon*, a spiritual body, which requires precisely that it not be *sarx*. This is why Paul states in Philippians 1 that being with Christ is not being in the flesh.

So although there is no positive evidence for immediate resurrection here, one can at least attempt to make a case for its consistency with the text, thereby fending off victory of the future resurrectionist.

This maneuver is weak, however. Paul's use of *sōma* in verse 20 strongly suggests that it is a synonym for *sarx*. Even if it is not, Paul's "spiritual body" in I Corinthians 15 is a *sōma* after all. But there is no mention of a resurrection *sōma* in Philippians 1, which leaves intact the contrast between being in the earthly body and not being embodied at all. There is only an argument from silence for a spiritual resurrection body here. Furthermore, our Lord himself explicitly states in Luke 24:39 that his own resurrection body consists of flesh *(sarx)* and bones. So either Paul has a different view or his statement that "flesh and blood cannot inherit the kingdom of God" is not to be taken as a literal description of bodily composition after all. In fact there are serious challenges to the assumption that Paul's distinction between the "soulish" and "spiritual" bodies of I Corinthians 15 has anything whatsoever to do with their substantial or anatomical composition. It is just as likely that "spirit" refers to the life-giving power of the Holy Spirit, who will confer on us the immortality which the earthly body, animated only by *psychē*, is lacking.[46] For all these reasons,

---

46. Cf. Ridderbos, pp. 540-544.

attempting to argue for an immediate spiritual resurrection in Philippians 1 is a case of special pleading.

G. The Time of the Resurrection in Philippians and Romans

In addition, the broader context once again enables us to focus the text more sharply. For Philippians 3:20-21 speaks about the resurrection and seems to correlate it with Christ's renewal of all things at the end. Verse 20 says that we await a Savior from heaven, where our citizenship is. That seems to refer to the future coming of the Lord. Verse 21 then proclaims that "he will transform our lowly bodies so that they will be like his glorious body."[47] The two events seem to share the same future. The immediate resurrectionist will have to argue that our future resurrection and the second coming do not necessarily have to go together or else that the second coming is not a future event in the history of this world. But that will not help us explain why Paul places them together and sees the parousia in the historical future.

And it will not help us understand why he also seems to do so in Romans 8:18-23, written between II Corinthians and Philippians. There he speaks of the groaning of the whole creation, which awaits the renewal it will receive when Christ's full glory is revealed. We, too, groan inwardly and eagerly await "the redemption of our bodies," which almost certainly refers to the resurrection (cf. v. 11). So here again, although he does not directly state that the resurrection will take place at the second coming, as he does in I Thessalonians and I Corinthians, he does appear to link them together. The generally strong connection between individual and cosmic eschatology is so central in Pauline and New Testament theology that most theologians have questioned separating them. If cosmic renewal is future, so is the resurrection.[48] Indeed, where would we be with new bodies if the

---

47. Cf. J. J. Müller, *The Epistles of Paul to the Philippians and Philemon* (Grand Rapids: Eerdmans, 1955), p. 134, on 3:21: "With the coming of Christ the transformation of our weak and corruptible bodies to the likeness of His glorious body will take place."

48. Cf. the discussion by Berkouwer of this theme: "Two-fold Expectation?", *The Return of Christ* (Grand Rapids: Eerdmans, 1972), pp. 32-64. "A legitimate doctrine of the intermediate state, despite what some have thought, need not shut the door to true perspectives on the coming Kingdom of the Lord" (p. 63). In addition, recall the correlation

new heaven and earth were not yet a reality? We would be all dressed up with no place to go.

The fact that both Romans and Philippians seem to correlate the resurrection with the return of Christ leaves the burden of proof on the immediate resurrectionist. He must show that Paul does not correlate them after II Corinthians. For failure to do so will leave him in the awkward position of having to explain why Paul would return to future resurrection, a position which he had previously abandoned. Just why would he jump from future resurrection to immediate resurrection and back again? As Ridderbos observes, "it would surely be very strange were Paul in the time between 1 Corinthians and 2 Corinthians to have come to this 'development,' and then to have returned, e.g. in Romans, to his original idea."[49] Furthermore, if he did return to a future resurrection as the last word, then in the formulation of Christian doctrine that would supersede the temporary aberration of an immediate resurrection even if it were taught in II Corinthians 5. Surely it is more reasonable, all things considered, to suppose that he did not make the leap in II Corinthians 5.

III. Conclusions

A. Paul

Our project in this chapter has been to identify as precisely as possible the personal eschatology taught by Paul in order to determine the anthropology embedded in it. If our three possible options for personal eschatology are intermediate state, immediate resurrection, and extinction–re-creation, the first is the most defensible conclusion for a number of reasons.

First, there are formidable problems with the other two. With respect to the immediate resurrection hypothesis, there is no text which definitely supports it while precluding the intermediate state hypothesis. In fact it conflicts with a number of Pauline texts which state or suggest that the resurrection will occur at the parousia. And its proponents must engage in somewhat strained argumentation in order to make it stick to

---

between individual and cosmic eschatology discussed in the chapter on intertestamental literature.

49. Ridderbos, p. 500 n. 33.

some of the texts with which it is logically consistent. As for the extinction–re-creation position, to be compatible with the texts at all this theory must require us to suppose that Paul is speaking phenomenologically, not realistically, when he says that at death we will be with Christ. Given the theological centrality of the notion of being "with Christ" and "in Christ" for Paul, and recalling his insistence that neither death nor life in the present or in the future can separate us from Christ's love (Rom. 8:38), it stretches credulity to plead that he was not speaking objectively or realistically in such passages. Besides, there is no evidence from the historical context that anyone Jewish or Greek held the extinction–re-creation view. In contrast to its rivals, the intermediate state theory is confronted by no significant counter-evidence. At worst it cannot be conclusively demonstrated in some texts. So the intermediate state interpretation might just win by default.

More positively, in the second place, it can be proven to be true by deduction from two well-established Pauline teachings: that "to be absent from the body is to be present with the Lord"; and that the resurrection occurs at the second coming. Together these entail that persons exist with Christ between physical death and resurrection.[50] This conclusion holds even in the unlikely case that it was not clear in Paul's own mind.

Third, there is the positive textual and circumstantial evidence that Paul was a proponent of the intermediate state–future resurrection eschatology. For several texts we were able to demonstrate that this is a more adequate interpretation, all things considered, than either of its rivals. And

---

50. This of course assumes what some theologians seem to reject, the legitimacy of inferring conclusions from premises known to be true from Scripture. Some scholars seem to think that only what Scripture explicitly says or what the human authors specifically intended can be trusted. What is logically entailed (necessarily implied) by biblical teaching or by combinations of biblical teachings yields no knowledge. These theologians usually mumble something about the weakness of human reason or complain about speculation. In response we of course admit that one must be careful in drawing conclusions from Scripture. We must identify as precisely as possible what Scripture is asserting. And we must see the difference between what is entailed by Scripture and what is merely consistent with it. What is entailed is definite, following necessarily and unambiguously from its premises. However, many claims which are merely consistent with Scripture are speculations precisely because they are not definitely known to be true. They might be true. But then they might also be false. Observing these cautions, it is no more speculation to draw inferences from what the Bible teaches than it is to infer Socrates's mortality from his membership in a mortal race. Such inferences hold even if the biblical authors did not fully recognize them.

there was no text with which the intermediate state theory appeared to conflict or for which grammatically or contextually strained arguments were required. At worst its preferability could not be demonstrated in all cases.

For all of the above reasons, therefore, I claim that the dualistic intermediate-state theory is not just one defensible interpretation of Pauline eschatology, but clearly the most preferable. It is what Paul meant to teach, not just his incidental mode of expression.

A final word about Paul's terminology. Nowhere does he use the words "soul" or "spirit" to refer to persons in the afterlife. But this is no more evidence against dualism than the fact that the Old Testament may never use *nephesh* or *ruach* to refer to the dead in Sheol. For Paul always contrasts *himself* with his body or flesh. He always uses personal pronouns. In II Corinthians 5 "we" are either at home in the body or away from the body. In chapter 12 he speaks of "a man" — himself of course (v. 7), "he," and later "me." In Philippians 1 it is perfectly clear: "if I am to go on living in the body"; "I desire to depart." Unlike other New Testament writers, Paul does not refer to the departed as "souls" or "spirits." But he always employs the grammar of persons: the "I," the self, the core person is what continues in unbroken fellowship with Christ during this life, from death to the second coming, and forever. If Paul is a dualist, he is strictly speaking a self-body, person-body, or ego-body dualist, not a soul-body dualist.[51] This is a matter of terminology, not of substance.

B. The New Testament as a Whole

In spite of variations of language and detail, therefore, Paul teaches the same general personal eschatology as the rest of the New Testament. There is fellowship with Christ during the interval between bodily death and the general future resurrection. It is true that Scripture does not pay much attention to the intermediate state and that what it does say is neither precise nor detailed. To a large extent it is *terra incognita* — unknown territory.[52] The resurrection, not the intermediate state, is the heart of Christian hope.

51. Cf. Bultmann's remark on II Corinthians 12: ". . . the self can separate from the *soma* . . . and this *soma* can only be the physical body." *Theology,* Vol. I, p. 202.

52. This is the thesis of Hanhart's book; cf. p. 239.

Even the nature of the resurrection is less easy to pin down than is popularly assumed. Nevertheless, the New Testament's few hints, whispers, and occasionally direct assertions are all consistent: saints enjoy fellowship with Christ between death and the final resurrection.[53] Christians are not faced with conflicting testimony from the New Testament. There is a consistent revelation which we can trust for our comfort. And there is an answer to the question which motivated our inquiry in these two chapters. It is clear that the case for the intermediate state eschatology in the New Testament can be vindicated on scholarly grounds. The implication of this result for the monism-dualism debate about biblical anthropology is decisive.

53. Even Harris, who prefers the immediate resurrection position, admits the defensibility of a disembodied intermediate state and insists on conscious fellowship of the saints with Christ during the interval between death and the second coming; cf. pp. 138-142.

Chapter Eight

New Testament Eschatology and
Philosophical Anthropology

I. Introduction

All our efforts to understand the New Testament picture of the human constitution and what happens to it at death have been expended in the belief that this would finally settle the monism-dualism debate. Do persons exist without bodies or not? If the biblical view of the afterlife includes personal existence apart from the body, it was claimed, then some sort of anthropological dichotomy or dualism is entailed. If, however, the separation of personal and bodily existence is avoided, as immediate resurrection and extinction–re-creation would do, then some form of monism or ontological holism is implied.

But has the debate been settled? Has the scoring been accurate? Do the various theories of the afterlife generate the implications I have claimed? These questions deserve careful answers. For even a brief encounter with the literature will reveal confusion about what these theories entail. Some commentators even deny the implications I have claimed. For example, some who affirm the intermediate state are squeamish about dualism. Others who hold the immediacy of resurrection fail to recognize that they formulate it in a dualist fashion, contradicting the monism they endorse. And some who are extinction–re-creationists have not wrestled with a most formidable problem in their theory — the problem of personal identity. In this chapter, therefore, it is necessary to reflect more carefully on the three theories of the afterlife in order to demonstrate precisely what they imply. This will enable us to do two things: test the coherence and conceptual adequacy of each theory; and render a final judgment regarding the monism-dualism debate about the anthropology of Scripture.

II. The Intermediate State and Dualism

Not everyone who holds the traditional view of the afterlife is willing to admit being a dualist. I can recall sermons, college lectures, and theological debates in which speakers confidently affirmed the hope of being with Christ between death and resurrection. A paragraph later, however, they roundly denounced the body-soul distinction as the illegitimate offspring of a Christian affair with Greek thought. Apparently these folks think that the two positions are not necessarily connected, that the intermediate state does not automatically entail dualism.

Their number includes not only pastors and laypeople, but biblical scholars and theologians as well. Herman Ridderbos, a master Reformed expositor of Scripture, clearly affirms the intermediate state as part of Paul's teaching, but has only negative things to say about dualism and "Greek dichotomy." He even refuses to admit "disembodiment" as an implication of II Corinthians 5 and Philippians 1, although he denies that they teach immediate resurrection.[1] Motivating Ridderbos, in addition to his anti-Hellenism, is the desire not to draw inferences or "speculate" beyond what Scripture says because its statements cannot be made "anthropologically transparent."[2]

The same aura of paradox surrounds Berkouwer's *Man: The Image of God*. He stalwartly defends the teaching that believers exist in fellowship with Christ between death and the future resurrection. Yet he vigorously rejects all suggestions of dichotomy or dualism, and dismisses as unedifying any attempt to unpack the biblical message conceptually:

> And this reality, so full of comfort, surely can hardly be expressed clearly through an anthropological "division" within man; and if we are not satisfied with the New Testament description, and wish to achieve more "reality" by postulating the "substantiality" of a "part" of man, the "ego," or

---

1. Cf. Ridderbos, "Death Before the Parousia: the Intermediate State," in *Paul* (Grand Rapids: Eerdmans, 1975), pp. 497-508, and pp. 548-550 of "The Resurrection."
2. Ridderbos, p. 550.

the "heart," or the "person," we contribute nothing to a deeper under-standing of salvation.[3]

In the final analysis Berkouwer is unwilling to say more than that the inter-mediate state is "God's mystery."[4]

Helmut Thielicke's *Living with Death* is a third example. On one hand he presents an anthropology in which there is "no division of the I into body and soul." But he also affirms an intermediate state with the Lord. Not unaware of the tension between the two positions, he chooses to aban-don "the principle of theological consistency" and retain both horns of the dilemma.[5] Surely no one can accuse Thielicke of insisting that logic binds the intermediate state to dualism.

Interestingly, Cullmann's "Immortality of the Soul or Resurrection of the Dead," often touted as a champion of biblical holism against Greek du-alism, is not an example of this sort of conceptual ambivalence. He de-fends an intermediate state of "sleep" with Christ, but freely admits that this is "a kind of *approximation* to the Greek teaching," that is, some sort of dualism after all.[6] The big differences between Socrates and Jesus turn out to be in their attitudes toward death and future bodily existence, not the separability of self and body.

Friend or foe of anthropological dualism, each of these theologians appears concerned about two dangers: reading unbiblical (Greek) philoso-phy into the Bible and engaging in illegitimate speculation about the inter-mediate state.

So the question arises, Does the doctrine of the intermediate state nec-essarily commit one to dualism or not? The answer in part depends on what one means by "dualism." The fact that this term has been used so pro-miscuously makes one despair of rehabilitating it to a helpful role in the discussion. Plato, Descartes, the Gnostics, and the Manicheans have all

3. G. C. Berkouwer, *Man: The Image of God* (Grand Rapids: Eerdmans, 1962), p. 265; his chapters "The Whole Man" and "Immortality" contain much valuable material for our discussion.

4. Berkouwer, p. 265.

5. Helmut Thielicke, *Living with Death* (Grand Rapids: Eerdmans, 1983), "Appendix Four: The Intermediate State," p. 173.

6. Oscar Cullmann, "Immortality or Resurrection," in *Immortality and Resurrection* (New York: Macmillan, 1965), p. 83. The dualism label is mine but self-evidently appropri-ate.

been called dualists. And in this book I have claimed that the Hebrews and Jews were dualists. But there are such striking differences among these anthropologies. What can "dualism" possibly mean? One problem with the term, therefore, is its lack of a clear definition. To make matters worse, many polarities which have been labeled dualism do conflict with the biblical view of human nature. That is certainly true where a metaphysical antipathy between matter and spirit is postulated. Given these difficulties with the term "dualism," one can understand why theologians wish to avoid it. Perhaps it should be abandoned altogether and another such as "duality" adopted.[7]

However, a little pondering will disclose that other labels are just as problematic. "Duality," for example, does not say enough, since monists and ontological holists are willing to admit a duality or plurality of aspects, dimensions, or kinds of functionality in human nature. They too eagerly acknowledge "duality." At the same time they deny that any of these aspects or dimensions of humans can survive separation from the others at death, which is precisely the issue.[8] So we must try to clarify positions and not waste time arguing about labels.

Let me outline my version of dualism once again and compare it with what some theologians seem to be worried about. If to be absent from the body for me is to be with the Lord — still "in Christ" and "living together with him" as I am already now — then I must exist between my death and the resurrection. And I must be able to enjoy fellowship with Christ in some way, and probably also communion with the saints who have died, since being in Christ is a corporate reality. That is all we know from the New Testament. It does not say more. It does not elaborate. It does not describe in detail. For anyone to say more than this is indeed to speculate.[9]

7. Cf. Berkouwer, p. 211: "duality and dualism are not at all identical, and . . . reference to a dual moment in cosmic reality does not necessarily imply a dualism." Cf. also A. A. Hoekema, *Created in God's Image* (Grand Rapids: Eerdmans, 1986), p. 217, where this term is recommended.

8. Hoekema, for example, a theologian who is correct about the intermediate state and about the human constitution, prefers the term "duality" to "dualism." But he also endorses the "duality" view of Donald MacKay, who is a dual-aspect monist and cannot admit a disembodied intermediate state. Obviously "duality" does nothing to remove confusion from the discussion; cf. Hoekema, pp. 217-218.

9. Cullmann puts it well: "The lack of New Testament speculation about this does not give us the right simply to suppress the 'interim condition' as such. I do not understand why Protestant theologians (including Barth) are so afraid of the New Testament position when

But certain things necessarily follow from this modest biblical teaching. If this doctrine is true, then other things must also be true, for they are contained in or entailed by its truth. Simply put, the doctrine cannot possibly be true if these other things are not true. For example, if I am with Christ, then I — my essential selfhood or core personhood — must survive physical death. The being or entity who I am must continue to exist. In striking ways that being might be different from the being who now lives embodied on earth. It might not be able to do some of the same things or have all the same sorts of experiences. It might be incapable of running or smelling roses, for example. On the other hand, it might be able to do other things and have other sorts of experiences than it now does. But the being or thing that I am must remain. Otherwise it would not be I but someone or something else that is with Christ. I must also be capable of experience of some sort. Perhaps it will be dream-like or in some other ways quite different from my present experience. But there must also be some continuity of content with present experience. I must still be able to know that my Redeemer lives and be able to respond to his love. I must somehow be aware of myself as the same person who formerly lived on earth, for that is essential to my self-identification as one of the redeemed. All of this must be possible without my bodily organism.

The list of necessary implications could be developed further, but the point here is that constructing this list is not philosophical speculation. It is not using the imagination to paint pictures beyond the point at which the Bible falls silent. It is merely unpacking the content of biblical teaching. It is explicating what is implicit in that teaching. It is no more speculation than concluding from the fact that John loves Sylvia that John and Sylvia exist, that John is conscious and capable of personal relationships, and so forth. So I agree with those who rule out speculation as a source of knowledge about the intermediate state, but the assertion that the person I am will consciously fellowship with the Lord apart from my earthly organism is not speculation.[10] And the ontological possibility of that mode of hu-

---

the New Testament teaches only this much about the 'interim condition': (1) that it exists, (2) that it already signifies union with Christ (this because of the Holy Spirit)." "Immortality," p. 80 n. 35.

10. Ray Anderson, *On Being Human* (Grand Rapids: Eerdmans, 1982), p. 213, dismisses the intermediate state as "hypothetical." If he mistakenly takes "hypothetical" to mean "known by inference from other true propositions" as opposed to "known directly," he is correct that the intermediate state can be known by inference. But then he should not dis-

man existence is all I mean by dualism. Personal existence apart from earthly-bodily existence is possible. When we die, there is a dichotomy of ego and the earthly organism. We are constituted in such a way that we can survive "coming apart" at death, unnatural as this may be. This is all that I mean by "dualism."

Any theory of human nature compatible with the Bible must provide for this possibility, that is, must be a case of this minimal, generic dualism. There are a number of philosophical anthropologies which qualify, so the Bible is not teaching a particular philosophical position. The generic dualism entailed by the intermediate state is much too underdeveloped to be a philosophical theory. It is much more like the worldviews of pre-reflective peoples or commonsense experience. It is a picture which merely sets the parameters for philosophical theories. Any Christian philosophy should account for the possibility of this vision of the afterlife. Thus my claim for the truth of dualism does not violate the maxim that the Bible is philosophically unsophisticated and not a philosophical textbook. We get no philosophical definitions of "ego," "person," "body," "soul," or "spirit" from the doctrine of the intermediate state. We have no information about what sorts of experience are possible without bodies. There is nothing here to help us explain the body-soul or mind-brain relation. No data are given for a theory of organisms. We need philosophy and science for addressing those questions. All we know from Scripture is that in God's providence human beings can exist in fellowship with Christ without earthly bodies. But we can easily see that any philosophical anthropology which accounts for this possibility must necessarily be dualistic. For that is minimally what dualism means.

Obviously, therefore, dualism as I use the term does not automatically entail a Platonic or Cartesian dualism of essentially different substances. It does not necessarily require adoption of Aristotelian form-matter or Kantian noumenal-phenomenal categories. The usefulness of these conceptual schemes to Christian anthropologists is open to evaluation. My definition of dualism certainly does not imply the antithesis

---

miss the intermediate state, for what is known is true. I suspect that he takes "hypothetical" instead to mean "speculative." Speculation is guessing beyond what may definitely be inferred. The intermediate state is no more "hypothetical" in this sense than is the inference that there is no milk in the refrigerator from the knowledge that the milk is on the table and that there is just one container of milk in the house. The confusion between inference and speculation plagues much theology, not just biblical anthropology.

and essential disharmony between body and spirit which are characteristic of Orphic and Gnostic dualism. It does not require viewing body and soul as self-contained, independently functioning entities, at least not during earthly life. These are the sorts of unbiblical dualisms which theologians are rightly worried about.[11] In fact, the dualism of biblical anthropology presented here is part of the same picture which yields functional holism, as has been emphasized throughout this study. So asserting only that biblical anthropology is dualistic is a half-truth which distorts the scriptural picture of human nature. But so is the unqualified claim that it is holistic. Only some combination like "holistic dualism" will tell the whole story.

In conclusion, it is clear that the doctrine of the intermediate state logically requires the possibility that persons can exist without earthly bodies. This follows from the teaching of Scripture; it is not a Greek import. Christians who affirm the doctrine are committed to this general anthropology whether they admit it or not. Denying this is simply being incoherent, not modestly refusing to speculate. The view of the human constitution implied by the doctrine may be labeled "dualism" or "ontic duality," if one prefers, for it has to do with the structure of human nature and a mode of human existence. In itself it is a general pre-philosophical point of view, not a developed philosophical anthropology. Thus it is only a framework for doing philosophical anthropology, a project which will also require data from ordinary experience, science, and philosophical reflection.

III. Immediate Resurrection: Monism or Dualism?

In considering St. Paul's eschatology we encountered two versions of the immediate resurrection theory. One proposes the immediate possession of a new body. The other views resurrection as an immediate spiritual transformation of the inner self, either counting this event as receipt of a spiritual body or speaking of permanent disembodiment. We saw that proponents of the second position — immediate spiritual resurrection — are not typically embarrassed to acknowledge Paul's anthropological dualism, since their theory obviously postulates everlasting separation of personal

11. These and similar problems are discussed helpfully in the chapters on "The Whole Man" and "Immortality" in Berkouwer's *Man*.

existence from the earthly body. At least some immediate resurrectionists are dualists.

It may come as a surprise at this stage in the discussion, but many in the other group, those who defend the theory of immediate bodily resurrection, do so in an implicitly dualistic manner also. Only a few of them seem to be aware of this, however. Most appear to assume that since there is no time of disembodiment, persons are perpetually embodied and thus there is no person-body or soul-body dualism. According to the theological anthropology of Ray Anderson, for example, "it would appear that the concept of a disembodied personal existence which experiences duration and extension in time is difficult if not impossible to hold." For Anderson, a person is an ontological "unity," although he will admit a certain non-ontological "duality." Instead of the intermediate state, he opts for "death as an immediate experience of presence with God, and resurrection of the body" as "part of that immediate experience."[12] Anderson is assuming that immediate resurrection avoids dualism.

A moment's reflection, however, will highlight how dualistic the immediate resurrection theory really is. Although there is no time at which the soul or person is disembodied, we nevertheless suppose that one and the same person switches from one body to another. So we have one person and two bodies, one earthly and the other resurrected. Not only is the person distinct from her earthly body, she is separable from it. She puts off the old tent and puts on the new dwelling, to paraphrase II Corinthians 5. And that entails dualism. For it is not a time of disembodiment which is the distinguishing mark of dualism, although that would certainly suffice. Merely the separation of the person and her earthly body is enough for a diagnosis of dualism.

If monism or ontological holism were true, then there would be an unbreakable connection between a person and her body, the same body she ensouled throughout life. For holism, persons are simply body-soul unities. For materialistic monism, a person or soul is the set of human mental capacities generated by the human body and brain — a "mentating" or "personating" organism. On either view, body, soul, mind, spirit, person, ego, and self are all inseparably linked as interdependent parts, aspects, or capacities of one and the same thing.[13] The death of the

12. Anderson, p. 213.
13. The connection is ontological, i.e., required by the nature of the beast. It is not logically necessary. Even mind-brain identity theorists — materialistic monists who hold that

organism thus ontologically necessitates the decease of the whole person. Only if the earthly body itself were transformed into the heavenly body would the "whole" be preserved. But the reality of corpses rules out that possibility. Something of the former totality is obviously left over.

So it is clear that if a person can survive the decease of the earthly organism, then we have dualism by definition. Human beings can "come apart" at death. There is a dichotomy. According to immediate resurrectionists, there is an instant transportation from one body to another. The person does survive disengagement from the earthly body, which is forever left behind. Therefore she was not inseparably connected with it. And that is dualism. Anthropologically speaking, the only difference between an intermediate state and an immediate resurrection is the absence of a temporal gap between embodiments. On both views a single person leaves a natural body and receives a spiritual body. One person is contingently related to two bodies.

Not all immediate resurrectionists have failed to notice this completely. Murray Harris is a good example. Although he too pays lip-service to the allegedly monistic anthropology of Scripture, the formulation of his position clearly distinguishes and separates persons or egos from bodies: "the link between the Christian's successive forms of embodiment — the physical, then the spiritual — lies in the same identifiable *ego*." "One and the same person finds expression in two successive but different types of body. There are two dwellings but only one occupant. There is an identity of occupant but not of dwelling."[14] Harris's construal of an immediate resurrection presupposes that the ego (the person or self) is neither identical with nor essentially related to the earthly body. They are separated at death. Even though we have no period of disembodiment, we obviously have dualism. His explanation is clear enough, but Harris stops short of identifying it as dualistic. That label he reserves for those who defend the disembodied intermediate state.

All of this means, of course, that the dualist side in the debate is further augmented and enhanced; many of those who have moved from the

---

the mind is just some brain functions — recognize that there is a logical-conceptual difference between a person and a brain. But although mind and brain are not logically identical, they are in fact identical. Thus it is not in fact possible for the mind to exist without the brain. The same is true for the theory that the mind is a product of the brain.

14. Harris, *Raised Immortal* (Grand Rapids: Eerdmans, 1985), p. 126.

traditional position to instant resurrection in order to avoid dualism and defend monism have failed to achieve their goal. Unbeknown to themselves they have elaborated another dualist interpretation of the New Testament. So even if in the last chapter we were unable to demonstrate beyond doubt the truth of the intermediate state instead of an instant resurrection — even if immediate resurrection is a defensible view, dualism is still implied by the New Testament.

Or are we moving too fast? Doesn't the immediate resurrectionist have another option, a genuinely monistic or ontologically holistic one? Suppose that persons are the centered fields of self-conscious agency generated and supported by or holistically integrated with human organisms — complete with beliefs, commitments, memories, and personality characteristics. In either case a person is not a thing, an entity, or a substance which is separable from its organism. Instead a person is a unique and stable set of patterned mental states, dispositions, and behavioral capacities — a part of a single bodily whole.

Now imagine that at the instant of a person's death, God creates a new single mental-physical whole so constructed that the very same set of mental states and capacities would be present in the resurrected human being. The same self-conscious person would instantly change from one embodiment to the other without requiring any transfer of a mysterious soul substance or spiritual entity. Resurrection would be similar to switching on a new TV the instant the old one broke down.[15] The program would continue uninterrupted even though the picture tubes projecting the program were distinct. By analogy, the very same person would continue to exist even though she switched bodies.

This scenario is consistent with monism or ontological holism, because a person is not a thing which separates from the body, but remains integral to it. Isn't this a coherent account of an immediate bodily resur-

---

15. Donald MacKay, *Brains, Machines, and Persons* (Grand Rapids: Eerdmans, 1980), pp. 101-102, suggests the example of a computer which breaks down. The same program can be lodged in a new computer. So it is with persons and their bodies.

I am ignoring the well-known caterpillar-into-butterfly analogy. There we have an outer shell–inner body duality. The new body develops out of the old, leaving a cocoon. Nothing physically analogous would occur in an instant resurrection. The emerging "butterfly" (resurrection person) would be a spiritual being, leaving behind a physical shell. This would simply be another version of dualism, as immediate spiritual resurrectionists readily admit. This metaphor is useless to the monist.

rection? If so, then the dualist ought to refrain from too quickly adding the instant resurrectionist's points to his own score.

Before rushing out to celebrate, however, monists must answer one more question: What justifies the claim that we have the very same person after death as before, rather than merely an exactly similar copy? Here we slam into the formidable problem of personal identity, which any adequate theory of the afterlife must solve.[16]

The problem is easiest to see if we continue to use the monist's analogies. Lots of different TV's can show the same soap opera. Lots of different computers can run the same program. Lots of different projectors can show the same movie. But as we move from set to set, from computer to computer, from projector to projector, we do not have the very same — the numerically identical — instance of what they produce, but merely something which is exactly similar. One set's display of *General Hospital* is distinct from another's, although both simultaneously reproduce the same episode. The analogies suggest that we have two exactly similar persons implied by this account of the resurrection, not the very same one.

But suppose we think of two projectors simultaneously showing the same movie on the same screen. One or the other could be switched on or off and the very same display would cover the screen. Here we have two sources and just one display. Doesn't this illustrate the possibility of one person and two bodies? Even here the actual light waves and images are distinct. They are causally connected either to one projector or the other, even though our eyes might not distinguish them. We still have two differ-

16. This problem has a long history. It was first raised by Joseph Butler against John Locke's claim that personal identity is located in states of consciousness such as memory rather than in a substance such as the soul. Cf. John Locke, *An Essay Concerning Human Understanding,* Bk. II, Ch. 27, and Joseph Butler, "Of Personal Identity," and *The Analogy of Religion,* "Of a Future Life." Both are found in Anthony Flew, ed., *Body, Mind, and Death* (New York: Macmillan, 1964). Recent discussion has been sparked by John Hick's "replication theory," the idea that resurrection is God's creation of a spatio-temporally distinct psychophysical unity which is nonetheless identical with the psychophysical unity which existed on earth. Hick spells it out most fully in *Death and Eternal Life* (San Francisco: Harper and Row, 1976), Ch. 15, "The Resurrection of the Person." Reichenbach addresses this problem in *Is Man the Phoenix?* (Grand Rapids: Eerdmans, 1983), pp. 87-97. Two recent discussions which intelligently survey and evaluate the debate and provide more extensive bibliography are: Gerard Loughlin, "Persons and Replicas," *Modern Theology,* I, 4 (July 1985); and Stephen Davis, "Is Personal Identity Retained in the Resurrection?", *Modern Theology,* II, 4 (July 1986).

ent though superimposed instances of the same general kind, not a single instance.

How is it different for persons in the monistic-holistic version of immediate resurrection? In both monism and ontological holism, persons are essentially related to and integrally part of particular entities — earthly organisms. If the numerically identical person can switch bodies, she is separable from that body, and we have dualism. But if persons are essentially tied to particular bodies, and if we have two bodies — one earthly and one resurrection body, then it logically follows that we have two persons, not one and the same person.

Unless the immediate resurrectionist can solve this problem, his account must be rejected because it is conceptually incoherent, not just because it is incompatible with biblical anthropology. Since the extinction–re-creation theory likewise raises the problem of personal identity, we will probe them together in the next section.

IV. Monism, Re-creation, and the Problem of Personal Identity

To see that all monists — immediate resurrectionists and extinction–re-creationists alike — have the problem of personal identity, let's think of immediate resurrection as an instantaneous re-creation.[17] In both theories a distinct entity is created. One asserts that this occurs immediately; the other that there is a temporal gap between death and re-creation. So both must explain how this new personal being is numerically identical with the earthly personal being.

What arouses suspicions about personal identity is the fact that we do not have a single entity with a continuous history. Where we have such substantial and existential continuity, there is no question about identity. My childhood toys are the very same things now as then because they are the same organizations of atoms and molecules which have existed uninterrupted since then. Even the oak in the yard, which has grown and changed in material composition as well as appearance during these many

17. As noted at several points above, idealist or panpsychist monism does not generate this problem because it can account for the intermediate state. What it cannot consistently account for is the corpse.

years, is self-identical because it has an unbroken history as a single organized entity. It seems impossible that these things not be self-identical through time.

But where such continuity is lacking, questions arise. If my toys were utterly reduced to atoms and then remanufactured from them, would they be the numerically identical toys or new and different toys made from the same matter? If the oak tree died and decomposed and years later one of its acorns were planted at that spot; and if that acorn absorbed all and only those atoms from the soil which had belonged to its parent; and if it grew into exactly the same size, shape, and appearance as its parent; would it be its parent? Would we have self-identity if a branch from the dying tree were preserved and another tree indistinguishable in appearance were grown from it? Or what if a magician made that tree disappear and five years later made one exactly alike appear in the same place; would it be the very same tree or an exact copy? Or what if the magician made my oak disappear and one just like it appear in your yard; would the trees be numerically identical or only exactly similar? People may have different intuitions about these cases. But the question is a real one. In just this way the problem of personal identity arises for monistic theories of the afterlife.

It is worth noting at this point that the dualist has absolutely no problem. For his case is like the first example of the toys and oak tree. The person who survives death and undergoes future resurrection is a continuously existing reality. Whether philosophically conceived as consisting of spiritual stuff or as an organization of personal and mental states and capacities, the soul or person is a continuously existing entity or being. Although her properties and capacities may change due to disembodiment or divine sanctification, she remains the self-identical person from life, through death, and into the life to come. The possibility of nonidentity cannot arise. I know of no one who has suggested that the dualist has any problem with self-identity in the afterlife. The problem confronts those who cannot accept dualism.[18] It does not arise if dualism is true, for continuity of existence guarantees continuity of numerical identity.[19]

18. Cf. the remarks on the problem of personal identity by Stephen Davis, p. 335: "temporary disembodiment . . . seems to me a perfectly viable alternative for Christians (who have no trouble accepting dualism). . . . My aim is to defend the other alternative for Christians, viz., temporary nonexistence." Only the monist alternative raises the problem.

19. I recognize of course that continuously existing things can become other things, as when Moses changed Aaron's rod into a snake. This would involve changing form in Aris-

It is precisely the lack of continuity which raises questions for the monist, although it does so in slightly different ways for each of the two theories. If re-creation is immediate, then we clearly have two distinct psychophysical unities with no substantial or causal connection between them. For an instant resurrection is not like a magician's moving a tree from my yard to yours. Nor is it like the transporter on *Star Trek* by which someone's molecules are instantly shipped and reconstituted. It is more like the magician's putting a tree in your yard just as my tree died; or a malfunction of the transporter which leaves a dead Kirk on the Enterprise as it beams a living Kirk onto the planet's surface. We unavoidably posit two different entities on this theory, a dead earthly body and a resurrection body. If persons are essentially connected to particular bodies, we have two different persons.

The extinction–re-creationist is not trapped so quickly. For his theory does not postulate two bodies which exist simultaneously in different locations. The mortal body dies and an immortal one is created at a future time. It is therefore possible that the resurrection body be in some way identical with its earthly counterpart. There may be cases like Jesus and Lazarus where the very same body is raised. Or perhaps God preserves some part of the body — a bit of backbone, the Rabbis thought — as the locus of identity. Or possibly God might gather some or all of the atoms which had once constituted a human being and re-create the very same person in this way. In each of these cases there is some basis for holding that the identity of the body is preserved because there is some continuity of its substance. If persons are essentially linked to particular bodies, then by extension we have reason to claim that the very same person has been re-created. Re-creation is not ex nihilo, but from what that person was before.

This does not guarantee identity, however. For recall the examples above in which the toys and the oak tree were totally disintegrated and re-

---

totle's sense and thus identity. Persons do not change this way in the afterlife. So the problem of identity does not arise. I am also not dealing here with the epistemic question of how much change in a person or thing is possible before doubts about identity will arise. Obviously there are limits to change beyond which recognition will be difficult. But identity is an ontic matter and identifiability is epistemic. They ought not to be conflated. A person can remain ontically identical even though neither he nor his associates recognize this, as cases of amnesia coupled with facial disfiguration will demonstrate. The repulsive toad might really be the handsome prince, whether anyone knows it or not.

constituted from the same matter. Or suppose that one branch of the tree or one axle of the toy truck continued from the original to the reconstituted version. It seems no less reasonable to think of these as examples of exact copies than to claim self-identity. My own intuition leans heavily toward the copy theory. The point is that this response by the re-creationist plausibly illustrates possible identity. It does not demonstrate actual identity.

The key issue here is whether there is any connection between a collection of matter or even a body part and personal identity. It is one thing to claim that preserving a brain would preserve a self-identical person if that brain were to regain its functions and reanimate what appeared to be the same person. We know that there are important connections between persons and brains. But preserved brains are not the stuff of which resurrected persons are created. Why should a new body made of someone's ashes or built around one of their vertebrae count as the same body as previously existed? And why should it be the very same person? Perhaps it could be. But matter and body parts can be transplanted without altering personal identity. So where is the crucial connection required between the body parts and the person? We are back to the same point. We have at best an account of possible identity. But we cannot be sure of actual identity.

As a matter of fact, however, most extinction–re-creationists do not wish to rely on the continuity of bodily substance as the guarantor of identity.[20] An obvious reason is that physical composition is not even essential to bodily identity during life. Biologists tell us that because of ingestion, growth, and excretion, the matter in our bodies changes several times during a normal life-span. Although I have the very same body as I did years ago, hardly any of the atoms and molecules of which my body now consists were part of me when I was a child. Thus it is not the physical substance which gives my body its identity over time in the first place. So using that substance to re-create my body might not make it the same body after all. Another problem is the possibility that over the ages the same matter has belonged to a number of persons. Our bodies decay, returning to dust. That dust then becomes part of the ecosystem and might well reenter the human food-chain, eventually incorporated in someone else. So to para-

20. Hick, *Death*, pp. 281-283, rejects the dependence of bodily identity on material identity. Instead he adopts Norbert Wiener's view that a body is a system or a code which organizes matter. Cf. also Reichenbach, p. 87.

phrase the Sadducees' question, Whose will it be in the resurrection? Although this query smacks a bit of angels dancing on pinheads, it raises a genuine problem for those who would tie personal identity to material substance. Most extinction–re-creationists do not rely on this connection.

On what then do they base their identity claims? Rather than proposing a criterion, let's begin with a thought-experiment. Suppose Bill Jones died and passed out of existence, his corpse cremated and ashes scattered forever. On the Last Day God creates out of nothing a human being similar to Jones, although sanctified and perfected. His physical and personal deficiencies are removed along with his sinful nature. Although he has been modified, all of his friends recognize him as Bill Jones. His physical form has not substantially changed, and his personality, though much improved, is unmistakably Jones's. Furthermore, Jones himself believes he is Jones. He is elated with the improvements. But he remembers his earthly life, recognizes his friends, and never wonders who he is.

In this imaginary situation, Jones appears to be himself both from the first-person and third-person points of view. There is no doubt in anyone's mind that this Jones is identical with the person who formerly lived on earth. So even if the re-creationist cannot formulate a clear and distinct criterion of identity, why should he have to? Isn't this illustration sufficient to dismiss the problem? There are many things which we intuit as self-identical without having a clear criterion or procedure of verification.

But the monist does have an operative criterion: a set of identity-making characteristics which we could call "Joneseness." Jones is a certain sort of person with a certain physical appearance. What makes us sure that he is Jones is that he looks, acts, and thinks like Jones. And that is also why Jones himself has no identity crisis. In this account what makes Jones self-identical is not his being a single, continuously existing entity, either spiritual or physical. Rather, it is exhibiting "Joneseness," looking and acting like Jones. Identity is not located in an entity but in a set of properties — an essence. It does not inhere in a subject but in a set of predicates. A being which exemplifies "Joneseness" is identical with Jones.

If viable, this theory of identity would solve the problem for all monists. It would not matter that the immediate resurrectionist is forced to posit two bodies, because the instant the earthly being would cease exemplifying "Joneseness," the heavenly being would begin. If having "Joneseness" is a sufficient condition for personal identity, then the two beings are numerically identical. Similarly, the extinction–re-creationist would have no need to show material continuity between the earthly and heavenly bodies. If God created a being who exemplified "Jonesness" even after thousands of years of nonexemplification, that new creation would be the real Jones.

But there are significant doubts about the viability of this solution. The problem has frequently been illustrated by the scenario of multiple replication. What if God created a whole crowd of resurrected persons each of whom perfectly exemplified "Jonesness?" Each of these persons would look, think, and act like Jones. Even more confusing, each would be certain that he is Jones, having all the Jones' memories, commitments, hopes, and an incorrigible sense of self-identity.[21] Each would have an identically strong case for being Jones. But obviously it is impossible that all of them be identical with Jones. At most one could be. All the rest must be deluded. But since all of them are exactly similar in all regards (except bodily location), then if all but possibly one are deluded about being Jones, most probably all are deluded in that belief. Obviously something has gone wrong here.

The issue is the essential uniqueness of persons. All of us know intuitively that we are single individuals and that it is impossible that there be two or more of us. This is a matter of necessity. It doesn't just happen that there is only one of me. It is absolutely impossible that there be more than one. This is part of the essence of being a person. Numerical identity and exact similarity are different properties.

But the necessity of individual uniqueness is exactly what is forfeited in the monist's criterion of identity. Numerical identity is a special case of exact similarity. It is where there just happens to be one of a kind. On this account, multiple replication is a logical possibility. God could make more than one. Of course the monist will argue that this whole idea is

21. Since the content of all of their memories would be identical, like so many prints of the same movie, memory would provide no basis for selecting the real Jones. So while it is true that veridical memories would be a sufficient condition for picking out Jones from the counterfeits, we have no way of telling which memories, if any, are veridical. For there is no continuity between the mind or body which had those experiences and any one of the persons who now claims veridical memory. There is no basis for determining which apparent memories were caused by actual experience and which were not. There is no way of telling which is the original print and which are the copies. As early as Joseph Butler it was pointed out that veridical memory presupposes personal identity and cannot therefore be the basis for it. Cf. Loughlin, pp. 308-309 and 317 n. 24. Nevertheless, monists such as Reichenbach finally base their case on the possibility that having memory-contents of a previous existence is veridical memory. Cf. Reichenbach, pp. 92-95.

foolish and irrelevant, for the God who resurrects his children is not the prankster we have imagined.[22] However, this avoids the issue, which is not about God's faithfulness but the analysis of personal identity. Even if God did not replicate multiple Joneses, the point is that unique individuality is contingent, not necessary, on this view. It would be within God's power to perform multiple replication; it is ontologically possible. And so each of us would just happen to be a single individual at the resurrection, we wouldn't have to be. Individuality would be accidental, not essential to personhood.[23]

A response might be that since uniqueness is essential to persons, it is not logically possible that God perform multiple replication. We have dreamed an impossible dream. God could only create one human with Jonesness at the resurrection even if he wanted more. For Jonesness is not a universal capable of multiple instantiations; it is an individual essence. But this seems rather arbitrary. It is easy to see that God cannot create round squares and married bachelors. Such are impossible "nothings." We can say the words but they are meaningless and inconceivable. The possibility of multiple replication, however, is quite easy to conceptualize. One need only adopt the account of a single resurrection offered by monistic eschatologies and reproduce it a few times. Of course it is true that only one person can have the property of being Jones. But it seems intuitive that lots of people could fully exemplify Jonesness. Each Volkswagen Beetle is an essential individual, but Wolfsburg has produced lots of exactly similar ones. Denying the possibility of multiple replication seems to be special pleading. So perhaps that unique property of being Jones is not identical with the conglomeration of Jones-like properties after all.

In conflating numerical identity and exact similarity the monist has also confused ontic and epistemic issues. Being the self-identical human being is one thing; being recognized or identified as that human being is another. Ordinarily we are justified in thinking that persons who look the same are self-identical. It never occurs to me to doubt that my mother is herself even though I have not seen her in months. Usually being recogniz-

---

22. Cf. Reichenbach, p. 95.

23. Davis, p. 338, attempts to solve the problem of identity by adding God's intention that Jones be Jones to Jones's exemplifying Jonesness. I certainly agree with Davis that "God's will is the glue of the universe," but I don't see how this makes uniqueness an essential rather than an accidental property or why it is plausible to think that God intends to conflate numerical identity and exact similarity.

able is sufficient to warrant the judgment of identity. But there are those hard cases where this does not hold. An amnesiac who became disfigured would not know his own identity and would not be recognized by his old acquaintances. Here recognition and identifiability fail, but this is the numerically identical person nonetheless. Conversely, a striking look-alike trained to imitate an absent person and then hypnotized to believe he is that person would meet all the conditions of first- and third-person identifiability, but not be the same person at all. There is an important distinction between being identified as Jones and being Jones. But the monist must consider the latter a case of the former.

This is not merely a philosophical problem. It is existential for those children of the Lord who have been severely handicapped both mentally and physically during this life and for those who have died in infancy or been aborted. When they are raised by God on the Last Day they will be made whole. No longer will they suffer the deformities or loss of possibilities which crippled them. But in these cases resurrection will involve such a radical transformation that even their parents will not recognize them. And they are too severely undeveloped to have any sense of self-identity. So no one will know who they are. But if numerical identity is just defined as being similar enough to an earthly person to trigger first- and third-person recognition, these folks will not be the numerically identical human beings who existed on earth. That implication is not just false, it is cruel. No one will defend it. The monist could again appeal to God's intention that they be identical. But that once more begs the question of identity in the first place.

When the tale is told, the monist's attempts to solve the problem of personal identity at the resurrection are tenuous at best. I know of no one who claims to have given a definitive solution. Many philosophers have concluded that monism is simply incapable of an adequate response.[24]

---

24. Cf. Loughlin, pp. 315-316: "The idea that a replica is or could be the same person as its original, when the original is conceived as a mentating material entity, does not make good and coherent sense. . . . It is thus to be hoped that the replica theory may be laid to rest, and left undisturbed." Loughlin does not endorse an alternative, although he recognizes that dualism provides one. The impossibility of a solution leads Peter Carruthers in a much more wild and sinister direction: "we ought to think in terms which will allow a person to survive as two distinct people; and the fact that we presently employ a concept of survival which implies identity, is an error." Cf. *Introducing Persons: Theories and Arguments in the Philosophy of Mind* (Albany: State University of New York Press, 1986), p. 218. Some people will stop at nothing to hold on to monism.

Even the most optimistic monists judge their answers to be no more than possible solutions. What they claim, in other words, amounts to this: while it is possible or plausible or reasonable to think that re-created persons are identical with their earthly prototypes, it is also possible that they are not.[25]

If this much optimism is warranted, this is a useful apologetic contribution for defending against charges that the truth of monism inevitably renders belief in an afterlife incoherent or that Christian monists are necessarily irrational. Even if anthropological monism or holism is true, in other words, Christian eschatology is not necessarily false. That is worth knowing. And often this is as much as the Christian use of reason can manage, demonstrating the coherence of Christian belief but not its truth.

There is still a problem, however. For the monist's defense of the possibility of personal identity is not exactly like defending the possibility that God exists or that Jesus Christ is the Second Person of the Trinity incarnate, beliefs we know to be true from Scripture and defend by reason. The monist's defense is more like taking the truth that Jesus loves me, analyzing it, and coming to the conclusion that possibly Jesus loves me, although possibly he does not. For the monistic account can raise reasonable doubts even in the minds of believers that we are really the same persons at the resurrection. The certainty of biblical revelation is somehow diminished by the analysis.

That is the bad news. The good news is that there is a more comforting way of construing the Christian faith about the afterlife. There is a way of moving beyond the meager hope that possibly the person who dwells forever with the Lord will be oneself. If a theory of the resurrection which guarantees one's presence is preferred, I recommend anthropological dualism.

V. Conclusion

Previous chapters have made the case that the intermediate state and the anthropological dualism it implies are the most defensible interpretation

---

25. According to Reichenbach, p. 95, "it would seem most reasonable to conclude that he can be and probably is identical with the deceased." Davis, p. 340, can do no more than conclude that personal identity has not been disproven.

of the personal eschatology taught in Scripture. In itself that should provide sufficient reason for Christians to endorse these positions. This chapter has strengthened the case for the superiority of dualism in other ways. We have shown that most immediate resurrection theories actually entail dualism, not monism as is commonly supposed. And it has been demonstrated that dualism fully accounts for the self-identity of persons in the afterlife, whereas the best any monistic theory can do is argue for the reasonable possibility of personal identity. At worst monism may entail nonidentity. This would seem to be a relevant consideration in the final evaluation of the monism-dualism debate.

Chapter Nine

Practical and Theological
Objections against Dualism

I. Introduction: The Case Is Not Completely Closed

If it is true that anthropological dualism is implied by the Bible and is conceptually superior to monism as an account of the afterlife, why should anyone hesitate a moment to embrace it? What possible objections remain to give one pause? The fact is that a number of other significant arguments against dualism have been raised. Defending monism is not just a matter of stubborn prejudice. If the dualist is to emerge triumphant in this debate with the monist, he will need to defend his flanks against these assaults as well.

Some problems which thoughtful people have raised against dualism have already been addressed. A major charge is that dualism is an imposition of Greek philosophy and Hellenistic religion on Christian anthropology which distorts the biblical picture of human nature. Our defense has been that dualism is implicit in the biblical account of what happens at death, that the New Testament employs an anthropology already developed in Judaism and rooted in the Old Testament. This anthropology superficially resembles Hellenistic views in that it, too, affirms personal survival of death, but its functional holism and affirmation of bodily existence set it sharply against them. Affirming dualism does not commit one to endorsing Greek thought or claiming that the New Testament has been shaped by Hellenistic religion. It is maintaining something inherently biblical.

A second objection already answered focuses on the relation between

179

Scripture and philosophical anthropology. Some argue that since the Bible is not a theory book or even concerned with theoretical questions, it cannot teach dualism. To infer anthropological dualism from Scripture is to engage in unjustifiable speculation. In response we have endorsed the nontheoretical nature of the biblical message and denied that it teaches a philosophical anthropology. Instead we have insisted that Scripture presents a nontheoretical, "commonsense" vision of the afterlife which nevertheless has ontological presuppositions and implications. We have argued that it is legitimate and nonspeculative to identify these assumptions and to make inferences from the teachings of Scripture using the laws of logic. Finally, we have claimed that the framework of beliefs necessarily connected with the teachings of Scripture ought to govern a Christian philosophy of human nature. So although Scripture does not teach philosophy, it provides a normative framework for a Christian anthropology. And this turns out to require some sort of ontic duality or dualism.

Thus two important objections to dualism have been given respectable answers. But there are a number of other tough questions and alternative suggestions which a traditional Christian anthropology must face up to. In this chapter we will identify some of the hard questions put to dualism by theologians and practitioners of Christianity. In a study of this sort it will be impossible to answer them exhaustively. But unless an initial response outlining a reasonable answer is provided, the dualist position will remain open to charges of inadequacy serious and numerous enough that judges of the debate might award a draw to monism after all.

II. Objection One:
Dualism Undermines Christian Orthopraxis[1]

A. The Problem

In the opening chapter we saw that an important reason why many Christians have an aversion to anthropological dualism — a veritable "dualophobia" — is their suspicion that an ontic body-soul distinction inevitably leads to other dualisms and dichotomies which not only conflict

---

1. Cf. John Cooper, "Dualism and the Biblical View of Human Beings (2)," *Reformed Journal*, Vol. 32 (October 1982), pp. 16-18, for an earlier discussion of this objection.

with the biblical view of human nature, but are downright harmful to people. Traditional anthropology undermines Christian orthopraxis. Theologians have linked body-soul dualism to a nature-grace or sacred-secular dualism which views part of human life as religiously neutral, thereby cutting it loose from the claims of the gospel and the Kingdom. Ministers have charged the body-soul distinction with promoting intellectualism in theology and quietism in the lives of ordinary Christians. Evangelists and missiologists have claimed that anthropological dualism has led to a truncated witness of the gospel — saving souls without ministering to whole human beings in their life-contexts. Liberation theologians are convinced that traditional anthropology is implicated in fostering an individualistic, spiritualized Christianity which has nothing to contribute to the practical quest for social justice. Educators trace the negative features of traditional curriculum and pedagogical methods to the body-soul distinction — the fact that children were allegedly treated as pure intellects and made to memorize a lot of abstractions irrelevant to life. Traditional anthropology has been suspected of blinding psychologists and physicians alike to the psychosomatic dynamics of bodily and emotional illnesses. The list of problems blamed on dualistic anthropology could be expanded. But the point has been made. There is a deep concern among some Christians that belief in the intermediate state is harmful because it leads to conditions and practices which conflict with the biblical vision of what human life ought to be. Faithfulness to Scripture therefore demands the abandonment of dualistic anthropology.

The response to this objection is not difficult but will require some discussion to spell out. What we must show is that there are no necessary connections between the body-soul distinction and this catalogue of false dichotomies. In fact, some who hold a traditional anthropology have been the most heroic in combating them. And some who boast a monistic anthropology have been guilty of supporting them.

In order to elaborate this defense clearly it is necessary to make some distinctions, since a wide variety of very different dualisms, dichotomies, and otherwise objectionable separations have been lumped together and the whole batch has been associated with the body-soul distinction. This has left the appearance of a strong cumulative case for the evil consequences of dualistic anthropology and has generated untold confusion. Many have concluded that the body-soul distinction must be rejected. To straighten out this muddled situation we must distinguish at least four kinds of dualism besides the anthropological variety which has been the center of our attention: religious, axiological, functional, and social.

B. Religious Dualism

The body-soul distinction has often been faulted for conducing to an illegitimate division of life into two separate areas: those which are religious or spiritual and those which are not. We will call this sort of division "religious dualism." One example is the modern sacred-secular dichotomy, which many Protestant scholars have argued is a direct descendant of the nature-grace distinction of medieval theology, which they take as another example.[2] In this sort of dualism, religion pertains to the spiritual or supernatural realm and consists of theological beliefs, personal piety, and personal morality. But other aspects of life are said to be "natural" and "religiously neutral." As such they can be properly understood and successfully practiced without reference to special divine revelation or the principles of God's coming Kingdom. Thus science, philosophy, business, politics, art, and culture are considered inherently secular pursuits which can be engaged in on a common basis by Christians and non-Christians. Distinctively Christian principles have no bearing on the internal formation of these enterprises, only on the moral and religious uses and disuses they might have. Faith is external to these important human activities.

Twin dangers lurk in religious dualism. On one hand, Christians may overlook points at which biblical principles and the transforming power of the gospel can be brought to bear on important human activities. On the other, Christians might be blind to the ways in which these allegedly neutral areas are actually being shaped by un-Christian principles. By relying uncritically on what is historically available in academia, political opinion, economic values, business practices, popular culture, and lifestyle options, Christians may unwittingly surrender to the kingdom of this world areas which Christ has claimed. Religious dualism would therefore lead to unholy alliances.

Caution must be exercised in identifying and evaluating religious du-

2. Cf. Arvin Vos, *Aquinas, Calvin, and Contemporary Protestant Thought* (Grand Rapids: Eerdmans, 1985), pp. 124-133.

alism, however. As H. Richard Niebuhr's classic, *Christ and Culture*, reminds us, since the early church Christians have simply disagreed on the extent to which conversion to Christ puts one out of harmony with the rest of the fallen world. We have not all discerned the frontier between the kingdom of Christ and the kingdom of darkness in the same place. One tradition's illegitimate dualism is another's radical obedience. Furthermore, it is often difficult to determine just where genuine faith can make a difference and where it cannot. Christians and non-Christians all digest food, do arithmetic, and speak American English the same ways. But they operate quite differently in other regards. The line between what is legitimately common and what ought to be transformed by one's commitment to Christ is sometimes an exceedingly difficult one to discern.

Nevertheless, there is an appropriate concern that neither the Christian community nor the public at large illegitimately cut off important areas of human existence from their religious and spiritual roots either in theory or in practice. This sort of secularistic dichotomy is what I am calling "religious dualism." In defining it as illegitimate, I am agreeing with all those who believe it is a bad thing.

But where did religious dualism come from and what must be done to eliminate it? Already in Chapter One we encountered those who claim that a nature-grace or sacred-secular dichotomy in life and culture is incriminatingly linked to the traditional body-soul dualism. On this assumption, since the former must go, so must the latter.

In response it would be foolish to deny that some anthropological dualists have been religious dualists. Some who defend the intermediate state have endorsed the secularization of life. But it is hard to see why there is a causal connection between the two. Why should believing that I will be with Christ from death until bodily resurrection lead me to think that politics or intellectual activity or anything else in this life is religiously neutral? The idea that true religion does not reshape certain aspects of individual or cultural existence might presuppose a doctrine of common grace or a view about the extent of the fall's corruption of creation or an account of the image of God remaining in sinful human nature. It might involve a certain position on the relations among common sense, reason, and revelation. It perhaps assumes a certain understanding of the Kingdom of God and the kingdom of Satan. But it is hard to see how anything at all connected with the body-soul debate is involved. One could link an autonomous view of reason or too optimistic a prognosis of the fallen image of

God with the notion of a separable soul. But these positions could be held by a monist as well. The point is clear. Nothing in anthropological dualism per se in any way promotes an illegitimate nature-grace or sacred-secular distinction. Causally linking them is a straightforward case of a non-sequitur argument. Not the separability of the soul, but the extent of its fallenness is relevant to religious dualism. The solution to the problem is thus to find the correct view of creation, fall, and redemption, not to deny the possibility of the intermediate state.

In fact anthropological dualists have been among the most vigorous transformers of culture in the history of Christianity. Consider Calvin and the Reformed tradition, for example. Few historians would dispute the fact that Calvinism has self-consciously undertaken to shape society and culture according to its understanding of biblical principles. It has raged against rationalistic secularism. Its impact has been formidable. But John Calvin, the New England Puritans, Westminster Confession Presbyterians, and the Dutch Neo-Calvinists Kuyper and Bavinck have all affirmed the doctrine of the intermediate state and the anthropological dualism it entails. Whatever the sociocultural sins of this tradition, they have not been motivated by a body-soul distinction.

Furthermore, past and present history offers many examples of Christians and non-Christians who boast monistic-holistic anthropologies and also promote the secularization of worldly existence. Some of the radical Anabaptists and John Dewey are very different examples of holists who believe that religion ought not to shape public affairs.

My point is neither to praise Calvinism nor to criticize the Anabaptist tradition. It is, rather, to point out the lack of determinism between views of the body-soul distinction and the issue of religious dualism. There is no necessary connection either logically or historically. So repudiating anthropological dualism is neither necessary nor sufficient for eliminating religious dualism.

C. Axiological Dualism

The body-soul distinction has often been blamed for the tendency of historical Christianity to postulate a polarity of value within the created order itself. In a variety of ways Christians have considered some dimensions of life to be intrinsically more worthy than other dimensions which, if not downright evil, are clearly inferior. This illegitimate polarization or hierarchy of value or worth within creation is "axiological dualism."

If there is evidence of Hellenistic religion and Greek philosophy in Christian views of human life, it is here. The Orphic cults, the Gnostics, and Platonic philosophers all embraced a worldview in which matter and spirit or the material and the ideal are in metaphysical antipathy to each other. Matter is the principle of chaos, disharmony, decay, imperfection, and irrationality. The realm of the ideal and spiritual is just the opposite — rational, harmonious, perfect, and eternal. Since the human soul is from one realm and the body from the other, there is an essential contradiction built into human nature itself which can only be resolved by transcending one of the antithetical dimensions. Salvation is attained when the soul is wholly freed from the influence of the body and the material world. The means of salvation might be provided by religious practice or philosophical contemplation. In either case, attaining salvation required striving to overcome the encumbrances of bodiliness already in this life. Asceticism and the devaluation of participation in ordinary worldly existence are implications of this ethic. Undeniably, Hellenistic thought propounds an anthropological dualism which is also an axiological dualism.

The fact that there is evidence of axiological dualism within traditional Christianity may be an indication that elements of the Hellenistic worldview were uncritically adopted. Although the church fathers polemicized against Gnosticism, it is not difficult to find passages in their writings which are reminiscent of the anticorporeal biases of their pagan contemporaries. A low view of sexuality and a tendency toward asceticism can be found in as intelligent and culturally aware a Christian as Augustine. The flavor of axiological dualism can still be discerned in the attitudes of some contemporary Christians. In subtle ways we consider the soul superior and the body inferior. Some people who are morally and spiritually fastidious disdain physical fitness. In some circles ministers, doctors, and professors are still esteemed more than plumbers and farmers simply because they are highly educated and work primarily with their minds rather than with their hands. There are Christians who regard the world not just as secular, but as "dirty" and not a proper place for the involvement of a truly spiritual person. Regarding sex, we may all ridicule stereotypical Victorian morality, but there are still millions of Christians who have emotional difficulty with the idea that a good orgasm is a possible way of glorifying God. There are traces of dualism in the Calvinistic circles of my youth regarding Sabbath observance. The nonreligious mental game of chess was permissible on Sunday afternoon, but the nonreligious physical game of baseball was not. Examples of axiological dualism in the attitudes and practices of traditional Christians could be multiplied at length. It is undeniable that we have operated in terms of value hierarchies and polarities tied to the body-soul distinction.

What is deniable is the claim that axiological dualism is necessarily correlative with anthropological dualism. Some Greek monists were as ascetic as the dualists. And there is nothing in the simple belief that persons exist temporarily without bodies which makes bodies less valuable. It is the ontological dualism of matter against spirit in the Hellenistic worldview which led to an axiological dualism in its anthropology. But we have argued repeatedly that the body-soul distinction of the biblical worldview positively rules out axiological dualism. The Bible suggests a holistic dualism. Scripture emphasizes the goodness of bodily life as God created it. It tells us that bodily life can be enjoyed and lived to God's glory even in this fallen world. And it frequently depicts God's coming Kingdom and our future existence in worldly, bodily ways. Even Paul's antithesis of flesh against spirit is not a form of Hellenistic dualism, but refers to life as a whole either in Christ or outside of him. Furthermore, Jews and Christians who believe in the intermediate state regard it as an ontologically deficient mode of existence precisely because bodiliness is essential to existence as God created it. Resurrection of the body, not the immortality of the soul, has been the biblically based confession of most of the Christian tradition since early times. All of this is quite foreign to the anticorporeal anthropology and ethics of Hellenistic thought. Clearly the biblical worldview embraces anthropological dualism without axiological dualism. One need not abandon the former in rejecting the latter.

Even in diagnosing axiological dualism within the tradition we must be careful, for it could very well be that much Christian asceticism was and still is motivated not by an anticorporeal ontology, but by a certain ethic of the Kingdom. Self-denial and noninvolvement in broader culture are not always symptomatic of the belief that bodiliness is intrinsically inferior, but that some things are more important than others if one is to seek first the Kingdom of God. Paul himself advised that although all things are lawful, not all are expedient. Bodily exercise is beneficial, but not as central as other pursuits for Christians living in a fallen world. And sometimes the world is so anti-Christian that disciples of Christ ought not to participate in its activities and organizations. Should a Christian participate in Soviet politics if that requires membership in the Communist Party? Developing a hierarchy of values, deciding on priorities in one's life, denying oneself, nonparticipation in worldly activities — none of this automatically indicates an axiological dualism. It could be fully compatible with the holistic dualism of biblical anthropology. Once again we see that there is no connection between a body-soul distinction and a pernicious form of dualism.

D. Functional Dualism

This third category of dualism includes a wide variety of views which consider some kinds of human functions and capacities in isolation from others. Certain dimensions of life are "compartmentalized," abstracted, and treated as if they were independent of and uninfluenced by others. The intellect or reason has been a favorite for privileged status. It has been treated as though it functions unaffected by religion, the emotions, various personal and social interests, and culture or as if these influences are regrettable accidents of ordinary human life which can be overcome through proper education and self-discipline. But functional dualism can be found in many other places as well. Religion has been treated in isolation from reason and social-cultural dynamics. Some psychotherapies have attempted to treat individuals in isolation from their family and social groups. Others fail to consider organic factors in emotional disorders. Economists have viewed the behavior of individuals and social structures as mere producer-consumers, not attending to the complexity of human motivation. Educators have attempted to teach children without regard to their psychological development. Missionaries have preached the gospel oblivious to crucial cultural differences. Examples of functional dualism are myriad and can be found in virtually every discipline, theoretical or practical.

Functional dualism sets up another mistake. It allows one dimension of life to be accorded an absolute or definitive status while the importance of others is underappreciated. The intellect has been a favorite for privileged status. Many traditional theologians and philosophers have focused on rationality as the essence or defining feature of human nature, ignoring the affections, bodiliness, and sociality. But the genes, instincts, pleasures,

187

economic interests, social ties, and practically everything else under the sun have been given determinative status in human life by some school of thought. Each of them gives a one-sided picture of human nature which proceeds by isolating one dimension of life from its embeddedness within the whole.

But what does all of this have to do with anthropological dualism? In the first place, many of these dichotomies have little relation to the body-soul distinction. Intellect, emotions, will, and spiritual orientation are all capacities of the soul. Separating them is dividing the soul itself, not dichotomizing soul and body. Abstracting individuals from their interpersonal, social, economic, cultural, and political contexts can certainly be damaging, but what possible connection does this mistake have with the body-soul distinction? It turns out that many functional dichotomies have nothing to do with anthropological dualism.

A second response is that there is nothing inherent in anthropological dualism as such which makes it incompatible with a holistic view of life. Holism and dualism address different questions. Holism — the functional holism we have discussed — emphasizes that during this life body, mind, and spirit are functionally integrated and constitute an existential unity. Dualism claims that persons can survive and function in some ways apart from organisms. Scripture seems to affirm both holism and dualism. So why suppose that dualism unavoidably generates functional dichotomies?

Of course it is true that traditional theologians defined the soul as primarily rational, a possible instance of functional dualism. But this could have been done without positing its separability from the body. Conversely, it is possible to hold the soul's separability without defining it rationalistically or ignoring how the intellect interrelates with other aspects of human existence.

There is also the infamous Descartes, whose dualism views mind and body as functionally self-contained entities which interact externally at a single point in the pineal gland. This is the paradigm case of an anthropological-functional dualism. But Descartes fully recognized that phenomenologically body and mind appear to be a unity within which the distinction is hard to discern. His anthropology was based on philosophical reasoning, not existential phenomenology. And since he worked with the science of his day, it can be argued that had he known more about brain physiology and physiological psychology, his account of physical-mental interaction would have been much wider in scope.

188

In any case, why suppose that Descartes's definition of body and mind is the only possible formulation of dualism? Why suppose that anthropological dualism must entail functional dualism? After all, the biblical view includes both dualism and functional holism, as do the anthropologies of most pre-theoretical peoples. The Thomistic tradition has provided a theoretical anthropology which is holistic and yet allows for the separate existence of the soul. And as we will indicate in the next chapter, there are contemporary dualists who fully recognize the functional interdependence of body and soul in normal human life. Thus while it is true that some anthropological dualists have championed some forms of functional dualism, it is simply false that most functional dualisms are rooted in a body-soul or body-mind distinction and that an anthropological dualist is unavoidably committed to functional dualism. There is no necessary connection between them.

Furthermore, there is no guarantee that anthropological monism will automatically generate a proper holistic model of human beings. Spinoza, Hegel, Marx, Freud, Dewey, and Skinner are just a few major thinkers who have monistic anthropologies and who nevertheless end up isolating and overemphasizing one aspect of existence while reducing the roles of the rest. There is simply no reason to believe that denying the separability of body and soul will avoid dichotomizing human existence.

Finally, Christians ought to exercise caution before baptizing generic functional holism for at least two reasons. First, although many aspects of human life are interconnected, neither science nor phenomenology yields the conclusion that every structure and function of existence is causally connected with every other one. It is not clear, for example, that one's particular genetic makeup has an important influence on one's religious beliefs or certainty that *modus ponens* is reliable, or that these mental states influence the speed of neural impulses. Some subsystems of existence are more autonomous than others. There are links between some, but apparently not between others. Science does not justify an unqualified functional holism.

A second reason for caution about holism: it is no more distinctively biblical than dualism is distinctively Greek. In fact, it has become a shibboleth of some very unbiblical spirits of this age, as the ideological holism of the New Age movement will demonstrate.

In conclusion, although some anthropological dualists have championed some forms of functional dualism, it is simply false that most functional dualisms are rooted in the body-soul distinction and that anthropological dualism per se inclines its adherents toward functional dualism.

E. Social Dualism

Among the sins in which anthropological dualism is allegedly implicated are the illegitimate separation and devaluation of certain groups of people. This can be labelled "social dualism." Its most blatant examples are classism, sexism, and racism. Victims and critics of these evils have justifiably lashed out at their perpetrators. But they have also charged that the body-soul distinction has been an agent of oppression. For a standard rationalization for the subjection of the exploited group has been that they lack fully human souls. Historically some white males have claimed that women, Black Africans, and American Indians lack rational souls. Since the body-soul distinction has been a tool of oppression, these critics argue that it ought to be destroyed.

It is our duty to condemn all forms of social dualism as unjust and unChristian. But it is not easy to make this charge against anthropological dualism stand up. The problem here is not that souls are thought to survive bodily death, but that certain kinds of people are said to lack them. So the solution is not to deny that people have separable souls, but to affirm that all people possess them to the very same degree. It is the prejudice of social dualism which leads to claims that some people lack souls. The reverse is not true. Affirming that souls are separable has nothing to do with any form of social dualism. Racism, sexism, and classism thrive just as readily among monists. Rejecting anthropological dualism because it has been used as a tool of oppression is like throwing away a hammer because someone's finger was hit. The fault lies elsewhere.

F. Conclusion

In its most basic form, anthropological dualism is simply the view that human nature is so constituted that persons are beings who can survive organic death. While some formulations of this position have been connected with illegitimate religious, axiological, functional, and social dualisms, these connections are accidental and can easily be avoided. Iden-

190

tification of these sorts of dualisms with one another exemplifies the crudest form of equivocation. It is perfectly possible to affirm the intermediate state and at the same time to hold that religion permeates human life, that all aspects of existence and all kinds of people are created good and have full value, and that life as we live it is a complex unity of interrelated functions. The compatibility of all these assertions is not merely an abstract possibility. Many Christians down through the ages have actually held them all without any hint of intellectual bad faith.

We set out from the objection that anthropological dualism is strongly inclined toward various sorts of unbiblical, life-distorting dichotomies — that traditional orthodoxy undermines orthopraxis. That charge turns out to be false. The diagnosis fusing illicit dualisms with the body-soul distinction is mistaken. Some traditional Christian anthropologists do avoid false dichotomies. And some monist-holists perpetuate them. Now if the diagnosis is mistaken, so is the prescribed cure. It is not necessary to give up anthropological dualism. And giving it up will not eliminate false dichotomies.

III. Objection Two:
At Death We Pass out of Time;
There Is No Intermediate State

The main pillar on which our case for dualism rests is the claim that New Testament eschatology teaches a sequence of an intermediate state and resurrection. There is an interval, a period of time between death and resurrection, during which persons exist without bodies. But this presupposes that the dead remain on the same time-line as the living, that eschatological time is historical time.

It has often been suggested that this view of time is mistaken. When we die, we depart from the spatio-temporal conditions which are the constitutive framework of the physical world. We are no longer in time, but pass into eternity. So the question of time between death and resurrection is irrelevant and meaningless.[3] Both the intermediate-state and extinc-

---

3. I am ignoring a popular weaker version of this argument which I sometimes hear from the pulpit or in discussion groups — that we no longer *experience* time and thus that the problem of disembodied existence does not arise. This strategy focuses on our experi-

BODY, SOUL, AND LIFE EVERLASTING

tion–re-creation eschatologies allegedly presuppose an improper view of time and eternity. If this is true, then our entire argument has been built on a foundation of sand — a naive assumption about time. The case for dualism crumbles. Or does it?

Whoever follows this strategy must move in either of two directions on final eschatology. Either he must suppose that the second coming of Christ and the renewal of creation are events in future earthly history which Christ will bring about by once again leaving eternity and breaking into time, or he must hold that the resurrection, judgment, parousia, and new creation are ever-present eternal realities which become real for us when we transcend time at the moment of our death.

The first option is no help. In fact, it is self-defeating, for although in eternity there is no time between one's death and resurrection at the second coming, there certainly is a temporal interval in earthly history between those two events. Someone dies in 1988 and is resurrected when Christ returns in 2056, let's say. The question about this person's condition in the meantime is perfectly intelligible. It is the question of the intermediate state. Fumbling to define it according to this theory, one would have to say it is a temporarily timeless disembodied existence, or something like that. Obviously this has neither avoided nor helped to solve the problematics of eschatology and anthropology.

What of the other option, that resurrection, the second coming, and the new heaven and earth are eternally present realities accessible to each individual in the time-transcending event of death? The first thing to notice about this objection is that it amounts to an argument for immediate resurrection. The other two theories are excluded because they hold that the resurrection will be a future historical event. So the proponent of the timelessness at death account must be able to live with some version of an immediate resurrection. Now as we demonstrated above, many immediate resurrectionists are dualists, whether they admit it or not. Those who propose an immediate spiritual resurrection, acknowledging that the earthly body and all embodiment is permanently transcended, usually embrace dualism without embarrassment. Of those who insist on a new body im-

---

ence, not on what is actually the case. In so doing it evades the problem rather than solving it. For if we do not experience time, it can be because (1) we are in eternity; (2) we are extinct for a time; or (3) we exist for a time without being aware of it. Those who employ this tactic either must pick one of these options or they have nothing to say on this question. It is a non-solution.

mediately upon death, at least some recognize the dualism implied by the switch in bodies. Of those who offer a consistently monistic account of immediate resurrection, few have squarely faced the problem of personal identity. So after the dust of the time-eternity objection has settled, we find the dualistic anthropology still standing.

But what about this objection itself? Is it biblical to hold that resurrection, parousia, and the new creation are eternal realities? This is a question to which numerous learned volumes have been devoted. I shall not attempt to enter the debate. I simply record my opinion, argued in previous chapters, that the writers of the New Testament clearly believed that Christ's return and the advent of the new heaven and earth are future historical events, not realities already actual in the transcendent eternal now. As Revelation 21 envisions it, the New Jerusalem, which does already exist with God, will descend from heaven to the new earth, where the Lord will dwell with his people forever. That teaching ought to stand as normative unless, like certain cosmological beliefs of those writers, it can be shown to be culturally relative or "merely metaphorical." But viewing Christ's return as a future historical event is not like viewing heaven as "up" — imaginatively valid but literally false. Nothing in philosophy or science has rendered a historical second coming either unlikely or conceptually impossible. Future eschatology is part of the biblical view of reality and ought not too easily be jettisoned in favor of some other worldview. And if the last things are historically future, the question of the meantime has not been avoided.

In fact the time-eternity distinction itself has come under scrutiny from various quarters during the past several decades. Cullmann's *Christ and Time* and Barr's *Biblical Words for Time* have led the way for biblical scholars.[4] Philosophers and theologians have also raised questions. Does the Bible represent God as eternal, that is, literally nontemporal, or everlasting, that is, enduring for all times without beginning or end? Process thinkers are not the only ones who have argued for God's temporality against classical theism's Greek notion of divine eternity. Nicholas Wolterstorff, a Calvinist, has argued that biblically and philosophically it makes more sense to think of God as everlasting than as eternal.[5] If this is correct, then even God himself is

---

4. Oscar Cullmann, *Christ and Time* (London: SCM, 1951, 1964); James Barr, *Biblical Words for Time* (London: SCM, 1962, 1969).

5. Nicholas Wolterstorff, "God Everlasting," in C. Orlebeke and L. Smedes, eds., *God and the Good: Essays in Honor of Henry Stob* (Grand Rapids: Eerdmans, 1975), pp. 181-203.

not wholly timeless, much less those of his human creatures who have departed this earthly vale of tears. Of course, the traditional Boethian view of eternity has its competent defenders as well.

But even if God in himself is atemporal and time is something he created, why should we think that we humans share that timelessness when we die? Isn't that attributing a divine property to a mere creature? Aren't we essentially temporal beings, dead or alive? Furthermore, is time a dimension only of the physical universe? Why absolutize Einstein's correlation of time and space? Why would time not remain even if matter and space passed away? Could nonphysical beings experience no boredom, no memory, no communication, and no hope or anticipation? But all these mental states require simultaneity and succession, before and after. They are essentially temporal.

When all is considered, therefore, the notion that there is such a state as eternity and that humans enter it at death is itself quite open to debate. Thus, appealing to the time-eternity distinction to embarrass those who hold to the intermediate state and anthropological dualism is a ploy which might backfire.

IV. Objection Three:
The Whole Person Does Not Die

A frequent objection to dualism is the charge that it limits death to the body. Persons do not really die, only their bodies do. The soul, self, ego, or person survives the death of the organism and is in that sense immortal, that is, not-dying. As Reichenbach puts this objection, "since the soul is not subject to death, no individual person ever dies."[6]

The problems with this implication are both philosophical and theological. Philosophically it seems counterintuitive and defies our ordinary way of speaking about death. Ordinarily we assert that persons do die. "John Smith" is the name of a person, a self, not just of a body. But it is John Smith who dies, and that is exactly what we say. Dualism, however, denies that the person John Smith dies. So dualism contradicts ordinary language and experience, according to this line of attack.[7]

6. Bruce Reichenbach, *Is Man the Phoenix?* (Grand Rapids: Eerdmans, 1983), p. 52.
7. Reichenbach, pp. 53-54.

There are also alleged incompatibilities with Christian theology. In implying that persons do not die, dualism contradicts the clear biblical assertions that "in Adam all die" (I Cor. 15:22) and that "it is appointed to man once to die" (Heb. 9:27). Furthermore, if persons do not die, then the person Jesus Christ did not die and we remain in our sins.[8] Finally, since the whole person has sinned against God, the whole person must die, not just the body.[9]

What is there for the dualist to say in response? The best answer is simply to point out that these objections beg the question. They all assume that dying must mean going out of existence. If the soul does not cease to exist, the person has not died. But that is precisely what the debate is all about: what happens when we die. These objections are real challenges only if the monistic-holistic extinction theory is the true account of death. Otherwise they present no insurmountable obstacle for dualism.

The Christian dualist holds that death is the unnatural separation of the person from bodily life. Whether traumatic or desirable, painful or pleasant, dying is making the transition from this life to the next, breaking earthly and bodily connections and inheriting a new set. Whatever this is like, that is what death is for the dualist. Human persons — psychophysical unities during life — are dichotomized at death, but nonetheless are held in existence by God.

In this way the philosophical objection from common sense is completely blunted. Extinction is not what the dualist means when she says, "John Smith died." She does not deny that the whole person, John Smith, died. She just means that he was torn from natural bodily life to enter another mode of existence. If that is what death is, then she is speaking quite correctly. Appeal to "common sense" would work only if all people were monists, and many are not. For many of the world's peoples, "John Smith died" means something dualistic.

The same response should work against the theological objections. The dualist has no trouble accepting that Scripture teaches personal mortality. He does not deny that Jesus died. He just thinks of death differently than the monist — not as extinction — and even claims to have solid bibli-

---

8. Reichenbach, p. 54; cf. also Oscar Cullmann, "Immortality or Resurrection," in *Immortality and Resurrection* (New York: Macmillan, 1965), p. 63.

9. Cf. G. C. Berkouwer, *Man: The Image of God* (Grand Rapids: Eerdmans, 1962), pp. 250-254, for a discussion of this "fruitful" argument in contemporary theology.

cal reasons for doing so. Of course people die. Of course death is the wage of sin. The issue once again is the definition of death. If it is extinction, the dualist is in trouble. If it is personal separation from earthly existence, the monist is. While God could have annihilated people as punishment for sin, he chose instead to remove them from earthly life. That is death, and it is undergone by the whole person. It is not that the body dies and the soul or person continues to exist as if nothing happened. That would indeed be a case of trivializing death. However, the dualist can list as many negative things about death as the monist, short of extinction.

Finally, if the monist wishes to accuse the dualist of denying that Jesus really died — a serious heresy — he should be prepared to show how his own theory avoids heresy. For if Jesus was extinct between Good Friday and Easter, then some doctrinally illicit separation took place, either of the divine and human natures or perhaps even of two implicitly hypostatized persons, one divine and one human.[10] In short, the objection that dualism takes death less seriously than monism begs the question. The dualist can meet this challenge easily.

V. Objection Four:
An Immortal Soul Is Postulated

Closely related to the previous discussion is the issue of the soul's immortality. The dualist is often charged with defending this position as though that by itself were proof of his wrongheadedness. After all, it is said, the Greeks are the ones who taught the immortality of the soul. The Bible proclaims the resurrection of the body. Moreover, Plato thought that the soul is inherently or necessarily immortal, whereas the Bible teaches that the whole human being — soul and body — is radically dependent on God for existence. Doesn't affirming the intermediate state commit one to Platonism after all?

This objection calls for a number of responses. Some have to do with definitions of terms. If "immortality" means "not dying," then the dualist would deny that the soul possesses it. For we just pointed out that souls do undergo death, although that does not involve their extinction. If immor-

---

10. Cf. Chapter Six above in connection with Jesus' location between Good Friday and Easter.

tality simply means "surviving physical death," then the dualist does think of the soul or person as immortal. But this does not automatically indicate illegitimate reliance on Greek philosophy. For we have made the case that it is a biblical teaching.[11]

This immediately suggests another response. The choice between continuous personal existence ("immortality of the soul") and resurrection is a false dilemma. The "either-or" which some wish to force into the discussion is illegitimate. The New Testament affirms both. Thus the famous essay of Oscar Cullmann, "Immortality of the Soul or Resurrection of the Dead," may have a point for those Christians who are Platonists and believe in everlasting disembodiment. But the title does not express an exclusive disjunction between continuous personal existence and extinction until the resurrection, as can be seen from Cullmann's own position. He posits an intermediate state for the "inner man," who "sleeps" until Christ's return.

In the third place, affirming continuous personal existence does not necessarily commit one to the soul's inherent or essential immortality. Plato argued that the soul is metaphysically indestructible because it is a simple spiritual substance and cannot therefore undergo decomposition. It is true that some Christians, including Augustine and Thomas Aquinas, have adopted this argument in defending biblical teaching.[12] But no Christian holds that the soul is necessarily immortal, can exist independent of God, or is impervious to destruction by God. Some may think that God created souls as inherently simple substances which are not therefore naturally disposed to disintegration. But these Christians affirm that if the soul is immortal by nature, it has this property as a gift increated by God and is in essence therefore dependent on him. The soul is not an absolute substance, as Plato taught. And many other Christians believe that the soul is no more inherently immortal than the body.[13] They know of nothing about souls or disembodied persons which would naturally tend to keep them in existence. Souls are radically contingent and dependent on God's continuing providence for their very being. Total extinction at death is

11. Cf. Murray Harris, "A Comparison of Immortality in the New Testament with Immortality in Plato," *Raised Immortal* (Grand Rapids: Eerdmans, 1985), pp. 201-206.

12. Cf. Reichenbach, *Phoenix*, Ch. 7, for a fine summary of the philosophical arguments for human immortality.

13. Even the arch-dualist, Descartes, emphasizes the contingent and dependent nature of created human souls. Cf. *Meditations on First Philosophy*, III and V.

thus a very real possibility. It is just that God does not will to destroy people in death completely. He chooses instead to maintain them temporarily in disembodied existence. For all of these reasons, Christian dualists are not committed to the Platonic view of immortality.[14] There is nothing unbiblical about affirming the immortality of the soul in the sense of continuous personal existence between death and resurrection.

VI. Objection Five:
Dualism Is a Result of the Fall;
It Is Not Inherent in Creation

In response to a paper I once read, someone admitted that my case for dualism is well grounded in Scripture, but suggested that dualism is really a result of the fall. It is not how God originally created us. In other words, he was suggesting that monism or holism is really the structure of human nature as God intended it. The metaphysical possibility that persons can survive the disembodiment of death is really a consequence of sin.

This is an ingenious strategy for preserving the normative status of monism-holism, even though it admits the temporary validity of dualism. It deserves a careful response. To begin we should admit that death and its consequences are a result of the fall and punishment for sin. Death is not "natural" for humans in God's creation.[15] Further, it might be true that if human beings never fell and came under sentence of death, we might never have become aware of the potential disconnection of body and soul. There would in fact be no separation of persons and earthly embodiment. There would not be any of the functional aberrations such as crippling diseases which make the distinction between persons and their bodies so painfully obvious. The functional holism we have stressed as a biblical theme would have characterized human existence fully. Perhaps nothing would have aroused our suspicion that an ontic duality or dualism is inherent in our constitution. Of course we would have noticed differences between the physical, mental, and spiritual aspects of life. It might have oc-

14. Cf. Harris, *Raised Immortal*, Ch. VII, "The Immortality of God and Man in the New Testament," pp. 189-205.

15. I do not agree with those theologians who claim that physical death is natural and that the consequence of the fall is that it became a punishment. Cf. Harris, pp. 191-194, for a sound exegetical response to those who hold this view.

curred to us that persons are more than merely organisms and that, conceptually speaking, minds and brains are distinct. But the separability of human persons from their bodies may never have dawned on us. So our knowledge of this possibility might in fact be based on the consequences of the fall.

But knowledge of this possibility is not the same as the possibility itself. It does not follow from the fact that our awareness of possible separation comes from the fall that the possibility itself does. It may have been there since the beginning. And the dualist holds that it was there. The duality is ontological. It is a feature of our original created nature.

The reason is formidable. Suggesting that dualism stems from the fall requires that God re-created human nature after the fall. If separation of body and soul were not possible in the beginning, then God would have had to redesign and rebuild human nature after the fall in order to preserve persons without bodies in death. But there is no evidence from Scripture that God did this. To the contrary, Scripture emphasizes that the very creature who sinned was punished. It is humankind as created which sinned, was subjected to death, and is being redeemed and restored through Jesus Christ. Creation, fall, and redemption are the biblical sequence. Human nature fell when it rebelled against God. But human nature was not ontologically altered. Its created essence did not change, or so every orthodox theologian since Augustine has insisted. But the idea that dualism is a result of the fall would imply that the ontological structure of human nature was revised. Fallen humans would not have the same essence as pre-fall humans. They would therefore be some other sort of being than the one which was created and sinned. And that is a thesis with many problematic implications.

The dualist sees death as parallel to sin. Just as God created humans able to sin although he did not make them sinful, so he made humans able to die although not inevitably mortal. And while creating them able to die, he also made them able to continue existing as persons beyond physical death. The separation of soul and body is thus an ontological possibility even for created human nature. We do not know why God made us this way. Perhaps in foreseeing sin and death he already was planning for our salvation. Then again, perhaps human persons are not the sort of thing which can be constructed from purely physical material. Whatever the reason, an ontic duality is implicit in God's original blueprint for human beings. The claim that monism-holism is original and dualism results from the fall is provocative, but makes sense neither theologically nor philosophically.

VII. Objection Six:
The Bible Depicts the Dead as Bodily Beings,
Not Immaterial Spirits

If persons exist between death and resurrection, they are temporarily disembodied. But they are not represented as wholly incorporeal in Scripture. In both Testaments as well as in Jewish apocalyptic, the dead are represented as quasi-bodily beings. They lack flesh and bones but still appear in bodily form. That is true of Samuel, the rich man in Luke's parable, and the martyrs in Revelation. How is it possible to maintain this idea and avoid a Platonic-Cartesian dualism in which the soul is completely incorporeal?

This is an interesting question which forces us to confront the notion of discarnate persons. It is not a challenge to the doctrine of the intermediate state, but only to our ability to give a philosophical account of quasi-bodily spiritual existence. Failure at the latter would not disconfirm the former.

There are two approaches which can be taken. One is to question whether the image of the dead as bodily beings is a Scriptural teaching which must be affirmed metaphysically. The other is to develop a theory of discarnate persons which includes bodily form.

In the first approach we could argue that although the biblical writers represent the dead as bodily, they do not teach that this is so. Rather, this is an imaginative depiction of the dead which was common to their way of thinking and in fact is a disposition of all humans. All of us tend to picture our departed loved ones as the bodily beings they were on earth, not as immaterial spirits. The Bible is written in common language and sometimes figurative genres, not in philosophically refined terminology. While Scripture sometimes represents the dead in the intermediate state as bodily beings, it does not intend to teach this view and thus we are not obligated to affirm it. In fact when we read Paul, the most philosophically educated of the biblical writers, we do not find the idea of quasi-corporeality. He simply contrasts being in the body and being away from the body.

When it comes to philosophical anthropology, therefore, we must do what was done by Christian philosophers in other ages. We must attempt to represent biblical teaching as faithfully as possible as we move from the Scriptural images of ordinary life and literature to clear and distinct philosophical ideas. We must use the best understanding we have of the constitution of the body and define personal existence in the intermediate state as existence without that body. If it does not appear that the organism is formed or shaped by the soul but instead by genes, for example, then the soul need not be thought of as the form of the body. And if the essential notion of a self-identical human person need not include reference to bodily form, then, too, the soul could be purely incorporeal as Plato and Descartes thought. This would not be abandoning a view taught by Scripture, but would be the legitimate result of moving from an imaginative mode of discourse to a more philosophically precise one.

It would still be possible to account for the quasi-bodily appearance of those who returned from the dead. Samuel and the transfigured Moses could have been provided temporary visible form by God even if their ordinary condition is totally incorporeal. This is apparently also what happens when angels are sent to visit humans on earth.

The other way of handling the corporeality of the disembodied dead would be to develop an analysis of the soul which included bodily form. One place this has already been done is in the Aristotelian-Thomistic tradition. As we saw in previous chapters, this tradition defines the soul in part as the form of the body. A human is a unity of form and matter. The matter is that of which she is constituted. The form or soul organizes, directs, and energizes the matter to actualize the bodily person in all her levels of functioning, from the biological all the way up to the rational-volitional-spiritual capacities. At death the soul no longer actually constitutes an organism. But it retains the capacity for doing so. It is then potentially the form of a body.

While the Thomist account does conceptually retain the notion of bodily form in the definition of the soul, it does not fully explain how someone could return from the dead in visible form without temporary reacquisition of a material component. It is closer than Platonism to Hebrew holism, but not yet the common idea of the dead as ghosts. It would need the same sort of explanation as the Platonist theory to account for appearances of the dead — that they are given temporary bodily appearance like the angels.

Perhaps there is another way of conceiving of the dead as ghostly, quasi-bodily beings. After all, even modern students of psychic research regularly encounter the notion of an ethereal body among people who have had near-death experiences.[16] This might be conceptualized using the contemporary idea of energy. If matter is a form of energy, perhaps spirit is another kind of energy. The human spirit might not be wholly incorporeal, but a kind of structured substance which, although it is not physical, is analogous to matter in that it can manifest spatial and empirical properties, at least under certain circumstances. Why think that physical energy is the only kind of energy there is which can impinge on the senses? During earthly existence, according to this approach, a human person or soul — an entity of spiritual energy — would be combined with physical matter — earthly energy — and be physically embodied. In the intermediate state it would continue to be the same organization of energy which not only retains the capacity for experience and mental action, but also the potential for appearance and interaction with the earthly environment under certain conditions. I'm not sure this can be worked out coherently. But if it can, it would be another account — more in line with traditional spiritism — of quasi-bodily persons during the intermediate state which would answer this question for dualism.

VIII. Conclusion

No doubt a host of additional objections to dualistic anthropology could be raised. But I believe responses to them would continue the pattern which has emerged in this chapter. Either these questions would not stand up as very substantial challenges or reasonable rejoinders would be ready to hand. Above we have addressed some of the most frequently encountered theological objections and put them to rest. Anthropological dualism does not commit us to unbiblical dichotomies or cripple orthopraxis, it cannot be avoided by appealing to the time-eternity distinction, nor is it a result of the fall. And it does not make us closet Platonists in any sense incompatible with biblical teaching.

We have spoken a great deal of Christian philosophical anthropology and even attempted to sketch a couple of possible lines in this chapter. One formidable challenge which remains is developing more fully what we

16. John McDonagh, *Christian Psychology* (New York: Crossroad, 1982), pp. 62-63.

have been talking about. Is it possible to articulate a philosophical anthropology faithful to the biblical depiction of human nature which is also sophisticated enough to participate in contemporary philosophy and science? Or is a Christian view irremediably naive and anachronistic?

Chapter Ten

Holistic Dualism, Science, and Philosophy

I. Introduction: The Final Topic of Debate

It's one thing to work out a comprehensive and coherent interpretation of a teaching of Scripture. It's another to assert the compatibility of that position with current science and philosophy. For the results of reason do not always appear to confirm and support the truths of revelation. Some beliefs based on readings of Scripture are inconsistent with contemporary knowledge claims. Creation science's affirmation that the world is no more than a few thousand years old is a prime example.

So the question arises for holistic dualism: Is this anthropological model one which can be given expression in terms of current philosophy and science? Or is the claim that we have separable souls more like creation science, a reading of Scripture which is basically at odds with the methods and conclusions of contemporary thought? This question is the final issue in the monism-dualism debate. We have already seen that dualism is the more reasonable position with respect to the biblical data, the conceivability of self-identical resurrected persons, and in answering stock theological objections. But as we saw in the first chapter, one of monism's cardinal claims has been that it is supported by the development of modern science and philosophy, whereas dualism has been ruled out by these disciplines.

If monism's claim is true, then Christians will be left in a dilemma. They will have to pick between an anthropology based on revelation and one based on reason. This will be a difficult choice for the majority of

204

Christians who believe that revelation, although it need not be vindicated by reason, is nonetheless consistent with if not confirmed by the results of reason properly achieved. Some will remain biblical dualists at heart, although they must operate as though monism were true when doing science and philosophy. There will always be a sense of intellectual bad faith for them. Others, convinced that science and philosophy are on the right track, will continue to argue either that Scripture is not dualistic or that its dualism reflects the prescientific cultural beliefs of its human authors and is not what the Holy Spirit wishes to teach the church in the modern world. A minority of Christians may affirm both, relishing yet another paradox between the deliverances of reason and the tenets of faith.

If it turns out that holistic dualism is compatible with contemporary science and philosophy, the dilemma does not exist. The best exegetical option will be one which can also be held by contemporary Christians who work in biology, psychology, and philosophy. There will be no need to repudiate the anthropology and eschatology of traditional Christianity in order to be a respectable participant in the modern academic enterprise. The last of monism's charges against dualism will have been deflected and, all things considered, dualism will have won the debate. This will not be because science and philosophy prove or render more probable the truth of dualism. All along our argument has been that our knowledge that persons can survive separation from their bodies comes from biblical teaching about the afterlife. Our certainty of life everlasting is based on the content of revelation, not the judgment of reason. But like our certainty that God exists, it will be consistent with reason and at points supported by it.

In this chapter, therefore, we will undertake a brief survey of the compatibility of holistic anthropological dualism with the findings of several sciences which study the human constitution. Thereafter we will consider some philosophical expressions of holistic dualism.

II. Dualism and Science

A. Brain Physiology

As suggested in the first chapter, one of the severest blows to classical dualism was the discovery that states of consciousness and mental events are heavily dependent on what goes on in the brain. Thoughts, sensations, and emotions can be influenced by chemicals and electrical stimulation of the brain, it was learned. Further, in the absence of certain functions of the brain, whole classes of mental states and conscious activities are not even possible. This dependence of the mind on the brain seemed to many to preclude the existence of a distinct self-activating entity such as the mind or soul. Many scientists operated with the assumption that brain science would eventually be able to map a one-to-one causal relation between particular states of the brain and specific states of mind. Some actually postulated the identity of mental states and brain states, assuming that science would vindicate that hypothesis.

But science has not turned out that way. In the first place, it is not even certain whether there is complete correlation between brain events and specific states of consciousness. The brain seems to function like a vast corporation in which millions of specific events all connected in large networks are required for a single thought or feeling. Reexperiencing the same thought or feeling does not necessarily involve the very same brain cells linking up in the same way. And if a certain part of the brain is damaged, other parts can take over to make mental activities still possible.[1] Furthermore, the sheer number of brain cells and complexity of the brain itself, as well as the complex interactions of brain cells connected with any particular mental state, make the mapping of mental states onto clearly defined brain states a practical impossibility.[2] So the thesis that all mental events are correlated with specific kinds of brain events has not and may never be empirically demonstrated. Nevertheless, the evidence does point in this direction. As Donald MacKay summarizes: "I am peaceably open-minded as to whether a complete correlation exists; so far from being established fact, this is no more than a working assumption which we brain scientists make as a basis for the design of experiments."[3]

But suppose there is a strict correlation of mental and physical states and events. Does this demonstrate that the correlation is always between brain events as causes and mental states as effects? Not at all. The numerous ways in which consciousness can be affected by injury, disease, electrical impulses, and chemicals are impressive, although humans have been

1. Donald MacKay, *Brains, Machines, and Persons* (Grand Rapids: Eerdmans, 1980), pp. 33-34.
2. MacKay, pp. 18-32.
3. MacKay, p. 37.

aware of this connection at least since they began overimbibing alcohol and beating one another's heads. But it does not follow from the fact that many states of consciousness are caused by states of the organism that all are. In fact it seems as though mental states affect brain states just as frequently. A person can generate incredibly complex occurrences in her brain by forming a concept, meditating on God, or worrying about an exam. In all these cases it seems that mental activity produces brain activity, not the reverse.

This is a crucial point. Empirically scientists are faced with data which, strictly speaking, favor psychophysical interactionism. Researchers can determine that certain complex events are occurring in the brain and, if they have a conscious subject who reports her experiences, that at roughly the same time certain mental events are taking place. Thus there is some observable correlation. If scientists can cause changes in the brain which result in changes of consciousness, a causal connection is apparently identified. Subjects usually experience the resulting changes in consciousness as passive events — things which happen to them. Conversely, if subjects initiate some mental act like thinking or imagining something, changes in brain activity can be discerned. Here it is reasonable to assume that the mind has affected the brain. In other words, the hard empirical data are that there are two different kinds of events — mental and physiological — each of which appears to be able to affect the other.

It is reasonable to suppose that there are causal connections between them on the basis of their regular correlation. When *a* is initiated, *b* occurs. The actual mechanism by which the connection is made cannot be observed. It is no more possible to observe a brain event producing or secreting a mental event than it is to see a thought or intention stimulating a change in the brain. Brain-caused mental states have no privileged status here. In both directions, causality is postulated on the basis of a pattern of regular association: whenever *a*, *b*.

Beyond this point scientists and philosophers are interpreting the data, not reporting what is self-evidently true. All we can observe is this two-way correlation. The data are consistent with various philosophical theories. There could be causal interaction between two substances. It could even be that there are two sets of events, each possibly connected to a different substance, which are occurring in parallel, not really causally influencing one another. The former theory is dualistic interactionism and the latter dualistic parallelism or perhaps dual-aspect monism. But idealism and materialism can interpret the data as well. Idealism can devise ways of making all the brain events somehow dependent on the mental events, even though prima facie they appear to be on a par. And materialism has proposed numerous accounts of how mental properties are really identical with or generated by events in the brain even though they do not appear that way. No doubt the data have been interpreted in terms of other metaphysical outlooks as well. The crucial point is that the observable data from brain physiology and physiological psychology underdetermine all philosophical theories alike.

Since materialism is most popular, it is worth pausing over. Its main claim against dualism is that the brain as a physical system is closed. There is no toehold for mind or spirit to influence the brain. Furthermore, science can completely explain brain events in terms of other brain events, leaving no role for the mysterious causality of the mind. Because the brain is complete, neither soul nor mind nor exclusively mental events can influence it.[4]

But scientists and philosophers have pointed out that, given the fact of physical causal indeterminacy on the level of subatomic particles, it is perfectly possible for mental or spiritual energy, if such exists, to influence brain events on that level without violating any law of physics. If mind influences the behavior of billions of subatomic particles in the brain, this could result in great variation in the firing of neurons and in the networking of the millions of brain cells correlated with even the most simple conscious episodes. Mind could influence brain without actually supplying the physical processes with any new energy or introducing anything foreign on the level of causal physiological explanation.[5] This of course is speculative and does not prove the truth of dualism. But it does defend it from a priori exclusion by materialism. Both positions have much they cannot explain.

In the end, competent brain physiologists can be found defending a variety of philosophical positions or remaining agnostic on the body-mind issue. All who are honest must confess that there is a great deal of mystery surrounding it, a vast unknown which in principle may be beyond

4. Cf. Mario Bunge, *The Mind-Body Problem* (New York: Pergamon, 1980), p. 17.
5. Keith Campbell, *Body and Mind* (Notre Dame, IN: Notre Dame University Press, 1986), pp. 52-53; Jerome Shaffer, *Philosophy of Mind* (Englewood Cliffs, NJ: Prentice-Hall, 1978), pp. 66-67.

our finding out. Nevertheless there are highly regarded scientists whose contemplation of the mystery has led them to favor some sort of dualist anthropology. At the end of his career, Wilder Penfield, an internationally respected neurophysiologist and brain surgeon, confessed: "I conclude that it is easier to rationalize man's being on the basis of two elements than on the basis of one."[6]

Another dualist is Sir John Eccles, Nobel Laureate for his work in brain physiology and a Christian who places himself in the Cartesian tradition. In his view, the soul is the self capable of experience. Embodied during life, it is conscious of itself, the external world, and objective knowledge, although Eccles is not sure how it is attached to the brain. Since the soul is nonmaterial, it is not subject at death to disintegration. In his opinion, however, the possibility of experiencing anything other than the disembodied self is problematic.[7] Of interest here are not the details of Eccles's position, but the fact that a world-class brain scientist can openly profess dualism without being regarded as a quack by his colleagues.

No doubt there are problems in his anthropology. Problems and mysteries are inherent in any dualistic anthropology. But dualism does not face greater problems or more of them than any other philosophical outlook in accounting for the data of contemporary brain physiology and their relationship to the human mind. Being a dualist is not obviously irrational from the standpoint of modern brain science. A Christian who is convinced that Scripture implies dualism need not be double-minded when it comes to the scientific analysis of the human constitution.

B. Psychology

What has been said above in connection with brain science applies to psychology as well. Insofar as it deals with physiology at all, it is confronted by the very same data as brain physiology: seeing, hearing, emotional states, depression, motivation, learning skills, and the like all have roots in or-

6. Wilder Penfield, *The Mystery of the Mind* (Princeton: Princeton University Press, 1975), p. 114.

7. John Eccles, *Facing Reality: Philosophical Adventures by a Brain Scientist* (New York/ Berlin: Springer, 1970), pp. 173-174. Cf. also John Eccles and Karl Popper, *The Self and Its Brain* (New York: Springer, 1977), and Eccles, *The Wonder of Being Human* (New York: Springer, 1984).

BODY, SOUL, AND LIFE EVERLASTING

ganic states. But they also seem in turn to influence the functions of the organism. Once again the data suggest the intimate correlation of psychophysical phenomena. The mind-body problematics are the same.

Christian psychologists have engaged in serious reflection on the relationship between anthropological presuppositions and academic psychology. While some have concluded that dualism must be rejected as incompatible with the evidence of integrated human psychophysical functioning,[8] others have realized that this is not so. Mary Stewart Van Leeuwen has recently encouraged Christian psychologists to take responsibility for how their models square with the biblical teaching about the afterlife, including the intermediate state.[9] In formulating her own anthropology, she is concerned that crude Cartesianism be avoided. However, she does endorse "minimal dualism," the view that soul and body are not separate during life but are separable at death. This recognizes the intimacy — virtual identifiability — of mental and physical phenomena so evident in ordinary life and psychological research. But it also admits the possibility of an active disembodied existence during the intermediate state.[10] Van Leeuwen is another example of a Christian dualist who is also a competent and up-to-date research scientist, and who discerns no contradiction between the two.

C. The Question of Holism

One of Van Leeuwen's concerns about Cartesian dualism is that it posits too great a separation between mental and physical functioning, a fear which motivates many psychologists to reject dualism altogether. But we have seen that Eccles, who is highly aware of mind-brain intimacy, has characterized himself as a Cartesian. What is going on here? This issue ought to be confronted, for the thesis of this book is that the proper anthropology is holistic dualism. If biblical anthropology is expressible in terms of science and philosophy, functional holism must be preserved. Are

8. Cf. David Myers, *The Human Puzzle: Psychological Research and Christian Belief* (San Francisco: Harper and Row, 1978).

9. Mary Stewart Van Leeuwen, *The Person in Psychology: A Contemporary Christian Appraisal* (Grand Rapids: Eerdmans, 1985), Ch. 6, "Psychology and the Mind-Brain Debate."

10. Van Leeuwen endorses the position of C. Stephen Evans in "Separable Souls: A Defense of 'Minimal Dualism,'" *Southern Journal of Philosophy*, Vol. XIX, pp. 313-331.

a robust substantial dualism and functional holism incompatible with one another?

The fact is that Cartesian dualistic interaction could produce the phenomenological and scientific data of psychophysical intimacy and integration. Descartes himself pointed out that his dualism was based on philosophical analysis and not on the phenomenology of embodied personal existence. From the latter, he said, we can only conclude that we are single beings who are unaware of any transitions between the mental and the physical.[11] Yet it is the interaction of the mind and body via the pineal gland which results in the phenomenological, existential, and functional unity of embodied experience. Of course Descartes was handicapped by an extremely simplistic notion of psychophysical interaction, not having studied twentieth-century brain physiology.

But suppose there is pervasive interaction at the sub-atomic level of the brain. The hundreds of thousands of thoughts, memories, beliefs, feelings, moods, commitments, hopes, and loves which humans have will all correlate and interact with millions of patterned events in the brain, thereby interfacing with the numerous subsystems which network the various regions of the brain. The regional subsystems in turn monitor and regulate bodily functions and are likewise influenced by what goes on in the rest of the organism. If this model is incapable of accounting for the intimate coordination, harmonious integration, mental-physical "identifiability," and phenomenological unity of human psychophysical existence, I do not know what would. Minimal dualism, perspectivalism, and materialism have nothing more sophisticated to offer. Not only could this allow for experienced psychosomatic unity, it could also provide for the countless connections of mutual conditioning among religion, worldview, social and cultural values, language, perceptual skills, psychological characteristics, desire for pleasure, genes, hormones, and the thousands of other correlativities known to common sense, uncovered by the human sciences, and as yet undreamt of. How would sophisticated Cartesianism undercut a holistic approach to the study of humankind? How would this anthropological model suggest that in hurting my body I would not be hurting myself instead of some thing to which I seem to be loosely attached?

Involved here are two levels or issues which ought not to be confused.

11. Cf. the section on Descartes in Chapter One.

One is the functional holism and phenomenological unity of personal-bodily existence. The other is how that holistic unity is constituted or brought about. There is nothing about a contemporary Cartesian mind-brain dualism which would preclude the functional holism of life as I and my psychologist experience it. The issue, once again, is not pro or con a strong substantial dualism, but how intimately and extensively the two substances are thought to interact and influence each other. Very intimately and extensively indeed, apparently. The mind-brain relation is a complex of countless interconnected subsystems. If this is conceivable, the choice between substantial dualism and functional holism, as we have argued all along, is a false dilemma.

D. The Psychology of Near-Death Experiences

Thus far we have only claimed that dualism is compatible with contemporary science, not that science vindicates dualism against its rivals. There is a growing body of evidence, however, which some claim favors dualism — the strange out-of-the-body experiences some people have had when they were near death. If veridical, these experiences would go beyond biblical teaching and provide empirical data for body-soul separation. The data deserve to be evaluated.

A great deal has been collected and written on this topic, some of it by Christians and responsible investigators,[12] but a lot of it by uncritical prophets of the occult, Eastern religion, and the New Age movement. The whole issue must be approached cautiously and critically for the sake of both religious and intellectual integrity. I will consider two sorts of near-death experiences: those which involve perception of this world from a location other than the body; and those which claim experience of something trans-worldly.

With respect to the first category, I know of a case in which a person in a coma near death experienced himself as leaving his body and moving to another room in the hospital where he observed several relatives in prayer for him. Later he emerged from the coma and reported that experience to

---

12. Cf. Raymond Moody, *Life After Life* (New York: Bantam, 1975); Paul and Linda Badham, *Immortality or Extinction?* (New York: Macmillan, 1982), Ch. 5; Michael Sabom, *Recollections of Death* (New York: Harper and Row, 1982).

those relatives with great detail and accuracy, including the wording of the prayers and the arrival of the pastor. This case is typical of many in the literature.

What can we deduce from it? Is it just a case of imagination or hallucination, generated by a brain under great stress? Of course it is possible for a person even under normal circumstances to imagine, dream, or hallucinate an out-of-the-body experience. But this explanation is inadequate to account for the veridical experience of events wholly removed from the patient's body. He saw, heard, and perhaps even smelled things physically removed from his eyes, ears, and nose. Certainly his eyes were closed. If this was not an actual separation of the person from his body, it was at least a case of clairvoyance. It simply cannot be explained in terms of the normal mind-brain relation, even if the brain is operating under mental stress. But it is not necessarily a separation from the body or even a case of conscious experience independent of some brain function. Perhaps if the brain did not function at all, such an experience would not occur.[13] While this sort of out-of-the-body phenomenon demonstrates that there can be veridical sense experience without the use of the sense organs, it does not prove that the soul can completely separate from the body. It does not prove the truth of dualism, although it certainly seems to support it.

The second type of near-death experience involves encounter with what seems to be a transcendent dimension of existence. People feel themselves drawn from their bodies through a tunnel toward a bright light. They experience great joy, comfort, love, and peace. Sometimes they encounter other persons. I recently learned of a case in which a man who had a near-fatal heart attack not only underwent the standard experience but was greeted by an acquaintance of his who appeared in bodily form, wearing clothing. After this brief meeting he was told he must return and was drawn back into his body. Later he regained normal consciousness and related his experience. What is so striking about this case is that the acquaintance whom he met had died twenty-four hours previously over two thou-

---

13. Cf. Robert Almeder, *Beyond Death* (Springfield, IL: Thomas, 1987), Ch. 3. Almeder is a non-Christian philosopher who takes a tough-minded approach to this evidence. He, too, concludes, p. 52, that such experiences must at least be extreme cases of ESP or clairvoyance. They would prove dualism only if the subject's brain waves were flat at the time of the experience, for ESP involves brain activity. While some researchers claim to have demonstrated the absence of brain waves during such experiences, Almeder is not yet completely convinced; cf. pp. 90-92 nn.18 and 19.

sand miles away. His death was unknown to the heart attack victim until two months later. Many other accounts similarly report meeting persons whose deaths were unknown to the reporter. On the other hand, subjects do not report meeting people in this sort of experience who have not died.[14]

What are we to make of this? Does it vindicate dualism or provide evidence of what the afterlife is like? A great deal of caution is warranted. In the first place, similar experiences with white light and feelings of euphoria can be caused by depriving the brain of oxygen, as in drowning, or chemically induced by anesthetics or hallucinogenic drugs. The body itself secretes endorphins, the brain's own opiate, in great quantities under stress. These, too, can induce paradisal experiences. So there are a number of perfectly straightforward explanations of why people have such visions and sensations near death.

What cannot be explained are the encounters with dead persons, if these are genuine. But their authenticity is difficult to determine because unlike experiences of earthly people, whose presence can be verified, there is no way to tell if encounters with the dead are genuine or imagined. One can vividly dream of meeting a deceased spouse. What is uncanny is the fact that a number of cases report meeting persons whose deaths were unknown to the reporting subject. This phenomenon is too regular to be mere chance. But it need not involve more than an unusual instance of ESP or clairvoyance yielding knowledge of that person's death. This sort of thing does not automatically prove that the soul has temporarily left the body or actually met deceased persons. Once again it does not seem to occur without at least some brain functions continuing. Given the difficulties with verifying encounter claims, this sort of otherworldly out-of-the-body experience may provide even less hard evidence for body-soul separation than experiences of different locations in this world.

Even if experiences of the transcendent do involve the ecstasy of the soul, it is not clear that they provide us any information about existence after death. For how do we know that when people really die, that is, when they do not come back to tell about it, their experience is the same as near-death experience? Perhaps when people really die, something quite different takes place. It is in principle impossible for us who remain in this life to answer this question. It may turn out that dying is just as these reports in-

14. Cf. John McDonagh, *Christian Psychology* (New York: Crossroad, 1982), pp. 58-59.

dicate. But maybe not. In any case, the conclusions about the afterlife drawn by popular and occult writers on the basis of near-death experiences are really unwarranted. Agnosticism is the most responsible attitude.

In summary, then, while the evidence from different sorts of near-death experiences tends to support dualism and requires more than a standard physiological account of consciousness, it falls short of demonstrating the soul's ability to survive and function apart from the body. Responsible scholars are persuaded differently about what the evidence indicates.[15] It certainly does not conflict with a dualistic anthropology, however, and that is really all we need to establish.

III. Anthropological Dualism in Philosophy

A. Introduction

Although materialism and ontological holism are most popular today, an ontic body-soul distinction is defended by a number of contemporary philosophers, both Christians and non-Christians. Throughout this study it has been suggested that three types of anthropology could account for personal existence in the intermediate state: the robust dualism represented by Plato, Augustine, and Descartes; the softer dualism of Thomism which modifies Augustine with Aristotle; and spiritual monism or panpsychism, a view which sees the body as a contingent aspect of a more basic immaterial element. What follow are sketches of the anthropologies of contemporary Christian philosophers who represent each of these approaches. All of them recognize both the intimacy of the bodily and personal aspects of life and the possibility of personal existence apart from the

---

15. McDonagh has been persuaded of dualism and the afterlife by this material and has given it a Christian interpretation; cf. *Christian Psychology,* Ch. 4, "Metaphysics and Psychology: the Case for an Afterlife." Robert Almeder, a non-Christian philosopher, concludes the following in *Beyond Death,* p. 76: "We need a lot of evidence for belief in life after death. And I am urging that we have reached the point where a critical examination of all the evidence available makes such a commitment a good deal easier than it has ever been before in our history." Richard Swinburne, a Christian philosopher and a dualist, is more skeptical: "My conclusion on parapsychology is that it provides no good evidence that the soul continues to function without the brain to which it is currently connected, functioning." *The Evolution of the Soul* (Oxford: Clarendon, 1986), p. 305.

body. Thus all of them present examples of holistic dualism as we have defined it. Their methods and styles of philosophy are quite diverse. But together they illustrate my contention that a number of current approaches to philosophical anthropology can be used to articulate the holistic dualism implied by Scripture.

My purpose is to illustrate possible ways of linking biblical, theological, and philosophical reflection on the human constitution. My selection is intended to be suggestive, not necessarily to recommend these anthropologies as wholly unproblematic or as the best examples of their type or as exhausting the options. An anthropology must do much more than exemplify holistic dualism to be philosophically satisfactory. These cannot be extensively evaluated here. Nor can a full-blown theory of human nature be developed in this study. For now I only wish to illustrate some connections between biblical anthropology and the project of philosophical anthropology, not to undertake that project itself.

B. John Cobb and Process Philosophy

While some process thinkers have rejected the afterlife in general and the possibility of disembodied existence in particular, John Cobb is a theologian steeped in the metaphysics of Whitehead and Hartshorne who has defended the possibility of the soul's survival of death.[16]

Process thought is an unusual form of panpsychism, the thesis that all of reality consists of "soulish" stuff. For Whitehead, the ultimate realities from which the things in the world are constituted are not enduring substances or entities, but transitory bits of experience or sensation called "actual occasions."[17] Since sense experiences are psychic, all is psychic — "panpsychism."

These units of experience are not isolated monads but intimately linked with other actual occasions, both those which have preceded and those which occur subsequently. Each occasion is two-sided or bipolar. As

16. I am relying on Cobb's *A Christian Natural Theology: Based on the Thought of Alfred North Whitehead* (Philadelphia: Westminster, 1965), especially Ch. II, "The Human Soul." Cf. also John Cobb and David Ray Griffin, *Process Theology: An Introductory Exposition* (Philadelphia: Westminster, 1976).

17. For an introduction to basic concepts of process thought see Cobb, Ch. I, or Cobb and Griffin, Ch. 1.

it occurs or "concresces" it is affected by previous occasions in responding to or "prehending" them. This is its backward-looking, causally determined side, which is called its physical pole. But it also has a future-oriented mental pole which prehends its own possibilities and actualizes one as it concresces. Thus each unit of experience is both mental and physical, both causally determined and to some extent free for creative self-determination. (Process thought is also a dual-aspect monism.) Each experience is linked to all others, past or future, either immediately or mediately through the endless series of actual occasions of experience.

The enduring things we encounter in the world are constituted because actual occasions do not just link up randomly, but are coaxed to occur according to definite patterns or possibilities ultimately located in the mind of God. In forming the relatively stable existence of a molecule, for example, thousands of actual occasions concresce in regular patterns through millions of instants in a temporal series. The result is an enduring entity we call a molecule. A molecule or even an atom is not a real individual, but an enduring society of real but ever-changing individual bits of experience. These relatively small societies can in turn become organized into larger societies such as rocks and even more complex ones such as plants, animals, and human beings. Of course they can become disorganized as well and thus disintegrate into more simple forms.

Although every actual occasion has its mental pole and every molecule or rock has many of them, this does not mean that they have souls or are conscious. Freedom, creativity, and sensation or feeling do not require actual subjective awareness. The conscious soul exists only in entities constituted by layers of complex organization. Even many lower animals are barely conscious. But in higher animals and humans a complex society or organism of actual occasions emerges in which there can be a dominant or presiding occasion — a conscious soul. The organism is governed at least partially by a center of actual consciousness. Since this structure includes and dominates all the others, it is the defining feature of this sort of being. Thus Whitehead affirms that both animals and humans have souls. And he would rather say, with the Old Testament, that they are souls.

The human soul is distinct from that of animals because it has so many capacities that they do not, not because it has a different nature or origin. Human consciousness includes self-awareness and a sense of identity over time because it can remember or prehend its past and project into the future as well as engage the immediate present, as the animals do. The greater complexity of the human brain provides us much higher mental and spiritual capacities than the animals. This in turn enables us to do many more complex things with our bodies.

Strictly speaking, the soul is located in the brain. Occurrences in the brain are what the soul prehends immediately. Likewise the brain is the immediate recipient of the effects of the soul. Thus, given the process analysis of causality as prehension, there is causal interaction between soul and brain. Whitehead does allow for the possibility of mental telepathy and the immediate experience of God, however.[18] Mediation of the body is not in principle necessary. But that is how things ordinarily work.

This does not set up some crude Cartesian dualism, however. For the entire human being is a complex of interrelated and interacting functional systems. Mind and body are extensions of one another. Self and world are organically related to each other. Mediately or immediately all actual occasions are interrelated with all other actual occasions (except those which occur simultaneously with them). If a holistic framework is desired for philosophy and the human sciences, surely process thought can claim to provide one. In principle, all levels of existence both within a person and in her natural, cultural, and spiritual environment impinge on each other.

So we have holism, but in what sense is Cobb's anthropology dualistic? Since the mental and the physical are defined as two poles of actual occasions, the basic stuff of reality, one might expect that process anthropology represents a dual-aspect monism: the mental and physical are dimensions of a more basic unity. However, Cobb has employed Whitehead's categories to argue that the soul and the body are distinct organizations, and he holds out for the possibility that the soul can exist apart from the organism.[19] "That there is a soul or living person, ontologically distinct from the body, is the first condition of the possibility of life after death. This distinct existence has been established in Whiteheadian terms. . . ."[20] The reality of the afterlife cannot be demonstrated philosophically, however. Christians know it to be true by revelation — if not an intermediate state then certainly a resurrection. The disembodied soul could be conscious because its awareness of itself, its own past, the souls of other persons, and God himself is not necessarily mediated by the body. The location of this existence

18. Cobb, p. 54.
19. Cobb, pp. 63-70.
20. Cobb, p. 66.

might be some two-dimensional space other than the four-dimensional framework of our spatio-temporal world.

Cobb's process anthropology with its provision for disembodied existence is not without its difficulties, some of which he addresses. If souls are actually societies of ever-changing individuals, do we really have ontological self-identity over time even with accurate memory and a sense of self? That is a nagging problem which Cobb admits. A much more basic question is why anyone would want to buy the process assumption at the outset — that ultimate reality consists of atomic sensations. That is a curious starting point even if a coherent anthropology can be constructed from it.

But the key question for our present topic is whether Whitehead and Cobb have really provided a basis for asserting the possibility of disembodied existence. Cobb claims to have justified an ontological distinction between body and soul. I believe he has. But just because one can distinguish levels of being does not mean he can separate them. The entire process account of how human beings are constituted involves a series in which lower levels of complexity reorganize themselves to create higher levels. The new whole is more than the sum of the previous parts. In that sense it is ontologically different. The human soul is a whole which organizationally comprehends the human organism as it transcends it. Again, this transcendence is ontological — it is a new level of being. But just because the new whole transcends the sum of its parts and can interact with them does not mean that it could exist without those parts. It is organized from them. Is the soul anything more than a consciously centered functional level of the human body? Do we really have a distinct entity here, a society of actual occasions not constituted by the body or necessarily including it while transcending it? If not, this sort of soul does not amount to enough even for (the non-omnipotent process) God to hold in existence after the demise of the body in spite of their ontological difference. As Cobb himself admits, "clearly a psychophysical organism cannot survive the death of the physical organism."[21] He claims to have presented more than this. I am not sure he has or is able to with process categories.

If Cobb is successful in accounting for the possibility of disembodied existence as well as the intimate correlation of body, soul, and every dimension of human existence, then his process anthropology is an example of holistic dualism. Whether it is successful is a matter for further study.

21. Cobb, p. 65.

And whether process theology's views of God and the divine-human relation in creation, providence, and salvation are consistent with biblical orthodoxy is a matter about which I have serious doubts.[22] But those issues cannot be treated here.

C. Richard Swinburne and Dualistic Interactionism

A Christian philosopher who with some qualifications represents the Augustinian-Cartesian tradition is Richard Swinburne. His recent book *The Evolution of the Soul* articulates and defends an anthropology that views humans as consisting of two substances, body and soul, which causally interact with each other. In fact his position is quite similar to that of John Eccles, the brain scientist encountered earlier.

Defining a substance as "a component of the world which interacts causally with other components of the world and which has a history through time,"[23] Swinburne outlines his position as follows:

> [A] man living on Earth is a substance which consists of two substances, his body and his soul. The body is a material body, but the soul is not a material object or anything like it. . . . Body and soul are connected at present, in that events in the body affect events in the soul, and conversely. But the essential part of man is the soul. . . . This is dualism, the position which I shall defend.[24]

Although he pays close attention to brain science and physiological psychology, Swinburne does not offer a theory about the mechanism by which psychophysical interaction takes place. In fact he is skeptical that science will ever be able to do more than note the regular correlations between mental and bodily phenomena.[25] It will never solve the body-soul question.

Swinburne's dualism does not prevent him from recognizing the pervasive functional integration of human existence. He is aware of the complexity of brain and soul alike and hence the compound complexity of

22. Cf. Ronald Nash, ed., *Process Theology* (Grand Rapids: Baker, 1987).
23. Swinburne, p. 5.
24. Swinburne, p. 10.
25. Swinburne, pp. 183-196.

their interaction. The body and its states influence the soul in numerous ways both on the conscious and unconscious levels. The soul itself has an extremely complex structure which combines and integrates sensations, thoughts, purposes, desires, and beliefs and makes possible rationality, language, and genuine moral agency.[26] Personality, character, and intellectual outlook are relatively stable structures which are formed and function both consciously and unconsciously. Surely Swinburne's anthropology allows for the interplay of various aspects of existence and suggests the functional holism prized by practitioners of the human sciences.

What is the origin of the soul? Swinburne's acceptance of general theistic evolution might lead one to suppose that he sees the soul as emerging from or generated by the body. This is not so. He believes that souls, both human and animal, are created and infused by God.[27] Although the soul's existence does not depend on the body, its functioning does, at least as far as we can tell. It is like a light bulb and the brain like a socket. The bulb can exist apart from the socket, but not light up.

Here is where Swinburne departs from Augustine and Descartes. They believed that the soul can function on its own, at least in certain important ways. Further, science and philosophy do not suggest that the soul is naturally immortal, as traditional defenders of dualism have argued. For these reasons Swinburne is unwilling to identify fully with Augustine and Descartes.[28]

What then happens at death? Neither science, parapsychology, nor philosophy can answer that question. Although it seems that the soul cannot function without the brain, Swinburne must finally admit that due to the limitations of our knowledge, we really do not know whether this is so.[29] In any case, it is surely possible for God to keep the soul with its in-

26. Swinburne, Ch. 14, "The Structure of the Soul."

27. Swinburne, p. 199. William Hasker is a Christian dualistic interactionist who affirms the existence of the soul in the intermediate state, but who believes that the soul is generated by and emerges from the body. Cf. Hasker, "Emergentism," *Religious Studies*, Vol. 18, pp. 473-488; and *Metaphysics* (Downers Grove, IL: InterVarsity, 1983), Ch. 3, "Minds and Bodies."

28. Swinburne, p. 10. Although he lists Descartes as affirming the soul's natural immortality, Descartes actually believed in immortality on the basis of divine power, not the soul's own nature. It is a truth of revelation, not reason. Thus Swinburne's position is the same as Descartes's on this issue.

29. Swinburne, p. 196.

herent structures in existence and functioning if he so wills. "If souls exist ... without their bodies or with totally new bodies, they do so by special divine act, not under their own natural powers."[30] Thus Richard Swinburne's dualistic interactionism allows both for functional holism and the possibility of the intermediate state without defining the soul rationalistically or as naturally immortal.

D. Pope John Paul II and Lublin Thomism

Thomas Aquinas is still a major inspiration in Roman Catholic thought. Although some philosophers and theologians who appeal to him are really committed to quite incompatible systems of thought, many neo-Thomists like Jacques Maritain and Etienne Gilson are as faithful to Thomas and doctrinal orthodoxy as they are contemporary in their manner of intellectual expression. In this latter category are the scholars articulating Lublin Thomism, the intellectual framework of the vital witness of the Roman Catholic Church in Poland today. The general public does not realize that Pope John Paul II (Karol Wojtyla is his given name) is a trained philosopher who has authored numerous works on Christian anthropology and ethics.[31] He was a leading member of the school of Lublin Thomism before his election to the papacy. In what follows I will briefly describe the highlights of John Paul II's view of human nature as explained and elaborated by two of his fellow Lublin Thomists.

John Paul II's anthropology is a Christian humanism based on the metaphysics of Thomas Aquinas but articulated at least in part in terms of the method of contemporary European existential phenomenology. Although he utilizes and dialogues with the phenomenologies of Jaspers, Heidegger, Scheler, Marcel, and Sartre, he does not mistakenly equate phenomenology with ontology or metaphysics. Describing phenomena does not automatically disclose their underlying ontological structure. Identifying phenomenology with ontology can lead to subjectivism and the equation of persons with states of consciousness. John Paul II avoids these

---

30. Swinburne, pp. 311-312. He affirms this in spite of his not being inclined to hold that Scripture teaches the intermediate state.

31. Cf. Andrew Woznicki, *A Christian Humanism: Karol Wojtyla's Existential Personalism* (New Britain, CT: Mariel, 1980), pp. 72-80, for a partial bibliography.

pitfalls. As his former student, Professor Andrew Woznicki, summarizes his approach: "although Wojtyla uses a phenomenological method in his philosophical anthropology, nevertheless his philosophy of man is entirely based on St. Thomas' metaphysics of the human person."[32]

Following Aquinas, Wojtyla defines humanity in terms of substance, not just phenomena or functions.[33] "A human person is regarded as a substantial being because only as such can a person be the causative subject of his act and an efficient cause of all human values."[34] The person is not just the soul or consciousness, however, but is incarnate as being-in-the-world. People are bodily beings inevitably situated someplace in the world. Instincts, bodily feelings, and emotions are as much the stuff of motivation and consciousness as thoughts and volitions. In defining persons as substantial beings, moreover, Wojtyla does not think of substance as an inert subject supporting accidental properties, but as something dynamic and self-realizing, thus echoing Thomas. Unlike God's other earthly creatures, human persons are substances created to realize or develop themselves through their acts. This thesis is why Wojtyla's anthropology can be classified as a form of existential personalism. He does not, however, simply identify persons with sets of acts as some existentialists do, thereby denying that persons are substances. Persons are substances whose nature is to act and thereby to develop themselves.

John Paul II's anthropology is a Christian personalism. Humans do not just create themselves normlessly or from nothing, but have been created by God in his image. That gives us a definite nature. The most striking feature of God is his love, which of course involves his rationality, will, and creativity. Thus the central thing about the creature who bears God's image is love, which is the goal or meaning of all human capacities. "Love is the source of all humanity's various spheres of existence. Love, understood in these terms, becomes the ultimate and fundamental principle of self-realization of a man as a 'person-act.'"[35] Not just consciousness, but embodied human existence in its entirety is created and ordered for love. Nowhere is this more clear than in how human sexuality culminates in the expression of interpersonal love. Love is the ori-

---

32. Woznicki, pp. ix-x. Cf. Ch. III.B, "Phenomenology and Its Limitations."
33. Woznicki, Ch. II, "Metaphysical Structure of Man as a Person."
34. Woznicki, p. 9.
35. Woznicki, p. 30; cf. Ch. IV, "The Foundations of Christian Agapology."

gin and goal of human life, its first and final cause, to use the categories of Aquinas.

Love seeks and affirms the real value of things. God exists and is of infinite value. Thus he is to be loved for his own sake. And God has created the world as an ordered community of creatures each with its own value. Each human being therefore must love himself. But all of us find ourselves in relation to God's other creatures as well — other persons most valuable of all. Each of us must love God's other creatures according to their created natures, affirming their inherent worth. This is the basis for ethics as a whole. It is the foundation for proper treatment of the natural environment and animals as well as ourselves, cultural objects, and other human beings. Love is therefore the summary of our whole duty to God and the foundation for justice in human society. It is the purpose and definition of human nature. In essence a human is not just a rational animal but an animal who acts from love. However, just as all people do not behave in accordance with rationality, not all act from the right sorts of love, love which truly perceives and affirms the value of things. Genuine love does not negate the self, for the self has value. But neither does it negate the other or use another person merely as a means. Love is not opposed to happiness but is precisely what will lead to it, for happiness results from self-fulfillment, and love is the purpose of human existence. Love is from God, and all God's creatures are to love him according to their natures. Only humans can do so as self-actualizing persons.

Wojtyla's anthropology concentrates on life in this world as a foundation for Christian ethics. In fact, developing a sophisticated alternative to Marxist humanism has been his main concern, an enterprise in which he and his colleagues have been blessed with great success.[36] Functional holism and the possibility of disembodied existence are not issues of immediate concern. Nonetheless it is clear that his anthropology as formulated would imply the truth of both holism and dualism. Although he understands the notion of substance in a modern way, Wojtyla "accepts the doctrine of St. Thomas on the composition of the soul and body of man — understood in metaphysical categories."[37] This "leads to the acceptance of

36. The renowned Polish Marxist, Adam Schaff, has complained that "the greatest threat to Polish Marxism is Lublin Thomism, which is being taught in the Catholic seminaries and preached from the pulpits." Cf. Woznicki, p. v.

37. Woznicki, p. 17.

the existence of a substantial soul with its possibility of existing independently from the body."[38]

It is Lublin University's rector, Professor Krapiec, who has elaborated this anthropology in detail.[39] Following the approach of Etienne Gilson, Krapiec proceeds from the fact that we experience ourselves as unified psychophysical totalities and wishes to preserve the Thomistic insistence on the unity of human nature. Analysis of the entire bodily self or ego in terms of actuality and potentiality — the classic strategy of Aristotle and Thomas —leads to the conclusion that the soul is the form of the body. A human being is the unity of form and matter. It is this unity which functions biologically and psychologically as well as spiritually. Here is the standard Thomistic method of explaining the unity and functional integration of human nature.[40]

But pure Aristotelianism jeopardizes the separability of the soul and thus the Christian view of the afterlife. Thomas's solution — that the soul is a substance as well as the form of the body — is the one which best preserves the existential unity of life and the possibility of disembodied existence, according to Krapiec. Following Thomas he draws the conclusion: "If existence belongs immediately to the soul, and to the body only and exclusively through the soul, then the destruction of the body does not entail the destruction of the subsisting substance that is the human soul-ego."[41] In fact the soul is immortal by its created nature, not merely by a continuing act of God after death.

At this point John Paul II's analysis of humans as personal self-actualizing substances can be plugged in. Whereas Thomas defined the soul in terms of its rationality and rested his case for its substantiality and separability on this capacity, the Pope "tries to enrich the one-sided aspect of man's rationality by including within the definition of human reality the entire range of human actions."[42] In other words, we get a much more robust and many-sided definition of human souls as persons rather than treating them primarily as intellects. While the range of human actions

38. Woznicki, p. 64 n. 14.

39. Mieczylaw Krapiec, *I-Man: An Outline of Philosophical Anthropology* (New Britain, CT: Mariel, 1983), Ch. IV, "The Ontical Structure of Man."

40. Krapiec, Ch. IV. III: "Soul Organizing Matter (The Form of the Body)."

41. Krapiec, p. 117.

42. Woznicki, p. 17.

without a body will be limited, it is clear from John Paul II's analysis that persons can survive bodily death.

However one may evaluate contemporary Thomistic anthropology by other criteria, it is clear that the thought of John Paul II and the Lublin Thomists provides a Christian view of human nature which not only affirms holism and dualism, but is effective in the battle against such anti-Christian anthropologies as Freudianism, existentialism, and Marxism.

E. Herman Dooyeweerd and Neo-Calvinist Philosophy

Another anthropology nourished by the tradition of Christian Aristotelian Platonism and constructed to do battle with the spirits of this age has been developed by the late Herman Dooyeweerd of the Free University of Amsterdam. Dooyeweerd was shaped by the rebirth of a vigorous spiritual and cultural Calvinism in late nineteenth-century Holland under the leadership of Abraham Kuyper and Herman Bavinck. Desiring to reform all of life according to Christian principles, Dooyeweerd developed a systematic philosophy based on the premise that God's Word provides the lawful structure of all created reality and that human existence as a whole is a religious response to God.[43]

Philosophies express the inner spirits of cultures. Western philosophy has been shaped by spiritual "ground motives" which postulate inner tensions within human existence because they fail to acknowledge the biblical proclamation of creation, the fall into sin, and redemption and renewal through Jesus Christ. The Greeks saw a structural tension between matter and intelligible form. The medievals were Christian but posited a structural dichotomy between nature and grace. The modern antinomy is between natural determinism and human freedom.[44]

The biblical alternative, according to Dooyeweerd, is to recognize that the basic division is not within the structure of being human, but in the direction of human allegiance — either for Christ or against him. "Out of the heart are the issues of life," says Scripture. So Dooyeweerd holds that at

43. Cf. Herman Dooyeweerd, *A New Critique of Theoretical Thought* (Philadelphia: Presbyterian and Reformed, 1957), 4 vols. The best exposition is L. Kalsbeek, *Contours of a Christian Philosophy* (Toronto: Wedge, 1975).

44. Cf. Dooyeweerd, *Roots of Western Culture* (Toronto: Wedge, 1979).

bottom a human being is a religious "heart" in the biblical sense, which he also labels "soul," "spirit," "ego," or "self." The core of human existence is religious because it is essentially God-related — bearing his image, totally dependent on him, and inevitably responding positively or negatively to him.[45]

In its God-relatedness, the heart transcends time. But earthly human existence is also in time. The Word of God which addresses the heart is also the source of the cosmic order. As that creative Word passes from eternity through time to the creation, it is refracted into various dimensions of lawful creaturely existence just as light is separated by a prism into various colors. These dimensions are the numerical, spatial, physical, organic, psychic, logical, culturally-formative, linguistic-symbolic, social, economic, aesthetic, juridical, ethical, and pistic or faith-expressing. These are a priori modes of being for all possible creaturely existence. Thus temporal human life exists in all these different modes or displays all these different aspects. They express not only the ontological structure of the heart or soul as it exists in time, but also its religious direction for or against Christ. So all of life is literally a matter of religion. That emphasis expresses Dooyeweerd's strong Calvinism and is his alternative to the nature-grace distinction of Roman Catholic and much Protestant theology.

The deep, supratemporal core of human existence is the heart, soul, or spirit. The body, according to Dooyeweerd, is the entirety of temporal life in all its diverse aspects. For this reason he rejects those anthropologies which equate the body with the organism and the soul with the mental-spiritual capacities. Temporal existence does not consist of two entities or substances, each with its own operations.

In fact it is a unity of interrelated structures and functions. On Dooyeweerd's analysis, the various aspects or functional modalities of existence listed above are not merely parallel with one another, but are mutually bound together and rooted in one another for their very structure and meaning. They can be distinguished but not separated. They constitute a holistic unity of functionality.

But earthly existence is not merely a set of functions. Entities have inherent structures. The human body is a complex set of progressively more

---

45. My description of Dooyeweerd's anthropology is based on Kalsbeek, Chs. 37 and especially 38, "Outline of a Philosophical Anthropology"; and Dooyeweerd, "What Is Man?", in *In the Twilight of Western Thought* (Nutley, NJ: Craig, 1965).

comprehensive structures ultimately rooted in the human heart. The simplest are the physical structures, the atoms and molecules, which, even though they are included within the human organism, nonetheless retain their own structure and functions. The organism is the next most comprehensive structure. It, too, retains its own structure and functions as it is both encapsulated by and makes possible the next structural level, the psychophysical organism. This is mainly the neural-cerebral system of the organism and the passive consciousness of feelings and sensations which it makes possible. The psychophysical organism in turn is included within a yet more complex system, the act-structure. The act-structure is the interrelated set of intentional operations of the heart or soul, both internal — such as thinking and imagining — and external — such as bodily activity in work, socializing, creating art, loving one's neighbor, and overtly praising God. Human action involves the lower structures while it retains the integrity of their structures and functions. But even the act-structure is not the source of unity in life. For it is grounded in the heart or soul, whose deepest motives it expresses. The heart in turn is not the ground of its own being but is utterly dependent on God. So the entire human body in all its structures and functions is dependent on God for its being and as a whole either expresses love and obedience to him or rejects him.

Inasmuch as the soul structures and directs the body in its physical, organic, and psychophysical functions, as well as its intentional acts, Dooyeweerd's anthropology bears a striking formal similarity to the anthropology of contemporary neo-Thomism. The historical link is the scholasticism (use of Aristotelian categories) in Dooyeweerd's Reformed theological background.

Dooyeweerd's anthropology provides an excellent framework for diagraming and exploring functional holism in human life. All human functional levels are interconnected with all others. Similarly, the more comprehensive structures of existence have a bearing on the structures they encapsulate. But the substructures also enable and influence the operations of those in which they are contained. This model certainly offers the categories necessary for charting the functional interrelations we know from science and ordinary experience. The only question is whether the entire complex of earthly existence has any bearing on the heart or soul itself. Dooyeweerd does not seem to allow for this. His Kantian notion of the ego allows the supratemporal to shape the temporal but not the reverse. His scheme could be modified appropriately, however.

This anthropology is also very useful for combating scientific reductionism. None of the aspects of existence objectified by science can be used to define or explain human life as a whole. All are partial and correlative. So Dooyeweerd is a holist.

But he is also an anthropological dualist according to our definition of the term. For it is clearly possible that the soul or heart can exist without the body.[46] As indicated above, Dooyeweerd's use of the words "body" and "soul" is unconventional. The soul is the supratemporal heart, self, or ego and the body is the entirety of temporal existence. But granting his definitions, it is nevertheless true that the soul survives bodily death. "The soul, Scripture shows, is not affected by temporal death, but after the end of the body (i.e. of all the temporal aspects of man), it continues as a form of existence with an individuality structure."[47] The supratemporal self continues to exist in relation to God even though it completely ceases to function in time. The dualism is between temporal and supratemporal existence, not between physical and spiritual functions or substances. But human existence is clearly dichotomized at death. The whole person does not survive, unless human wholeness does not include temporal existence in the first place. Dooyeweerd is unquestionably an anthropological dualist who affirms existence with the Lord apart from bodily existence.

The only question is whether the disembodied self is subjectively active or in some kind of "soul-sleep." For if the soul is without the body and the body includes all temporal functions, then we seem to be left with an existent but nonfunctional soul. This is not the case, however. What is lost is the soul's functioning in earthly, temporal modes, not all of its capacities whatsoever.[48] The soul's relation and response to God are supratemporal, so presumably fellowship with God would still be possible. Furthermore, the capacities for imagining, thinking, and willing are rooted in the supratemporal heart, not in the temporal act-structure. They can still operate, although not in earthly modes. So subjective activity is possible supratemporally. Finally, even the communion of the saints is possible for those who have departed earthly existence. For the supratemporal heart is

46. Cf. G. C. Berkouwer, *Man: The Image of God* (Grand Rapids: Eerdmans, 1962), pp. 255-263.

47. Berkouwer's paraphrase, p. 257 n. 33, of Dooyeweerd's words in "Het Tijdsprobleem in de Wijsbegeerte der Wetsidee" (The Problem of Time in the Philosophy of the Law-Idea), *Philosophia Reformata*, Vol. V, p. 181.

48. Cf. Berkouwer, p. 257 n. 33.

not an isolated individual before God. Its membership in the human community is supratemporal as well. So fellowship with the saints is also ontologically possible apart from the earthly body in Dooyeweerd's anthropology.

Whatever the questionable features of Dooyeweerd's philosophy — time and supratemporal human existence prominent among them — it is clear that he offers a sophisticated Christian anthropology, expressed in a neo-Kantian and phenomenological style, which is both holistic and dualistic.

F. Summary

Cobb, Swinburne, John Paul II, and Dooyeweerd are four contemporary Christian philosophers who are holistic dualists. I do not mean to suggest that they provide the only approaches or even the best ones. All of their anthropologies require further evaluation on philosophical and conceptual grounds. In addition, one would have to determine how well they can elaborate other biblical doctrines such as the image of God and the nature of sin before endorsing them as fully Christian anthropologies. But they are at least sufficient to demonstrate that holistic dualism is a view of human nature which is still taken seriously by competent professional philosophers. It is not just intellectual quackery.

IV. Final Conclusion: Holistic Dualism Vindicated

Not all questions have been answered. Not all problems have been solved. Not all mysteries have been dispelled. But it seems reasonable at this point to assert that a holistic-dualistic anthropology is not obviously incompatible with the findings of establishment science or with various contemporary approaches to philosophy. A lot more work in these disciplines needs to be done. But Christians who are committed to a holistic dualism because they believe that this is the sort of anthropology entailed by Scripture can work out of their commitment and belief as scientists and philosophers with integrity. There is no need for pitting the truths of revelation against the current results of reason. One need not pick between biblical orthodoxy and an adequate theoretical model of human nature. Intellectual bad faith is not a necessary condition for Christians who participate in the contemporary academic enterprise.

Thus the last objection to a dualistic anthropology has come to nothing. Let's briefly recapitulate the others. Against the objection that Scripture is monistic our study has demonstrated that the biblical view of human nature is both holistic — emphasizing the religious, phenomenological, and functional integration of life — and dualistic — asserting that persons are held in existence without fleshly bodies until the resurrection. The monisms of materialism and ontological holism are simply incapable of allowing for this intermediate state. Nor can they give a reassuring account of personal identity at the resurrection. Thus dualism has won the debate about the nature of biblical anthropology and eschatology. That left a number of theological and practical objections to dualism which were laid to rest in the last chapter. And in this chapter we have seen that there is no obvious incompatibility between science and philosophy on the one hand, and holistic dualism on the other. So the objection that dualism cannot be defended by sophisticated intellectuals these days does not amount to very much either.

My final conclusion is that holistic dualism is more than merely defensible. All thing considered, it is clearly the correct position. It is the best reading of Scripture both in its ability to account for all the biblical data and in its conceptual adequacy with respect to the afterlife. Since there are no other unanswerable challenges to it, holistic dualism ought to be embraced by Christians without reservation. It ought to be part of our worldview, shaping this life and informing our hope for the life to come. Theologians, ethicists, pastors, and counselors ought to get over their embarrassment and confusion about the body-soul distinction in their teaching, preaching, and advising. And Christian brain physiologists, psychologists, and philosophers ought to stop insisting that traditional anthropology and eschatology are incompatible with the assured results of their disciplines. In fact we all ought to stop squabbling and get on with what we are called to do. For there is no incompatibility between the anthropology of Scripture and faithful, effective participation in the modern world. Just the opposite. God's Word is a light upon our path.

Index of Subjects

Duality, ontic/ontological: synonym for dualism, 53, 69, 160-61, 164

Ecstatic (out-of-body) experience: near-death, 212-15; in Paul, 149-51
Exegesis: Calvin's, 33-34, 94-95; dualistic, 25, 33, 94-99, 154-61, 177-80; monistic, 34-36, 95-99, 99-104; of New Testament anthropological terms, 99-104; of Old Testament anthropological terms, 38-43
Extinction (annihilation), 76-77; and re-creation (resurrection), 107-108, 121-122, 129-33, 137-38, 141, 145, 152, 154-55, 158, 169, 171-77

Functional holism: and dualism, 210-12; in intertestamental Judaism, 92-93; in New Testament, 97-99, 103-104; in Old Testament, 43-45; and ontological holism, 45-47. *See also* Holistic dualism

Gehenna (Hell), 88, 118, 124-25, 130
Greek mind (philosophy). *See* Hebrew mind vs. Greek mind

Hades (realm of death), 53, 86-89, 124-25, 130-31. *See also* Sheol
Heart *(leb, kardia)*, 41-43, 96, 97, 227-28
Heaven, 87-88, 149-50
Hebrew mind vs. Greek mind (philosophy), 25-26, 35, 67n.26,85-86, 118; in Paul, 134, 148-49, 150; in Bible interpretation, 159-61, 179-80
Holism, functional. *See* Functional holism
Holism, ontological. *See* Ontological holism
Holistic dualism, 37, 164; in Christian tradition, 72; in intertestamental Judaism, 91-93; implied by New Testament, 108, 118-19; in Old Testament, 70-72; in Paul, 148, 150-51; in contemporary philosophy, 215-31; and contemporary science, 205-15

Idealism (monistic anthropology), 20n.36, 47n.26, 48, 49, 208. *See also* Panpsychism

Identity, personal, 67-68, 167-78; and exact similarity, 168, 174-76; and extinction–re-creation, 171-77; and identifiability, 171, 175-76; and identity of body, 171-73
Immediate resurrection, 78, 106, 120-21, 123-24, 129, 133, 156-57, 164, 192-93; implying dualism, 156-57, 164; and monism, 171, 173, 177 195; in Paul, 138, 141-48, 152, 153, 154-55
Immortality. *See* Soul, immortality of
Intermediate state: entailing dualism, 104-106, 159-64; in intertestamental Judaism, 81-85, 125-26, 128, 130; Jesus', 129-32; in New Testament, 113-14, 116, 120-24, 126, 129, 132-33, 154-57; in Old Testament, 65; in Paul, 135-36, 137-41, 143, 145-48, 154-56; and quasi-corporeality, 200-202; and time-eternity distinction, 191-203
Intertestamental literature: as bridging Old and New Testaments, 73-74, 110-111; Hellenistic influence on, 85-86

Leb. See Heart

Materialism (monistic anthropology): Hobbes, 16-18; and the Old Testament, 48; in contemporary philosophy, 17-18, 208-209
Monism, 165, 167, 169, 171, 173-78; and the New Testament, 95, 99-104; and the Old Testament, 35-36, 47-49; and Paul, 139-41, 147-49, 151. *See also* Dual-aspect monism, Idealism, Materialism, Ontological holism, and Panpsychism
Monism-dualism debate: Christian reactions to, 3-4, 204-205, 230-31; *re* New Testament, 94-109; *re* Old Testament, 33-36
Multiple replication, 174-75

Necromancy, 57-60
Nephesh (soul), 39; in intermediate state, 82-83; as separable, 61, 67-69; in Sheol, 60-62. *See also* *Psychē* and Soul

Index of Authors

Index of Scripture References